T0381124

A PLAGUE ON YOUR HOUSES

A PLAGUE ON YOUR HOUSES

*How New York Was Burned Down
and National Public Health Crumbled*

◆

DEBORAH WALLACE
RODRICK WALLACE

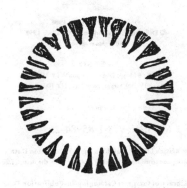

VERSO

London • New York

First published by Verso 1998

VERSO
UK: 6 Meard Street, London W1V 3HR
USA: 180 Varick Street, New York, NY 10014-4606

Verso is the imprint of New Left Books

ISBN: 978-1-85984-253-9

British Library Cataloguing in Publication Data
A Catalogue record for this book is available from the British Library.

Library of Congress Cataloging-in-Publication Data
Wallace, Deborah.
A Plague on your houses: how New York was burned down
and national public health crumbled / Deborah Wallace, Rodrick Wallace.
    p.   cm.
Includes bibliographical references and index.

    1. Public health—New York (State)—New York. 2. Fire depart-
ments—New York (State)—New York. 3. Social planning—New York
(State)—New York.   I. Wallace, Roderick. II. Title.
RA448.N5W34   1998
362.1'09747'1—dc21
                                                    98-43932
                                                       CIP

CONTENTS

ACKNOWLEDGMENTS

Support for writing this book came from an Investigator Award in Health Policy Research from the Robert Wood Johnson Foundation. This grant is also supporting further research.

DEDICATION

This book is dedicated to our mentors: Peter Gould, Norman Bailey, and John Ullman, who use their enormous talents and exquisite methodology for public good.

PREFACE

WHEN SYPHILIS experiments on a group of black men at the Tuskegee Institute came to public attention in 1972, public outcry forced greater regulation of research on human subjects. This book recounts a far vaster experiment, one that continues to affect the lives and deaths of millions of residents in major metropolitan regions across the United States: the 1969–1976 Rand Corporation/HUD fire-service reductions in poor, overcrowded neighborhoods of aging housing in New York City. This experiment affected the poor neighborhoods it targeted, and their surrounding neighborhoods. It triggered citywide epidemics of homelessness, violence, and disease which diffused into the suburban counties around the City. Eventually, these epidemics hopscotched along frequently travelled routes to other major metropolitan regions of the USA.

PERSONAL POLITICAL HISTORY

In 1970, I met Rodrick Wallace on a picketline in front of a war thinktank, the Riverside Research Institute (RRI), which was conducting research for the Southeast Asian War as well as for nuclear and undersea warfare. The organization to which we belonged, Scientists and Engineers for Social and Political Action, targeted military research as an unethical use of science and as a means of oppressing nontechnological cultures.

Because of our regular picketing, many of the engineers employed at RRI came to know us and would speak with us. That is how we learned that one of RRI's founders, John Dunning (co-inventor of the gaseous-diffusion process that separates the two isotopes of uranium to make bombs), was close to then-Mayor Lindsay and served on his science-advisory board. This unpaid but powerful position allowed Dunning to direct city money toward RRI perfectly legally and helped boost the flagging morale there (a result of doing weapons research during an unpopular war) with potentially useful civilian work. Thus,

RRI received a contract from New York City to evaluate new voice fire-alarm boxes made by Norelco.

The City wanted to install these untried devices in its ghetto neighborhoods for a variety of reasons (see chapter 2). To instill confidence in them, the Fire Department had to have an "independent" review. In fact, RRI found serious problems with them: traffic noises made their use impossible in certain locations, their serial circuitry meant that use of one alarm box on a circuit rendered all the other boxes inoperative, and being electronic they were more prone to breakdown than the old electromechanical boxes. Nonetheless, RRI recommended that New York City go ahead and begin installing them because that was the recommendation the city needed.

In 1973, Rod visited the president of the Uniformed Firefighters Association, Richard Vizzini, to discuss the Emergency Reporting System (ERS) boxes and the involvement of RRI and Norelco, both mainly military firms. Vizzini gave him an armful of reports by the New York City-Rand Institute which included systems analysis of the fire service and recommendations on how to cut service to the ghettoes and bust unions at the same time. During these same years, Rand was shoring up the Indochinese War effort with its scenarios, models, and body counts (which later turned out to have been faked).

I am an ecologist and, at that time, was evaluating fish-population models in the Hudson river. Between battles over electric power and over Westway—a huge highway to be built on fill in the Hudson—striped bass and the modeling of their population were receiving great attention. The models evolved to extreme complexity both hydrodynamically and biologically.

Rod presented me with the armload of Rand fire-service reports. After scanning them, I felt literally ill. As I began to read through them, it slowly became clear that the data acquisition, analysis and interpretation, and the modeling methodology were much more primitive than those of the Hudson river fish population models. NYC Rand's level of science was inadequate for natural ecology and grossly inadequate for experiments on human populations.

Rod and I began to write critiques of the Rand models, to acquire and analyze Fire Department data, and to examine the impacts of the fire-service reductions using techniques of population and community ecology and environmental-impact assessment. In 1976, we were the first citizens to sue the City under the New York State Freedom of Information Act when the Fire Department ignored our requests.

By 1978, we discovered that the Rand-recommended fire service cuts had triggered an epidemic of building fires and heated up a related epidemic of building abandonment. We submitted a grant proposal to the National Institutes of

Health (NIH) to assess the public-health outcomes of this massive destruction of housing in New York's poor neighborhoods. The NIH did not even review our proposal. That research plan, carried out over a period of fifteen years without federal funding, resulted in this book.

Beginning with a 1977 book on the fire-service cuts and their fire-service impacts, we published a fountain of papers in peer-reviewed scientific journals on fire science, fire-system engineering, public health, geography, social science, criminal justice, and combustion toxicology. Our lack of significant funding allowed us to work without blinders: we could generate new paradigms, transfer approaches between disciplines, and come to conclusions about the precise roles of governmental agencies and private corporations in the ills we analyzed.

The results of our analysis were devastating and, unfortunately, accurate. In predicting the effects of the massive housing destruction and resultant loss of social community, we foresaw the tuberculosis epidemic, epidemics of sexually transmitted diseases, increases in substance abuse, and increases in mental-health and behavioral problems. We saw in this housing destruction the forces that fuel the process of homelessness and the roots of increases in low-birthweight newborns, in violent deaths, and in preventable diseases. Lately, we have raised our eyes from New York City and its neighborhoods to the metropolitan regions of several other cities and have seen the conditions in a central city like New York affect the public health of its entire metropolitan region, including the wealthiest of its suburbs.

The time has come to explain this line of research to citizens and policy-makers. Robert Fitch's book, *The Assassination of New York*, examined the policy behind the deliberate de-industrialization of New York and its consequences. Joel Schwartz's book, *The New York Approach*, described the relatively slow, planned clearing of slums and deliberate segregation by Robert Moses. In this book, we supply another piece of the puzzle: the very rapid, unplanned burning out of whole neighborhoods by withdrawal of fire-control service after slum clearance had become legally difficult and politically unfeasible. We have all begun to feel the effects of a generation of war on the poor, even if we are far from poor. The Red Death has entered Prospero's castle.

This book summarizes more than twenty years of pure and applied science to direct remedies and reforms that can stop these urban processes of destruction and disease. Free people can yet "stand between their loved homes and the war's desolation."

Deborah Wallace, Ph.D.

INTRODUCTION

Beginning in 1969, the New York City Fire Department targeted its poor, densely populated neighborhoods for service reduction. The technical rationale for these cuts came from the Rand Corporation Fire Project, then established as the New York City-Rand Institute. Early cuts included changing the number of fire companies sent to alarms and switching from the reliable electromechanical fire alarm boxes to the all-electronic and problem-ridden Emergency Response System voice fire boxes. By 1972, the Department was closing fire companies or moving them from poor to middle-class areas. The conclusion that such closings and permanent relocations were safe and the decisions of which companies to move or remove were dressed in a pseudo-scientific veneer of Rand's substandard, egregiously flawed mathematical operations-research models. These models effectively silenced community residents.

The expressed motivations for changes designed to kill off whole neighborhoods ranged from a perceived need for enlarged space to revive New York City's shrinking industrial base, to social-engineering schemes to segregate trouble-makers from the middle class. NYC Housing Commissioner Roger Starr and others took benign neglect, the recommended policy of then Presidential advisor Patrick Moynihan, a step further to active planned shrinkage (cutting vital services), with the overt goal of killing off "sick" neighborhoods. Starr denied the existence of the social networks that compose communities and mocked the idea of community, claiming that Americans can be arbitrarily shifted around without serious consequences. These schemes also resulted in—and may have sought—the political emasculation of marginalized communities much like Southern terrorism against blacks under Jim Crow.

About 10% of New York City's fire companies were eliminated, turning New York City into one huge fire-service network through temporary relocations and "move-ups" of companies to cover for each other. Previously, neighborhoods had functioned as relatively independent, self-sufficient fire departments. Subsequent reductions in staffing levels further depleted fire-control resources and guaranteed inadequate initial responses to a significant proportion of alarms. The inability to control individual fires on the initial alarm triggered a contagious fire epidemic with all the usual spatial and temporal characteristics such as geographic clustering and temporal peaking of fires. This epidemic in turn set off a separate but related epidemic of housing abandonment by landlords.

Many poor neighborhoods simply collapsed from the spatial concentration and temporal peaking of these modes of housing destruction. Health areas of the South-Central Bronx, for example, lost 80% of both housing units and population between 1970 and 1980. About 1.3 million white people left New York as conditions deteriorated from housing overcrowding and social disruption. About 0.6 million poor people were displaced and had to move as their homes were destroyed. A total of almost two million people were uprooted, over 10% of the population of the entire Standard Metropolitan Statistical Area. (The SMSA consists of the central city and its economically linked counties; New York's SMSA is comprised of 25 counties.)

Housing overcrowding temporarily declined as the poor filled the larger housing units vacated by the fleeing middle class. As soon as the emigration stopped—around 1980, the year of lowest prevalence of extreme housing overcrowding—the trend in overcrowding reversed. By 1990, the number of extremely overcrowded housing units had reached about double the 1970 number, the initial condition of the fire epidemic. The number and size of fires depend on prevalence of extreme housing overcrowding.

Out of the overcrowding and the social unraveling of the community came epidemics of contagious disease and contagious behavior problems both in the remnants of the burned-out neighborhoods and in the newly crowded neighborhoods receiving refugees: tuberculosis, measles, substance abuse, AIDS, low-weight births, and violence. Life expectancy of elderly blacks declined between 1970 and 1980 after decades of increase and in contrast to that of elderly whites which increased uninterruptedly.

The temporal changes in the geographic distribution of cases and of high incidence for the diseases and behavioral pathologies link them to the burnout and to each other. They correlate with overcrowding, change in an area's socioeconomic status rank (an index of social disruption), or change in population or population density.

The neighborhood disease dynamics determined citywide trends in disease. The tuberculosis epidemic most clearly illustrated how citywide incidence grew as secondary epicenters became established in the Bronx and Brooklyn from earlier primary epicenters of Central Harlem and the Lower East Side. The burnout, overcrowding, and mixing of populations rendered whole boroughs susceptible to the tuberculosis epidemic, and the primary and secondary epicenters spread the high-incidence area across whole boroughs through the 1980s and early 1990s. The 1990 geography of measles cases indicates a similar diffusion process. The poor neighborhoods with high housing overcrowding and social disruption came to determine the public health of the whole city.

The contagious processes operated via three mechanisms: hierarchical diffusion (leap-frogging from the primary epicenters to hard-pressed neighborhoods which then became secondary epicenters); spatial diffusion from the epicenters to surrounding areas; and network diffusion within neighborhoods through social networks of friends, family, and co-workers.

The tuberculosis and AIDS epidemics within the city demonstrated the lack of respect for jurisdictional boundaries, class, ethnicity, sex, age, and sexual orientation held by contagious processes . AIDS jumped from largely white, middle-class gay communities concentrated in Greenwich Village and the West Side, to intravenous drug users and minority heterosexuals. Tuberculosis fanned out from primary and secondary epicenters across whole boroughs and claimed white middle-class victims, even a few wealthy ones. Even white children, by 1990, were drawn into the contagious-epidemic process.

Examination of the metropolitan region, the Census Bureau's Standard Metropolitan Statistical Area (SMSA), also demonstrated the failure of containment. Linkage among the counties, indicated by the percents of the workforce living in a given county and working in the various SMSA counties, predicted patterns of AIDS, tuberculosis, violent crime, and low-weight births. Introducing county poverty rate into the equation, the index of vulnerability to these pathologies, raised the predictive power of the model to over 90%.

Our analysis made clear that a pathology can be introduced into any county and will make its way to the inner city rapidly along the commuting paths; there it will incubate to high incidence and be broadcast back out to suburban counties proportionate to their linkages with Manhattan. The mixing of workers from the five boroughs and all the suburban counties in Manhattan is one mechanism, although it may merely indicate overall mixing in Manhattan at a variety of sites besides the workplace (recreational, cultural, religious, etc.).

The Manhattan dispersion effect negates local county conditions and produces parallel correlations for AIDS, tuberculosis, and violent crime. In other words, the relationship between pathology incidence, and the components of linkage and vulnerability, is the same for the three pathologies. The linkage must thus be tight, and the pressure from the decaying city, great.

Analysis of eight SMSAs and four pathologies showed that the history and structure of each fashioned a somewhat different picture of public health and public order. But all eight showed that a single socioeconomic system operated throughout the SMSA: at least one marker—pathology—was regionalized in each SMSA. Pooling data from all eight SMSAs (54 million people) rendered a national picture of urban America. Poverty determined low-weight birth and violent-crime incidences more than commuting pattern. Commuting pattern determined AIDS incidence more than poverty. Commuting pattern and poverty rate had nearly equal weight in the determination of tuberculosis incidence. However, all three independent variables were associated significantly with all four markers: commuting pattern, county, poverty rate, and effect of SMSA.

A fairly complete picture of the spread of AIDS within and between the metro regions of the 25 largest cities emerged from a migration analysis. The three factors which explained over 90% of variation in number of AIDS cases were contact with New York, contact with San Francisco, and regional incidence of violent crime (an index of social network disruption).

Violent crime also spread nationally. Just as New York and San Francisco act as the primary AIDS centers, Miami and Los Angeles act as the primary epicenters of violent crime. The national pattern of AIDS reflects interaction between these four metro regions and the local metro-regional conditions, particularly population, economic opportunity structure, and level of social organization.

In our last analysis, we found that the US metro-region network was so tightly linked that it had an amplification factor of nearly 50. The amplification factor indicates how brittle and stressed a system is and how close to drastic change due to stresses. A natural ecosystem is considered resilient only if its amplification factor is less than one. Thus, perturbations readily ripple out and amplify through the network of US metro regions. Within the three metro regions with the most suburban counties, linkages are as tight as or tighter than those between metro regions. New York and Washington had amplification factors two to three times than those of the 25-region system. Philadelphia's was nearly the same as that of the 25-region system. Thus, the individual metro regions and the national system of metro regions are unstable and brittle—unable to "roll with the punches."

Drawing from all of our research into the New York City metropolitan area, as well as regional and national studies, we reach the stunning conclusion that the keystone populations that determine the national public health and public order are poor inner-city neighborhoods of population scales in the thousands to hundred-thousands. Even more astonishingly, these neighborhoods communicate over long distances between cities. The pathologies we discuss in this book reach high incidence in susceptible poor neighborhoods and diffuse out to entire metro regions. About three-quarters of the country's population lives in metro regions (cities and suburbs) and is more or less subject to these contagious processes.

The three parts of this book focus on the public-health and public-order disasters caused by the application of planned shrinkage in New York City. First we look at fire, then epidemics, and finally we present a policy to heal the wounds.

PART ONE

◆

BAPTISM BY FIRE

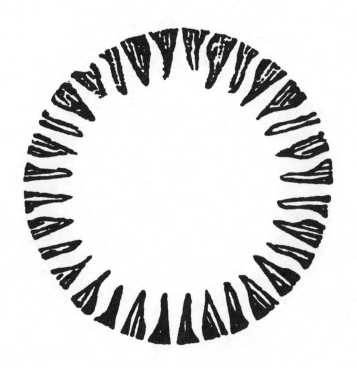

BAPTISM BY FIRE

HOW FIRES IN BUILDINGS BURN

Fires happen when three factors come together: fuel, oxygen, and heat or an ignition source. Every combustible or flammable substance, typically a carbon-based material (natural, like wood, or synthetic, like polyurethane foam) has its ignition temperature, the temperature at which it oxidizes fast enough to produce energy in the form of flames. However, each fuel also has its temperature of mass decomposition, also called pyrolysis. At this temperature, the chemical bonds break, and gaseous products of pyrolysis diffuse off the surface of the fuel rapidly. These gases are easily ignited (methane, for example), highly toxic, or corrosively irritating and incapacitating (hydrogen chloride from polyvinyl chloride, for example). The pyrolytic products usually ignite first and spread the fire.[1]

Fires grow exponentially in time. This means that the early flame stage grows slowly until a critical size is reached, and then growth accelerates rapidly. The exponential pattern of growth makes every second count in terms of hazard to life, health, and property. Fires in buildings are constrained by the building materials and design. Heat and smoke are trapped by ceilings and roofs, accumulating under these barriers and moving outward from the fire along them. The toxic fumes from decomposition and burning may reach great distances from the fire itself. People on the floors above the fire may be poisoned or killed by the smoke and fumes which rise through the various openings for plumbing and electrical systems, elevators, and heating/cooling systems. People who don't even know there's a fire and see no flames are often the ones to die from smoke inhalation. In the 1980 MGM Grand Hotel fire in Las Vegas, the great majority of the 85 people who died were on the top floors, though it was the ground floor that was burning.[2]

ADEQUATE FIRE SERVICE RESPONSE

The object of designing a municipal fire control system is rapid assemblage of an adequate team to control most fires quickly. The definition of an "adequate team" differs with varying conditions such as building use (residential, industrial, commercial), building size and age, the building code in force when it was constructed, crowding, whether the people can get out, and whether the building contains an especially vulnerable population (schools, hospitals, nursing homes, and jails).

For most multiple dwellings, three engines and two ladders plus a battalion chief is an adequate team, as long as the staffing of these units is also adequate. Five firefighters and an officer per engine company, and six firefighters plus an officer per ladder company constitute adequate staffing for New York City conditions. The first engine and ladder should arrive at a multiple dwelling in a multiple-dwelling neighborhood within 3–4 minutes after the alarm is turned in. The entire team should be assembled within 5–6 minutes. The dispatcher must be able to find enough nearby units to do this quickly; for each address in the city, the following units are assigned for response: first-due engine, first-due ladder, second-due engine, and second-due ladder.

The first-due team enters the fire floor. The second engine and ladder companies enter the floor above. Engine companies extinguish the fire, usually with water from a hose and nozzle, with the company officer acting as nozzle-man. Ladder companies effect entry, vent the smoke, search, and rescue. An engine company may arrive very quickly, stretch and charge the hose and be totally useless if the ladder doesn't arrive to effect entry. The third engine "stands fast" (is available just in case) unless the fire requires such lengthy firefighting that the first-due engine company needs relief or unless the fire is so large that it requires two nozzles on the fire floor for control.

Multiple dwellings present more problems than one- or two-family homes: finding the fire, stretching many lengths of hose, gaining entrance, evacuating large numbers of people, potential for huge fuel loads, and prevention of fire spread both from apartment to apartment within the building and between abutting buildings. Older buildings have no standpipes, so that hose must be stretched all the way from the street hydrants to the fire. New buildings have steel doors to the apartments and oven-like, tight, low-ceiling construction. Entry is time-consuming and exhausting, and the heat and smoke debilitating and impenetrable. Multiple-dwelling fires require a much more rapid assemblage of a larger team than one- and two-family residence fires.

Fire-control resource levels also determine fire-prevention inspections and training-and-familiarization programs. If the busy units are either out on alarms or resting between frequent alarms, they can't inspect very much or go on training drills. If the area is busy, the dispatchers will keep the companies from going out on inspection and training. Companies have to be available in busy areas if there aren't enough of them, so they essentially train on the job. The neighborhood residents become unwitting teachers.

NOTES FROM THE FRONT

The following 1976 interview with a veteran battalion chief shows how these factors come together on the fireground and how fire-response policy became disconnected from fire-company workload. Chief X, now retired, had served in the South Bronx during its famous ordeal-by-fire. The fires of the South Bronx attracted international attention and were the subject of a BBC-TV special, "The Bronx Is Burning," in 1976. This battalion chief participated in the Uniformed Fire Officers Association's workload committee, which also analyzed risks to citizens from inadequate levels of fire control resources.

Q When the dispatcher transmits the alarm to the station what happens?

A The house officer takes the alarm-box address or house address and turns the men out. The men get into their gear and onto the unit in an average of one minute, but at night it takes a little longer. We maneuver the unit into the street and go.

Q You say go. Is it that easy?

A It's not easy getting to a fire in New York City. We have to slow down at intersections because we used to have frequent accidents. Some streets are always jammed with double-parked cars. During rush-hour, all major streets are jammed, but some streets are jammed nearly all the time. Sometimes we can go the wrong way on a one-way street, but many times we can't because of traffic. The Fire Department doesn't always use the latest maps which show all the intersection obstructions such as subways rising out of the ground. Getting around a construction site can lose you half a minute along the way.

Q So you get to the alarm box. What next?

A Then we look for the fire. Usually we have someone waving us in the right direction. It we don't, we'll be lucky to see the fire or smoke from the street. If the fire's in the rear of a tenement and no one stayed at the box to show us where it is, we're in trouble.

Sometimes people who phone in alarms give the wrong address. It's hard to see addresses on tenements and the fire search can be slow. The one- and two-family houses in Queens and Staten Island don't cause this problem. You can see where the fire is right away.

Q After you find the fire, what happens?

A The engine maneuvers to the nearest hydrant. One man hooks up and waits for the order for water. The other men begin to stretch hose. If the fire's in front, the attack is simple, but if we have to stretch extra lengths of hose to the back or stretch up the fire escape, it just sends the men into the attack already tired and out of breath. It takes ten lengths of hose to get to the back of the top floor of a six-story tenement—that's 360–600 pounds. Each man wears 30–50 pounds of gear besides. The people who live on the top floor of Old Law tenements have the least fire protection of all. It takes longest to get the hose stretched and the men are already out of breath. We get a lot of civilians jumping out of windows of the top two stories because they can't take the heat anymore.

Q So you're stretching hose. You get to the apartment door. What then?

A That ladder truck better have rolled up by now or we don't get in. All the forcible-entry equipment, the rescue equipment, the venting gear, and all the manpower to do these jobs are on the ladder truck. An engine can do very little by itself, especially since the manning reduction of July 1975. A ladder can do very little by itself. Once the apartment door is open, that water has to beat back the fire enough for search-and-rescue. That little girl that died in East Elmhurst—the ladder rolled up and forced the door but had to wait for the engine. Fire activity was so heavy that the nearest available engine came from 60 blocks away and took 15–20 minutes.

It's hard to get into tenement apartments. Most tenants have several locks on the door, chains, wires, and bars. They have gates on the windows. It takes 1–3 minutes longer to get inside an apartment than into a private home. Some of the apartment doors are steel and deform from the heat so that you can't open them. Then you have to go in by the window or from above.

That fire is spreading all the time and raising the temperature of the air in that apartment. If you're lucky, it'll be only about 500° F when you go in. If it's been burning five minutes, it'll be near 1000° F in the room. According to the *Handbook on Fire Protection*, a human can take 300° F in dry air for a minute or two, or about 200° F in moist air. Then the pain gets too great. That's why people jump out windows. My men have been trained to go into 1000° F. I remember how we did it when I was a young firefighter. We'd put some water on the fire. Then when the steam came up and scalded us, we'd crawl along the floor until things cooled a little. We'd get some more water on the fire and hit the floor again. It didn't always cool down, and we'd be in trouble. We couldn't breathe. We'd stick our noses into our coats and breathe that way or look for a pipe projecting from the wall and breathe in the space between the pipe and the wall.

Q The time it takes to stretch hose and get at the fire in a multiple dwelling (3–4 minutes)—how important is that?

A If you don't get water on the fire within three minutes of ignition, you could have a problem. The National Fire Underwriters let a fire burn through an old abandoned tenement. Within three minutes, it had spread from the ground to the top floor. Within 47 minutes, the building was destroyed. We have areas of rapid-fire-spread potential not only within the building, but between buildings. Some buildings share a common cockloft. Others have less than ten feet of space between them, some only one or two feet.

Q The population density in some areas must be pretty high?

A After all these studies, no one came up with a standard for the maximum number of people who should be served by a fire company. In the South Bronx, the average number of people per engine is over 44,000. In Staten Island, it's 17,000. There is no standard for manning in areas of multiple dwellings as opposed to one- and two-family residences.

Q The fire situation of your area, the South Bronx, has become a proverb. What led to the present situation?

A The population in the South Bronx is one of the densest in the City, and the housing conditions among the worst. The alarm rate rose slowly during the early 1960's until 1968 when it simply took off. By 1966, the city-wide workload was so heavy that the state Public Employees Relations Board ordered the City to open 16 new fire companies, of which 13 were opened by 1970. This eased the load, but the alarm rate continued to climb. The Lindsay administration brought Rand in to analyze the situation. Rand began eliminating fire companies.

1

SETTING THE SCENE

THE DEBATE OVER SLUMS

It has often been observed that real estate is to New York what oil is to Texas. Indeed, since before 1850, the gladiators of New York City's political arena have waged battle over slums. Those who owned slum properties wished to exercise their property rights, which meant, for them, continuing to rent at as high a rate as possible and to invest as little as possible in construction and maintenance. The vast number of slum properties on potentially high-value land in Manhattan, Brooklyn, and the Bronx were seen as a paradoxical economic condition to be set right.[1,2] Banks, insurance companies, owners of other properties, and real estate entrepreneurs, on the one hand, took the stance that slum conditions lowered the value of their properties and limited their opportunities for future income. Reformers, on the other hand, wanted slums upgraded because they saw them as breeding disease, drunkenness, promiscuity, and violence.[3,4]

The battle lines were drawn: those who favored slum clearance for redevelopment versus those who defended owners' property rights and laws that limit evictions.[5]

At some point in their decay, slums can get out of hand and threaten the public health and order of outlying neighborhoods. Tuberculosis, for example, was the top-ranking cause of death for both the poor and the rich in most urban areas until about 1940 when the living and working conditions of the poor were improved to the point where even the poor experienced low risk of active disease.[6,7]

Historically, slums have often been defined by bias. The neighborhood of Bushwick, Brooklyn, for example, consisted largely of brownstones and rowhouses and was occupied by the upper-working and middle classes—bus drivers, plumbers, funeral home owners, etc. While the race of the residents,

9

mainly homeowners, remained white, the city planners saw it as a solid neighborhood. But when black bus drivers, black plumbers, black funeral home owners bought houses and moved into the pre-war apartment buildings in the late
1960s, suddenly the planners saw a slum.[8] Then the city policies proceeded to
turn Bushwick into a slum worthy of the name. Similarly, David Durk described
how police corruption, organized crime, and real-estate racial steering created a
slum in Crown Heights North.[9]

In fact, stable "slums," i.e. poor neighborhoods of old, mildly overcrowded
housing that are not experiencing rapid deterioration physically or socially, are
true communities, often with a history decades long. Clearance of this brand of
"slum" will do more harm than good both to the residents and to the metropolitan region as a whole. Loren Hinkle in 1977 co-edited a very important book on
public health and the built environment which was published by the United
States Public Health Service. Hinkle observed:

> It is the social environment and not the physical environment which is the primary
> determinant of the health and well-being of people who live in cities . . . . Within
> wide limits it is not the physical condition of the house, neighborhood, or human
> settlement that determines a person's health so much as his own social back-
> ground, his perception of his environment, his relation to the other people around
> him and to his social group . . . .
>
> The importance of the social milieu is such that the dislocation and disruptions of
> social relations that are produced when one moves a family from a dilapidated
> dwelling [within a functioning community] to a modern apartment [outside that
> community] may have adverse effects upon health and behavior that are not offset
> by the clean, comfortable, and convenient new dwelling. . . .[10]

Slums have long presented two distinct dilemmas: for government and citizens, the complex question of how to cure their physical and socioeconomic ills;
for the inner circle of financial leaders, planners, and developers, the simpler
question of how to clear them.

THE GREAT REFORM

After a slow beginning in the 1840s, the Great Reform entered its flowering in
the 1880s. In the large cities of the United States, patrician do-gooders allied
themselves with public-health physicians, religious leaders, labor union organiz-
ers, and community activists to develop and implement an agenda of uplift.
Living and working conditions of the time were targets of the reform. Building
codes were put in place. Sanitation standards, public-hygiene education, limits

on the workweek, and codes of workplace conditions were born during the Great Reform. The most intense period of this social movement was between 1880–1920.

The history of New York often seems like a series of battles over land. In this way, the Great Reform and other efforts at upgrading poor-people's housing rank as land-reform movements as surely as those in the various Latin American countries. Like them, the struggles in New York often left the poor in precarious conditions, as the hidden hand of the permanent government slowly corrupted reforms. Often, the consequence of slum clearance was a bigger, worse slum. On the other hand, the opportunities offered to the working class and working poor (but not the destitute) during these movements often gave them the social mobility to scramble into middle-class living and working conditions, relieving much pressure on the very poorest sector, so that some portion of it could position itself to make the leap.

Numerous histories recount the Great Reform in all its ambiguities: its rise, its dynamics, and its legacies. For our purposes, one important legacy was the precedent of setting limits to the property rights of landlords and the tenure rights of tenants when enough powerful factions moved to clear slums or to rehabilitate existing multiple dwellings.

One analysis of the Great Reform, *Hives of Sickness,* gathered chapters by several authors on different aspects of public health during various periods of New York's history. The debate described by Elizabeth Fee and Evelyn Hammonds between the sanitarian reformers and the "scientific" medical practitioners provides background for the debate now going on between those who demand an end to the war on the poor as necessary for general public health and public order and the medical establishment, which advocates control of diseases and mental health and public order problems by treatment of individuals medically, typically with drugs.[11] Another essay, by Elizabeth Blackmar, described the central role of stands of dilapidated, overcrowded, and unsanitary tenements as a threat to public health and public order.

John Griscom, the public-health physician who pushed hardest for reform, had the political dilemma of needing support from the large property owners.[12] He wrote the classic opening salvo in the very beginning of reform in 1845, *The Sanitary Condition of New York's Laboring Classes*, essential reading that established the impact of severe slum conditions on the health and well-being of residents. He described in detail slum living conditions and the role of the landlords not only in maintaining them but also in operating illegal grogshops right in the tenements. He created an agenda of physical and social reforms he believed would improve the health and intellectual status of the "laboring classes." [13] Subsequent enactment of his proposals has generally proven the young physician correct.

DEINDUSTRIALIZATION

However, by the 1920s, the Great Reform took a wrong turn in New York as the oil and auto industries teamed with the railroads and entered the New York real-estate market as major movers. Robert Fitch, in *The Assassination of New York,* describes the resulting programs of land clearance, beginning with the Regional Plan Association's 1929 Master Plan for New York City. [14] Besides slum clearance, this Master Plan called for clearing industries out of Manhattan and parts of Brooklyn and Queens. Office buildings for the financial industry and high-rent apartment buildings would replace the factories and plants. Instead of workers living near their jobs, armies of suburban commuters would enter the City every workday by railroad and by automobile via the vast network of highways laid out in the Master Plan.

Under the succession of plans from 1929 through 1969, New York was to metamorphose from an industrial caterpillar into a financial and cultural butter-fly. This change was motivated in part by a bias that saw manufacturing as a dirty undesirable way to use land, and by an invalidation of blue-collar, and especially minority, workers. [15] The new desired source of jobs, the financial sector, required educated, skilled, white collar (and largely white) workers.

So between 1959 and 1989, over 600,000 manufacturing jobs disappeared, [16] a loss that made New York the American city with the highest proportion of the population not in the workforce. It also transformed New York into one of the cheapest labor pools in America, with an average hourly wage below that of all major cities except for San Antonio. [17]

ROBERT MOSES AND THE HOUSING ACT OF 1949

Besides deindustrialization, the other driving force behind land clearance was the clearing of "slums." Robert Moses was the central figure in this movement, pioneering the use of a wide variety of condemnation and financing laws and instruments to raise the value of land and redevelop large swaths of it, especially in Manhattan. Because of the many books written about Moses, including several best-sellers, his history will not be described here. Such immense projects as the United Nations and its accompanying apartments and hotels, Lincoln Center and its accompanying apartments, Morningside Heights, and Stuyvesant Town were Moses projects. Because of the peculiar combination of racism and humanism endemic to New York liberalism, the "slum" clearances of his era resulted in both greater segregation and a larger number of housing units for the poor and middle classes, especially in public housing.[18]

Whether Robert Moses spearheaded this reshaping of New York or managed the process under orders from large financial and real-estate powers is subject to debate. Moses certainly didn't act in a vacuum. He bridged the interests of big real estate and the liberal middle class which viewed itself as humane and helpful to the poor. Perhaps his most important talent was seduction of the liberals into supporting his projects as helping the poor *and* arresting the spread of "slums." Liberals often saw the move of non-whites into their neighborhoods as "slum spread."[19] Joel Schwartz in *The New York Approach* paints him as the leader;[20] Fitch sees him as the flunkey.[21] There is little debate, however, about the results of his actions: he changed the color and class of many New York City communities by evicting poor and working-class blacks and Latinos; he ushered in the age of big ugly buildings; he planned and built the arteries which turned the car into a serious competitor with public transportation and into an urban plague.

Although Moses had a number of legal instruments at his disposal for condemnation and eviction, Title I of the Housing Act of 1949 was perhaps his favorite. He used it for many of his projects which cleared "slums" for middle-class housing. The federal Housing Act of 1949 gathered various housing programs into the Housing and Home Finance Agency and provided both funding and enabling legislation for new urban housing. Its two most important sections regarding new housing were Title I and Title III. Title I provided federal grants which would constitute two-thirds of a "write-down," with the other one-third provided by the local municipal government. A "write-down" was money provided to make up for the following costs: the dollar difference between market value of a land parcel in condemnation and the appraisal of the parcel's potential redeveloper, the cost of clearance, and the cost of site preparation. The market value nearly invariably exceeded the redeveloper's appraisal. Title I provided nothing for public housing but gave enormous support to private developers. Title III authorized 810,000 units of federally financed public housing.[22]

Title I required a local public authority to choose the development sites in conformity to a master plan, get approval from the local government for site plans and site-preparation plans (including relocation), condemn the property, and provide the one-third local contribution. The local authority would then clear the site, relocate the tenants, and auction the site to private developers. The local authority could coordinate Title I and Title III projects under the city master plan. The potential for abuse is obvious (cozy relationships with private developers, capricious evictions of tenants, bowing to political pressures) and was fulfilled in New York, where Title I projects never had an official master plan to which they had to conform.[23] The result was a vastly disproportionate targeting of communities of color for relocation.

The following projects were constructed between 1950 and 1964 under Title I, the percentages indicating the proportion of displaced tenants who were non-white: Corlears Hook (24%), Harlem (100%), North Harlem (100%), West Park (52%), Morningside Heights (65%), Columbus Circle (54%), Fort Greene (62%), Pratt Institute (36%), Hammels-Rockaway (67%), and Lincoln Square (7%). A total of sixteen Title I projects were realized out of 20 proposed.[24]

Under Title I implementation, New York became one of the most segregated cities in the United States. From integrated neighborhoods in Greenwich Village and on the West Side of Manhattan, black and Latino families were evicted and shuttled into Harlem and the Bronx. Like Stuyvesant Town before them (a pre-Title I super-project that flatly refused to rent to nonwhites until civil rights laws on housing were passed in the 1960's), the middle class Title 1 projects typically had less than 1% nonwhite tenants, whereas the public housing projects, especially in Harlem, were over 90% nonwhite.[25]

Title I projects built in Harlem uprooted old, solid black communities. The Protestant churches, especially the Episcopalian archdiocese, suffered greatly from the disruption of community. Poor members no longer lived near their churches, which would often be the only buildings left for blocks around after the old houses were demolished. The pastors decided to bear witness to the devastation of community and family which Title I brought to the poor of Harlem. This was the beginning of the end of Title I displacement.[26] From the reports, testimony, and sit-ins, by 1961, even the "liberal" racists could no longer avert their eyes and pretend that the poor were bene-fitting from "slum" clearance and were being properly rehoused. So-called "self-relocation" was not working for those who didn't make it into public housing; those who made it into public housing suffered from loss of old social ties and became behavioral problems which threatened the viability of the new public housing.[27]

During and right after World War II, but before Title I devastation, New York was one united city, relative to what followed. Everyone, by and large, wanted and tried to participate in civic duties. Judith Leavitt in *Hives of Sickness* described a smallpox outbreak in the city in 1947 and the massive vaccination program which kept it very small and brief.[28] The countless organizations in neighborhoods and citywide which had mobilized all sectors for the war effort also mobilized them for the vaccination program. Neighborhood leaders had their pictures in the newspapers as they were vaccinated. Houses of worship, political clubs, block associations, Masonic lodges, and other social enterprises brought residents to neighborhood vaccination sites in the mobile vans and public health clinics. Within two weeks after the discovery of smallpox in the city, 5 million people had been vaccinated (within one month, 6,350,000), an achievement which would have been impossible without the citizen's trust, commitment to the city and its society, and active participation in that society. Despite everything that was wrong and imperfect at that time, the city aspired to function and did function as a unity for the last time.

IMAGES, VISIONS, DREAMS

The name of Moses's special agency, founded in 1944, was the Committee on Slum Clearance, and he successfully cast its role as humanitarian and reformist. Moses ran the committee by skillfully coopting any local or citywide groups with enough muscle to count. Many do-good groups were seduced into supporting CSC programs and projects because Moses offered them the opportunity to hob-nob with the elite *and* help the poor at the same time. Moses knew how to flatter and make people feel as if they were wielding great power, even as he used them to create the illusion of popular support for his projects.

Even Hulan Jack, borough president of Manhattan in the late 1950's and early 1960's and a foxy politician himself, proved no match for Moses in the dickering over Lincoln Center. Moses had forged a vision: New York City as the world capital of culture. To take a stand against Lincoln Center meant being branded by Moses as anti-art, anti-culture, and grossly declassé. The most Jack could do was save a section of housing from the immense project as simply too much of an eviction to sell to constituents.[29]

The programs for slum clearance between 1945 and 1965 had taken a large toll in terms of family displacement, community disorganization, and loss of business and industry. Schwartz counted a displacement of between 100 and 200 thousand people from Manhattan and downtown Brooklyn (the main renewal areas), depending on how the process is viewed.[30] Reliance on re-housing the refugees in public-housing projects concentrated distraught families and individuals into small-er spaces, where they became "problems." The Housing Authority set up a social-services unit but was overwhelmed. A variety of methods were tried but the Authority had to settle for addressing grossly overt drug and prostitution activity.[31]

The land clearing had destroyed and weakened the community institutions which normally would have buffered the outfall of displacement: churches, political clubs, social clubs, merchants, and small factories. At the same time that the evictees lost their homes, they often lost their social anchors and their jobs. The prospect of replacing their jobs had been greatly diminished.

Some evictees were even relocated into city-owned tenements in worse slums than they had originally inhabited. These tenements had been acquired to be cleared eventually for later redevelopment. Thus, some evictees wound up displaced more than once and experienced extended uncertainty and a synergism of losses between the two displacements.[32]

Lopez in *Arctic Dreams*[33] and Stone in *Dreams of Amazonia*[34] related the history of European and American exploitation of vast wilderness areas and plans of exploitation, all driven by dreams, visions more bizarre than anything from a pipe or mushroom. The factories, homes, little stores, taverns—all these form an exploitable wilderness like the Arctic and the rainforest along the Amazon. The acme of this dreaming was the era of Robert Moses. Afterwards came the nightmares.

There is no doubt that Robert Moses inflicted great harm on the poor minority families and, possibly by himself, was responsible for the heroin epidemic of the 1950s and 1960s. But the health and crime statistics showed little or no effect of the disruption. The fundamental indicator of living and working conditions, active tuberculosis disease, continued its decline unabated. Violent crime such as murder, rape, and armed robbery simply followed population increase. Only heroin use showed that anything was amiss. Indeed, substance users formed the core of the pockets of new TB cases.

By the late 1960s, slum clearance had reached a standstill. What had been done during the previous two decades had strained public housing but did not cause any terrible outward signs of problems, especially problems which affected the other classes. The War on Poverty had created new organizations and funneled resources into poor neighborhoods. The black and brown neighborhoods watched the Southern civil-rights movement and waited for it to come north.

THE RISE OF COMMUNITY ORGANIZING

By 1968, the War on Poverty had been in operation only about four years but was yielding surprising results in public-health status, education, housing, and political participation of poor neighborhoods. In New York, by 1968, for example, the Tuberculosis Task Force looked on TB as possible to eliminate, just a matter of mopping up in the shrinking poverty pockets, especially among substance abusers (see Chapter 4). New fire companies were being opened, and fire inspections were keeping damage to a minimum. The Federal Model Cities programs of the mid-to-late 1960s included important tenant education modules on fire prevention, sanitation, and health.

Out of the multi-service centers, youth programs, senior-citizen organizations, churches, and clinics, organizing grew. Obstreperous political and community action grew. People from different neighborhoods and labor unions began visiting each other and pushing for needed programs along broad fronts. When the Vulcan Society (the organization of black firefighters) instituted a lawsuit against discriminatory hiring, a wave of broad support crashed down on City Hall. When Merrill Eisenbudd, Lindsay's first environmental commissioner, brushed aside an outcry about dead invertebrates coming out of the faucets in Harlem and the South Bronx, he didn't keep his position during Lindsay's next term.

By 1968, neither the local politicians nor the real-estate industry faced passive, disorganized low-income communities of color. Although the momentum began to slow by 1968, Sam Wright in Brownsville ignited the movement for community control of schools, and, in 1969, Herman Badillo, from a power base in the South Bronx, had a good run for the Democratic nomination for mayor (in 1973, he forced a run-off against Abe Beame). Voter-registration drives in the poor neighborhoods of Northern cities netted a rich harvest. In 1969, black mayors were elected in several cities, including Newark, just across the Hudson. The reins of power could end up in hands of the wrong color. In the view of politicians and the permanent government, something had to be done to develop poor neighborhoods and to disorganize the minorities and the poor. In this context, John Lindsay, who nearly lost his mayoralty in 1969, handed over vast powers to the New York City-Rand Institute, a public/private "thinktank."

THE NEW SLUM CLEARANCE

Although explicit policies of slum clearance ended in the late 1960s, the losses of both jobs and homes accelerated in the 1970s and remained rapid. Some abatement occurred during the 1980s but by 1990, job losses accelerated again[35] and housing overcrowding was at a very high incidence, about double that of 1970.[36] The poor communities suffered from a pincers movement with no relief or anchor. To our knowledge, no other urban scientists have seriously probed the withdrawal of municipal services from poor neighborhoods, although some have looked at various aspects of the loss of jobs.

The vision of the City Beautiful contains a rationale or assumption mentioned by Schwartz but more fully explored by Roberts[37]: that cities and their component neighborhoods have a life cycle. Indeed, Roger Starr supported his concept of "planned shrinkage" in terms of dying neighborhoods.[38] It is no secret that neighborhoods die because of public policies which kill them.

Successive mayors from Lindsay through Giuliani have enacted "slum" policies that make Robert Moses look good. They have cleared slums without any rebuilding policy, namely by targeting poor neighborhoods for the civilian version of firebombing. They reduced fire-control and fire-prevention resources to levels so inadequate that the effects even spilled over into the untargeted white middle-class neighborhoods. Jewish, Irish, and Italian neighborhoods which had thrived for nearly a century were dispersed into the suburbs. The political and social organizations based in these neighborhoods died and left the City armless, legless, and impotent. Between 1972 and 1980, we estimate that about two million people were displaced: 1.3 million whites documented by the Census as leaving the city (an unprecedented inter-census exodus) and about 600,000 African-Americans and Latinos driven out of their burned-out neighborhoods either to adjacent neighborhoods (for the very poor) or into the inner ring of suburbs (for those with some resources).

There is an extensive literature on migration and its disruptive impacts. South, for example, showed increased deviant behavior in communities with high rates of immigration or of emigration.[39] This disruption may lead to socioeconomic and behavioral deterioration. The community disruption from the Moses-era slum clearance programs, although documented as horrendous, was minor compared with the effects of policies of planned shrinkage which began in 1969. Fewer people were affected directly by the earlier clearance, and housing was built to replace what was demolished. But almost no housing replaced the 1970s destruction by planned shrinkage until about 1990. By then, hundreds of thousands of units had been burned or abandoned. A few tens of thousands of units were rehabbed to replace these, much too little, and much too late. The conditions which foster housing destruction remain in place even now, continuing to erode the remaining inadequate housing stock and generating increasing housing overcrowding and homelessness.

This new war on the poor had consequences which the previous planned and mitigated slum clearance did not: deterioration in public health, deterioration in public safety, and even serious decline in the life expectancy of elderly African-Americans citywide and of the young in particularly hard-hit communities. The housing destruction set contagious processes in motion which spilled over into middle-class neighborhoods, into the suburbs of the metropolitan region, and into the other metropolitan regions of the country. The following chapters depict the birth and growth of this nightmare.

2

BENIGN NEGLECT AND
PLANNED SHRINKAGE

DANIEL P. MOYNIHAN AND BENIGN NEGLECT

Not an arsonist at first glance, Daniel Patrick Moynihan burned down poor neighborhoods in cities across the country as surely as if he had doused them in kerosene and put a match to them. In January 1970, as President Nixon's advisor on urban and social policy, he sent the famous memo to the President which advised a stance of "benign neglect" and, key to this stance, used data on fire alarms and fires in New York City forwarded to him by the New York City/Rand Institute. Indeed, files obtained under a Freedom of Information Act lawsuit showed extensive correspondence between Moynihan and the Fire Project staff of the Rand Institute.[1] Fueled by the letters back and forth, Moynihan enthusiastically parroted the Rand misinterpretation of these data and gave the impression that a huge proportion of the alarms were "arson." Perhaps he was merely projecting his own intentions. In fact, alarms include fires in buildings, fires in means of transportation, fires in outdoor rubbish piles, emergencies requiring fire companies, false alarms, and emergencies to which other services have not responded in a timely fashion. Fires in buildings form only a portion of total alarms, and proven arson, even in slums, has never exceeded a small proportion of these. Moynihan's misrepresentation labeled the poor people of New York as lawless, pathological, and irredeemably locked into an antisocial behavior pattern.

The pathology Moynihan diagnosed from the picture of widespread "arson" led logically to his prescription for benign neglect and his broadcasting of the myth that large cities inherently cause social pathologies and should be made smaller. In recent years, Moynihan has reinterpreted what he meant by benign neglect, but in 1970 in the context of Nixon's Southern strategy and Spiro

Agnew's rhetoric, "benign neglect" could only have meant taking resources from poor urban minority communities. The actions of the Nixon Administration toward these communities included shifting money from the inner cities to the suburbs via block grants, dismantling the Model Cities programs, and violating the civil rights and civil liberties of organizations and individuals.

Since, to Moynihan, pathologies express themselves as malicious false alarms or arson, "benign neglect," when applied to fire service, meant not answering alarms in poor minority neighborhoods. In line with this philosophy, in 1978, Moynihan, as U.S. Senator, opposed federal housing construction efforts in the South Bronx burned-out zone by concluding: "People in the South Bronx don't want housing or they wouldn't burn it down. It's fairly clear that housing is not the problem in the South Bronx."[2]

The complete text of Moynihan's "benign neglect" memo was printed in the New York *Times* in January 1970.[3] Particular sections of this explosive document bear reproducing:

> You are familiar with the problem of crime. Let me draw your attention to another phenomenon, exactly parallel and originating in exactly the same social circumstances: Fire. Unless I mistake the trends, we are heading for a genuinely serious fire problem in American cities. In New York, for example, between 1956 and 1969 the over-all fire-alarm rate more than tripled from 69,000 alarms to 240,000. These alarms are concentrated in slum neighborhoods, primarily black. In 1968, one slum area had an alarm rate per square mile 13 times that of the city as a whole. In another, the number of alarms has, on an average, increased 44 per cent per year for seven years.
>
> Many of these fires are the result of population density. But a great many are more or less deliberately set. (Thus, on Monday, welfare protectors set two fires in the New York State Capitol.) Fires are in fact a "leading indicator" of social pathology for a neighborhood. They come first. Crime, and the rest, follows. The psychiatric interpretation of fire-setting is complex, but it relates to the types of personalities which slums produce. (A point of possible interest: Fires in the black slums peak in July and August. The urban riots of 1964-1968 could be thought of as epidemic conditions of an endemic situation.) . . .
>
> The time may have come when the issue of race could benefit from a period of "benign neglect." The subject has been too much talked about. The forum has been too much taken over to hysterics, paranoids, and boodlers on all sides. We may need a period in which Negro progress continues and racial rhetoric fades. The Administration can help bring this about by paying close attention to such progress—as we are doing—while seeking to avoid situations in which extremists of either race are given opportunities for martyrdom, heroics, histrionics, or whatever. Greater attention to Indians, Mexican-Americans and Puerto Ricans would be useful.

In this now-infamous memo, poor blacks and their families are portrayed as pathological, hate-filled, alienated and racist. Because of segregation, he also attributes racism to young educated middle-class blacks. They "catch" racism and other pathologies from their poor schoolmates and thereby become antisocial. According to the memo, the social pathologies of the poor blacks stem largely from female-headed households, and the antisocial behavior of the young black males "helps shape white racial attitudes," rather than the reverse.

The Rand Institute's correspondence with Moynihan provided the basis for his assertions that fires were the result of social pathology. Among the documents sent to Moynihan was Appendix B,[4] entitled *Incidence of Fire Alarms*, which gave Moynihan much of the wording for his memo's section on fire and arson. Appendix B blames a "substantial number of incidents" on behavior and asserts, "Among the most rapidly increasing alarm types in slums are false alarms and deliberately set fires." Alarm incidence is termed "an accurate and timely indicator of neighborhood physical and social conditions" and a "leading indicator of social change."

Rand paid great attention to racial composition of high-incidence and low-incidence areas: "These high-incidence neighborhoods are heavily Negro and Puerto Rican, mostly poor, with large numbers of poorly maintained and abandoned buildings. The neighborhoods unshaded, and shaded light blue and yellow [low-incidence areas], are overwhelmingly white and 'middle class.'"

Unsubstantiated statements in Appendix B accuse poor nonwhites of frequent arson. The authors asserted that set fires were almost as numerous then as "the traditional business of a fire department—residential and commercial fires, brush fires, accidents, and the like." "Typically, such 'nuisance' incidents do not arise out of carelessness or unavoidable accidents, but rather are the product of opportunity to create an incident and someone's desire to do so." These "nuisance incidents" are listed as fires in vacant buildings, abandoned cars, and rubbish piles. All are labeled as deliberately set without substantiation. In point of fact, many fires in abandoned buildings, cars, and large piles of rubbish are not deliberately set but can arise in a number of accidental ways. The Rand Appendix also never acknowledged the existence of landlord and business-owner arson. All arson is laid at the door of poor nonwhites, and nearly all fires are labeled arson.

Arson as an idea caught on in the late 1970s and became a political tool. Tenant groups and their allies pushed landlord arson as the big fire issue, and arson task forces were formed. The landlords and their allies made a big deal of tenant arson and arson-for-revenge or gang punishment. Huge amounts of time and money were drained by these efforts. Resources were made available to "fight arson" but not, unfortunately, to fight fires.

ROGER STARR AND PLANNED SHRINKAGE

"Planned shrinkage" was the New York City expression of Moynihan's "benign neglect." A form of triage, it dictated the withdrawal of essential services from sick neighborhoods which were seen as unable to survive or undeserving of survival. These services ranged from libraries to fire service to public transportation. Of course, the neighborhoods diagnosed as "sick" were all poor and nonwhite.

Roger Starr first articulated the theory of "planned shrinkage" in *Urban Choices: The City and its Critics* in 1966.[6] At that time, Starr had been executive director for a decade of the Citizens' Housing and Planning Council, a bogus "citizens' group," funded and governed by the real-estate industry. Starr cast himself as the rational, reality-based debunker of myths, prominent among them the "myth" of American community. He sneered at the thought of Americans living in communities. Consider the following quotes from the book's 1969 edition:

> Yet, no matter how lightly the word is used, the overtones of *community* refuse to die out, lending to the place or persons referred to, a significance they never earned. The overtones of the word suggest that, in the area described, people have thrown down their swords and spears; that they have created not only their own safety, but a web of love and kindness, understanding and mutual support, which it is sacrilege to tamper with. The careless abuse of the word *community* leads away from an understanding of the differences between people occupying a geographical area, and towards a veneration for kinship that may not even exist. The unearned veneration blocks changes that may, on other counts, be highly desirable. (pp 41–2)

> Provided only that a certain homogeneity of social class and income can be maintained, American communities can be disassembled and reconstituted about as readily as freight trains. (p 43)

> Since they have no property, their only marketable asset is hardship in a society pledged to eliminate that hardship which it is unable to ignore. Because this hardship is described to social workers and community organizers who are constitutionally disposed to believe the people they are listening to, and whose luck it is to listen only to the downtrodden and disadvantaged, it seems an immoral suggestion that some of the people displaced by urban renewal might just be exaggerating the sense of deprivation that they feel over their "lost homes." (p 46)

> We have advocated the continuation of urban renewal, in the course of which we may displace poor people to make room for middle-class people; and all in the hope of producing racially integrated models. We have recommended an increase in public housing on which we propose to spend far more money than ever before, urging extravagance as the way to provide more interesting design. We have urged dangerous flexibility in the civil-service system to provide stimulants for improved architectural design. We have urged taking an indeterminate number of children away from the homes of their natural parents or parent, to raise them in new,

small, pioneering institutions. We have conceded that some human city problems cannot be solved at all with knowledge now in hand. We have urged the expenditure of tremendous sums of federal money on sewerage systems and treatment plants. We have condoned the construction of new automobile highways that will destroy people's homes in the course of construction, and have scoffed at the possibilities of a greatly improved rapid transit system. (p 258)

These necessarily lengthy and numerous quotes reveal the ideology and techniques behind the selling of "planned shrinkage." He told a plausible story, a sheer fabrication, a theatrical selling of snake oil laced with poison. By denying the existence of the community social fabric and by evoking dysfunctional poor families, he helped provide the intellectual basis for massive demolition of the housing of the poor.

Roger Starr's ideology of sick communities did not become policy until 1976 when he was Mayor Beame's Commissioner of Housing Preservation and Development. Eventually, the outcry from black communities forced him from office, but by that time planned shrinkage had long been implemented and made part of municipal government culture.

A 1976 New York *Times* article characterizes Roger Starr's planned shrinkage proposal[5] :

The aim of such a policy, in the opinion of Roger Starr, the Housing and Development Administrator, would be to hasten the population decline already begun in these neighborhoods so that, ultimately, further cutbacks in city services could be concentrated in a limited number of areas.

This approach would be more efficient in the long run than continuing to "thin out services"—including police, firefighting, and subway services—in many areas across the city, according to Mr. Starr, who is urging consideration of the planned-shrinkage approach.

These recommendations on their face appear reasonable and humane, merely attempts to minimize the pain of service cuts required by municipal fiscal crises. They did not take into account, however, the huge numbers of people still living in these targeted neighborhoods—even after the burnout of the Bronx below Fordham Road, about as many people lived there as twice the population of Buffalo. And Starr also disingenuously pretended that "planned shrinkage" had played no role in the initial loss of population from these neighborhoods. In fact, what he proposed in 1976 was the coup de grace to neighborhoods which were victims of previous implementation of "planned shrinkage."

Particularly desirable in Starr's eyes was not repairing or rebuilding damaged housing. He urged letting the land lie vacant until a new use could arise. Among the new uses which he mentioned was industry.

Susan Roberts pulled together the sociology and urban studies literature on the concept of the city and the neighborhood life cycles and showed how this unproved notion led to "benign neglect" and "planned shrinkage."[7] In short, the life-cycle concept depicts cities and especially neighborhoods as organisms which grow, mature, age, and die. "Benign neglect" is a hands-off policy which allows neighborhoods to die on their own and proscribes resuscitation but allows unchanged levels of service. "Planned shrinkage" is a more aggressive policy of triage which actively looks for sick neighborhoods and pulls services from them to free the resources for healthy neighborhoods. Because the decline of a neighborhood is natural and inevitable, good public policy takes it into account and uses it. Because it is deemed natural and inevitable, no one seems responsible and nothing can be done to reverse it.

By 1969, legal urban renewal had come to a standstill because of entrenched resistance. Clearance of the housing of the poor had to proceed by other means, and "planned shrinkage" was that tool.

CLEARING LAND FOR INDUSTRY

In 1967, the Institute for Urban Studies of Fordham University published a report (*A Profile of the Bronx Economy*) with recommendations for "amelioration of the business climate in the Bronx." After noting the job losses, the report zeroed in on space availability as the crucial limitation for business and industry. Great was the lamentation: only 1% of the land was in light industry and only 1.6% in heavy industry. Moreover, the available plots were small and scattered. It asked the razing of the homes of 2,500 people in the South Bronx and their displacement into public housing to make way for industry. It called for relaxation of the zoning laws and of the building codes. It trumpeted the priority of industry over housing in land use conflicts. It called for designation of the South Bronx as a redevelopment area.[8]

In 1969, the New York City Department of Planning in its Master Plan for New York City described the South Bronx:

> It is an area of turbulence and change. . . . Frequent tenement fires force residents to move and leave gutted buildings or vacant lots. Residential densities are high, averaging 85 dwelling units an acre. Four-story walkups on 60-by-100 lots house as many as 21 families. Most of the housing—grim, crowded tenements—is concentrated between 134th Street and Bruckner Boulevard.

> The majority of residents are black and Puerto Rican. Mobility is high. Between 1960 and 1965, 64 percent of the black families in the Bronx and more than 75 percent of its Puerto Rican families moved. An estimated two-thirds to three-quarters of the dwelling units in the district will be vacated over the next five years.

This movement presents opportunities for needed industrial renewal if the City can act as change occurs.

"The South Bronx will be designated for industrial renewal, permitting the City to acquire small vacant parcels and empty buildings and to assemble sites large enough for growing manufacturing concerns. This would prevent the reoccupation of worn-out industrial buildings and lot-by-lot fixing up or replacement of burned-out tenements.[9]

Zones in Brownsville-East New York and East Harlem also received the "industrial" designation. Thus, one motivation for destroying the housing of large poor communities was to get land for industry. Again, the downturn in industry and the deindustrialization of New York was described as a natural phenomenon, divorced from both the national and global processes of which the loss of industry in the City was a local expression, and from the previous decades' policies of removing industry from Lower Manhattan. The burden of reviving industry in New York would fall on the poor who had the dubious taste to live on land that industry "needed."

CONTAGIOUS URBAN DECAY

Very early in their work, the Rand Institute staff had discovered that fires in poor neighborhoods had become a contagious disease on the housing stock. As the areas of high fire incidence spread, fire incidence rose within those areas. The Rand Fire Project staff knew by 1969 that the pattern of fire incidence in New York City had changed fundamentally. The fires ate away the housing in typical contagious pattern.[10]

Furthermore, in 1970, the Division Chief of the South Bronx, Charles Kirby, issued a report on the fire trends and background conditions in the South Bronx, arguing for the importance of new companies added just two years before in dealing with this rise in fire incidence. Under a workload arbitration, the Uniformed Firefighters Association and the Uniformed Fire Officers Association, under the leadership of a joint task force called the FLAME Committee, had forced the opening in 1968 of 16 fire companies in the ghetto neighborhoods, usually as second sections of existing overworked companies. The arbitration covered both engines and ladders. The Kirby Report noted that the opening of these companies would allow the City time to address the socioeconomic forces behind the growing fire incidence and its geographic spread, but it didn't stop there:

The major increases in fire companies recently added to the Bronx will assist in absorbing a large part of the expected fire rise. These units will also afford a

greater flexibility of Bronx operations. . . . These are capable administrative decisions and help us face our problems but not our causes.

As has been said 'trend is not destiny.' If we learn from examples of the past, a great
part of the expected fire rise can be averted. To do so rehabilitation must move forward at a greater rate than decomposition. Sanitation facilities in the Bronx must
be brought up to a level that exists in Manhattan; for example, the nonstructural-
to-structural-fire figures in the 11th Battalion are close to 1-to-2 while slum areas
of the Bronx are over 2-to-1. . . . There are many more physical and social changes
which must be planned to reverse the fire trend. If these are beyond the fiscal capa-
bilities of the City or inequitable with our economic structure, it does not relieve
us completely of our obligation to point up problems as we see and forecast them.
For this reason, I would recommend that a very high ranking member of the
Department be a full-fledged member of all New York City agencies dealing with
Housing, Redevelopment and similar functional groups.

It has been said that the major part of funds in the City should be allocated to
improvement of social conditions of the poor. The actual fires and the constant
threat of fire must surely be a devastating horror to people required to live in
houses in a deteriorating neighborhood. We also know that fire is a large component of the decay cycle and we can suspect that it adds to the uneasiness and inse-
curity of the poor. After years of fire experience, fire prevention and fire
investigation, I feel that it can be said that rather than being accidental, fire is largely a social problem and the Bronx has and will have its share of such problems.

Moynihan and Rand, who called fire a social indicator may seem to echo
Kirby, who called fire a social problem. Yet "social" means quite different things
in the two uses of the word. Moynihan and Rand accused the poor of arson and
mischief, but Kirby saw sanitation, housing, and economic development as part
of the social environment determining fire incidence and pattern.

The pace of urban decay suddenly increased with the 1968 rise of fire contagion (the simultaneous rise of fire incidence and spread of area of high fire incidence). Besides fire, another phenomenon destroyed homes in poor
neighborhoods, namely building abandonment. By 1969, the most densely
crowded neighborhoods, against intuition and logic, also hosted a growing number of empty building shells and partially occupied buildings. In most of these
"deaths," the landlord simply walked away, stopping all maintenance and not
paying the superintendent who, understandably, would also walk away when the
paychecks stopped. Because a report isn't filed every time a landlord walks, the
way a report is filed every time even one fire company responds to an alarm, the
incidence and geography of building abandonment went undescribed until the
late 1970's. The studies of Michael Dear in Philadelphia,[11] John Odland in
Indianapolis,[12] and The Women's City Club in New York[13] revealed that building
abandonment had become another contagious destroyer of the housing stock.

Dear described the contagious abandonment process in detail:

The process of abandonment as it operates in space. . .suggests an initial scattering of abandoned structures, characterized by the occurrence of many small groups of abandoned houses. With the passage of time, this pattern is intensified; the broad scatter is maintained, although the small groups now contain a greater number of structures. A two stage process is clearly suggested; the initial abandonments occur and later consolidation follows. . . . It suggests a 'leader-follower' sequence which resembles the propagation of a plant species or the diffusion of information. It is essentially a contagious sequence. . . . Only in very rare instances were larg[e] groups of abandoned buildings returned to the market. . . .

. . .[O]nce abandonment has begun it is likely to be very difficult to stop. It may become almost a selfsustaining process under the force of contagion. . .

It wasn't until 1970, when Owen Mortiz reported in the New York *Daily News* on the extent of building abandonment in the City ghettoes that the problem appeared on the urban-issues map. Neal Hardy, then Assistant City Housing Administrator, suddenly called for more federal funding to combat abandonment and predicted that sound areas would become "ghost-towns" as abandonment spread.[14] So it was clear that by 1970, the City knew about both fire and building abandonment contagion.

HOW RAND GUTTED THE
FIRE DEPARTMENT OF NEW YORK CITY

Let us now turn our attention to the men and women of the New York City-Rand Institute who, like the Rand Corporation technicians who gave us the false "body counts" and strategies for winning the Viet-Nam War, blandly manipulated fire death data, company response times, and fire-related destruction. Let us consider the actions of the behind-the-scenes, unaccountable team of technocrats from the New York City Rand Institute and the Fire Department: Bernard Gifford, Ed Ignall, Peter Kolesar, Warren Walker, Ed Blum, Grace Carter, Homer Bishop, and John T. O'Hagan.

If a medical device or drug is to be marketed, the Food and Drug Administration requires proof that the proposed treatments actually work and that they pose minimal risk to life and health. For public-policy prescriptions, no such tests are required. And this made the Rand fire-policy experiment possible. Nearly any plausible-sounding scheme can govern the fate of millions of people.

In medical treatment, efficacy is measured by how well the treatment returns a function or functions to normal. "Normal" is defined as a level and form of function characteristic of the healthy population. Sometimes defining which function indices to use as measures of efficacy arouses debate among the researchers, but the indices chosen must be tied to a real-life measure such as length of survival after treatment compared with length of survival without treatment, or level of disability after treatment compared with level of disability without treatment.

One of the first important decisions of the Rand Fire Project staff precluded the use of "global" measures of fire-service efficacy. "Global" measures include frequency and severity of fire damage, frequency of civilian fire fatalities and injuries, frequency and severity of firefighter injuries and line-of-duty deaths, and frequency and severity of domino effects where servicing of multiple fires during a single time frame causes slightly later fires to grow larger because of the Fire Department's inability to respond to the alarms swiftly and adequately. Instead, the staff decided to use "internal" measures: average response times of fire companies and average availabilities (the percent of time during which the company is not traveling to alarms or working at incidents).[15] This decision proved key to all that occurred later.

After choosing these limited measuring tools in 1969, the Fire Project undertook review of two policies: response policy and number and placement of companies. Let us first consider response policy which involves the number and kind of companies sent to alarms. In 1969, an alarm would receive a standard response of three engines, two ladders, and a battalion chief. That year, the Rand staff instituted scaled-back responses to alarms from fireboxes with high rates of false alarms (called "adaptive response").[16] Rand's aim was for stations to send nothing at certain times of day, but the firefighters objected, so, depending on how heavy fire traffic was, various less-than-standard numbers of companies were sent.

The scaling-back of response was also rapidly expanded through installation of voice fireboxes in place of the old simple pull-lever boxes. The new fireboxes were first placed in the South Bronx, East Harlem, and Brownsville. In time, all ghettoes received the Emergency Reporting System (ERS) boxes, and eventually all of Manhattan, the Bronx, and Brooklyn had them. The policy for these boxes was that if voice contact was not made between the person turning in the alarm and the fire department dispatcher, only one engine was sent. Policy was eventually changed so that during peak alarm periods, nothing was sent to no-voice alarms.[17]

The boxes were never truly independently evaluated (see the preface for a brief discussion of the Riverside Research Institute evaluation). Most people did not know how to use them and were not educated about them. They seem to behave like telephones in that when you press the activating button, you get ringing on the line. But you don't get an immediate dispatcher's voice. You have to wait until the dispatcher presses a button at the other end of the line and speaks. Most citizens don't know this, and many leave the box before the dispatcher speaks. In this way, many no-voice alarms occur which receive only one-engine responses!

Traffic noise makes these boxes nearly impossible to use rapidly. The dispatcher may speak to the caller but the caller has to say, "What? I can't hear you." Then they go another round while the dispatcher asks where the fire is yet again. Of course, when English is not the caller's primary language, turning in a fire alarm over these boxes can be a lengthy process. Although Spanish-speaking dispatchers are assigned to every shift, now significant portions of the population speak Chinese, Russian, Arabic, Haitian Creole, and many other languages which the dispatchers cannot accommodate quickly.

Very early on, it was clear that the ERS boxes attract false alarms. In an early experiment on the middle-class West Side of Manhattan, the number of false alarms zoomed specifically at the locations where the electromechanical fireboxes had been replaced by the ERS alarm boxes. Rand staff disguised this problem by labeling the false alarms "diverted alarms", and recommended rapid installation in the ghettoes.[18] Everywhere ERS boxes were installed, false alarm rates mushroomed.[19]

The idea behind the ERS boxes seemed logical: if someone can describe the situation to the fire dispatcher, the dispatcher can then send the appropriate number of each kind of company. If a single garbage can is on fire, one engine company could be dispatched to control the fire easily. In fact, legislators from the ghetto neighborhoods receiving the boxes were told that this method of turning in alarms would increase company availability. But the reverse was true: internal New York City-Rand Institute documents point to the ERS and its associated reduced response policies as mechanism for closing ghetto fire companies.[20]

By the end of 1975, standard response had been reduced to two engines, two ladders, and a chief; a bizarre system of non-standard response policies further reduced response to alarms in ghetto neighborhoods at certain times or under certain circumstances; a system of exchanging unfamiliar companies from less busy neighborhoods with familiar ghetto companies further reduced *effective* response; and a rise in no-voice ERS alarms due to expanded replacement of pull boxes with ERS boxes led to an increase in one-engine responses.[21] All of these changes translated into a higher frequency of inadequate initial responses to ghetto alarms.

The second major service change Rand shaped was the closing and permanent relocation of many fire companies (ten percent of the total), changes which largely reduced firefighting resources in poor, minority, overcrowded, high fire-incidence neighborhoods with very old housing. Table 2-1 lists the companies closed and moved in the several waves of cuts from 1972–1991. Figure 2-1 shows the 59 community districts of New York City and the traditional neighborhoods they comprise. As can be seen, the great majority of companies lost were from the traditionally poor neighborhoods. Those in white or integrated middle-class neighborhoods were often reopened.

The pattern of fire companies in the City in 1971 reflected the pattern of fires. The densest company placements arose in areas of the most frequent large fires in multiple dwellings. Failure to control fires in neighborhoods of multiple dwellings was serious: at best, it meant the destruction of large numbers of dwelling units; at worst, it would allow massive conflagrations in which many square blocks burned at once and firefighters could control further spread only by dynamiting a firebreak and thereby destroying even more dwelling units. Even without the knowledge that structural fires had become contagious in 1968, the Department knew from history that failure to provide rapid and adequate response to alarms risked both the housing stock and the lives of citizens and firefighters. Yet, the policy of planned shrinkage dictated running those risks, and Rand provided the pseudoscientific justification for cutting responses and cutting companies.

RAND'S DEADLY PSEUDOSCIENCE

The most complicated mathematical function in the two models which determined the shape of fire service in New York after 1972 is the square root. The Fire Department and Rand Institute represented these models to the citizenry as the latest, most innovative systems analysis—too complicated for citizens to understand. The sole criteria for closing or moving fire companies were response time and response distance. Response time was defined by Rand as the duration between the closing of the firehouse door and the arrival of the unit at the alarm box. Response distance was the simple geometric and geographic Euclidean map distance between the firehouse and the alarm box.[22] Response time is calculated in the Resource-Allocation Model as follows:

$$r_i = k_i \sqrt{\frac{A_i}{C_i - U_i}}$$

In words: response time in area i (r_i) is a constant (k_i) times the square root of area i (A_i) divided by the number of companies in area i (C_i) minus the unavailable companies (U_i).[23] The constant depended on the average velocity of the companies, and Rand *assumed* this to be 20 miles per hour during the early application of this model because they had no actual data. Of course, fire alarms are not uniform in time and peak sharply during the day, during certain days of the week, and seasonally. Average peak unavailability thus had to be calculated separately from average offpeak.

Unavailability depended on alarm rate and number of units sent to alarms. Because they did not bother to analyze fire records, the Rand fire project staff simply *assumed* that average offpeak alarm rate was 40% that of average peak and that two engines and two ladders were sent to alarms, although at that time three engines and two ladders were the standard alarm assignment until late 1974.[24] Several times in their reports, the Rand staff members explain that they calculated a number, made an assumption, or constructed a relationship because analyzing the real data would have been "too laborious"![25]

Rand then sorted the neighborhoods of the City into seven hazard categories. By use of the Resource-Allocation Model, they equalized response time between areas of like hazard designation. If an area had a lower-than-average response time for its hazard designation, it lost one company or more to bring it close to the average.[26] This process is known to engineers as suboptimalization because it degrades the better areas, rather than improving the worse ones.

For the 1975 cuts and thereafter, the Department coupled this Resource-Allocation Model with another model, the Firehouse-Siting Model. The Resource-Allocation Model determined which areas would lose companies, and the Firehouse-Siting Model determined which company or companies would be cut from each designated area. The Firehouse-Siting Model also uses nothing more mathematically difficult than the square root:

$$T(D) = 2\sqrt{D/a} \qquad \text{if } D \leq 2D_c$$
$$= V_c/a + D/V_c \qquad \text{if } D > 2D_c$$

where a = acceleration V_c = cruise velocity

D = distance T = travel time

D_c = distance to cruise velocity

In words, travel time for a given distance is two times the square root of the distance divided by acceleration rate if the distance is less than or equal to twice the distance needed to get to cruise velocity. Travel time is cruise velocity divided by the acceleration rate plus the distance divided by cruise velocity if the distance is more than twice the distance needed to get to cruise velocity. Distances were calculated by simple geometry and represent those between firehouses and *alarm boxes*.[27]

The Firehouse-Siting Model would look at each area on the Resource-Allocation Model's "hit list" and estimate average travel times for the area before any cuts and after hypothetical cuts and redrawing of the remaining companies' service areas to fill the service hole(s). The company whose removal resulted in the lowest average travel time of the hypothetical removals would be the one to be closed or permanently relocated.

Both Rand models contain many flaws of early ecological models: simplistic assumptions, omission of other simultaneous impacts, baseless assigning of a value distribution to a phenomenon, and the combination of an inadequate data base with inappropriate analysis and interpretation of the data. Table 2-2 contrasts Rand's simplistic assumptions with the complicated realities. Table 2-3 lists some of the neighborhood-specific variables Rand omitted from its models as well as typical workload policies which confounded the models. Finally, table 2-4 includes many of the policy changes in New York City from 1972–1976 which increased firefighting time per fire- or real-fire-alarm rate. Each of the factors in these tables held the potential for affecting company availability, velocity, distance, and effective service-area geometry.

The models projected only the time required to get from the firehouse to the alarm box, not to the burning building, and certainly not to the first stream of water on the fire. The difference in time between arrival at the alarm box and the first stream of water on a fire may range from two to ten minutes. Table 2-5 highlights the differences between fighting a fire in a tenement and fighting one in a one-family home. Longer additional times characterize overcrowded, poor neighborhoods, for obvious reasons, and the potential for both loss of life and loss of homes is greater in these areas than in others, partly because of fire-spread rate and partly because of the greater fuel loads due to the overcrowding.

"RAND LACKED REAL DATA"

To implement even these simple models, Rand should have acquired real data. The Resource-Allocation Model depended on the system of hazard regions and the seven hazard classes. The classes are:

1. valuable commercial

2. fireproof high-rise office

3. large industrial with lumberyards and oil tanks

4. high-density high fire-hazard residential

5. lower-density less-hazardous residential

6. mixed multi-story and one- or two-story frame

7. one- or two-story frame

Assignment to the classes allegedly depended on the fire and explosion hazards presented by the neighborhoods. Yet when the neighborhoods assigned by Rand to the same hazard class are considered, the data on which these class assignments were based aren't obvious. East Flatbush in Brooklyn and Astoria in Queens were placed in the same hazard class as Riverdale in the Bronx although the prevalent housing types, population densities, and presence of special hazards such as oil-tank farms were quite different in the three neighborhoods. Greenwich Village and Chelsea-Murray Hill (wealthy areas) were placed in hazard class 1 (valuable commercial) although the buildings and population densities were similar to the Westside and Inwood. The data on the likelihood and potential severity of fire and explosion hazard in the various neighborhoods were either not acquired, or not used properly for an objective hazard classification.

Rand's hazard regions were vast and so heterogeneous as to be essentially meaningless. The classification scheme failed to take spatial heterogeneity into account and led to underservice of areas of greater-than-average fire-incidence ("hot spots") within each region. Fire service cannot be designed for either geographic or temporal averages.

The only real data Rand acquired was firefighting-unit response time. In order to develop the formulae for the Firehouse-Siting Model, time and distance data were needed. Rand timed 2,000 responses by 15 units.[28] That sounds like a lot of data. However, eleven of the fifteen were in Lower Manhattan below 14th Street and two each in Brooklyn and Queens. Thirteen were ladder trucks and two battalion-chiefs' cars. No data were acquired on engines. Thus, both the geography and the unit types failed to sample the City properly.

What Rand then did with this non-representative data further guaranteed that whatever model was developed could not adequately serve the neighborhoods: Rand smoothed the data by plotting average response times against distance. This kind of smoothing is only acceptable during the exploratory phase of data analysis to get the basic underlying shape of the data. It is not an acceptable basis on which to build a prescriptive model for a life-support-system-like fire-control service. The Fire Department itself had timed several units just before Rand intruded into the scene and had seen that the velocity and response time of each timed unit depended on time of day and season and on incidents, accidents, and events which change traffic-flow rate.[29]

The entire Rand system of allocating fire-control service for New York City in the early-to-mid-1970's involved averaging and suboptimalization. Hazard regions of below-average response time for their classification were targeted for cuts by the Resource-Allocation Model; these response times were averaged over huge hazard regions which were in reality nonhomogeneous both in their demand for fire control service and in their potential for serious fire spread and explosion. This model used average and peak-average availabilities and never the smallest credible availability or smallest historic availability. The Firehouse-Siting Model was based on average response times for given distances and yielded average travel times for an area. Creation of a system based on such averages is not acceptable even for something as frivolous as delivery of beauty-parlor supplies, let alone delivery of fire-control service, for the simple reason that any area above average will be underserved. By the statistical Law of Large Numbers, if there are a large number of areas (over 200 engine response areas, for example), approximately half of the areas will be at least slightly above average and some will be outside the broad crest of the "bell-shaped" curve (well above average). Rand's use of averages in this way ensured gross underservice to a large number of neighborhoods. In particular, all neighborhoods at the boundaries of fire-company response areas necessarily suffered underservice due to their above average distances.

Rand's use of these models also ensured that the neighborhoods with the densest placement of firefighting resources would be the losers. These neighborhoods had dense resources because of the historic and projected demand for fire service, based on global measures such as fire incidence, lives lost, households de-housed, and firefighter workload. The Rand models, based largely on calculated internal measures of fire service, prescribed policy and actions opposite to those prescribed by the analysis of global measures.

The Rand staff itself knew that what they were doing was both bad policy science and unethical. In 1972 or 1973, Rand's Ed Ignall wrote an undated memo to ten people in the Rand Fire Project and the Fire Department (Arthur Swersey, Richard Urbach, Ken Rider, Mei Ling, Joan Held, Elmer Chapman, Frank Ronan, Homer Bishop, Ed Blum, and Hope Wong) with copies to seven other Rand or Fire Department staff members of note (Grace Carter, Warren Walker, Pete Kolesar, Jack Hausner, Tom Crabhill, Sandy Stevenson, and Rae Archibald) in which he proposed using actual fire records which report property damage and correlating the damage with the response distance. He wanted to construct the relationships between distance and damage with 1968–1969 data and validate them with 1970–71 data. Uneasy with the Resource-Allocation Model and purely internal measures of fire service, he asked the essential question: what is a minute of response time worth?

Ignall listed difficulties in relating damage to distance:

First: we do not have response times. The best we can do are Euclidean distances from an alarm box near the incident(s) to the house of the first arriving engine and the house of the first arriving ladder. . . .

Second: we do not have good measures of the extent of fire when fire companies arrive. . . .

Third: Delays in discovering fires are sometimes long, sometimes short. . . .

Fourth: Some fires grow quickly, others grow slowly. . . .

He discussed in great detail how local conditions influence unit speed and how a unit is not always in its house when its alarm comes in. He concluded: "Effects like these can cripple a naive approach to estimating the value of response time." Then he further detailed local conditions which may influence the speed with which alarms are turned in.

Thus, although nearly everyone of importance within the Rand Fire Project and the Fire Department knew of the technical and ethical objections to use of calculated average response time and of the need to correlate it with some global measure of fire service, fire-company permanent relocations and closings proceeded on the basis of the unvalidated Resource Allocation Model and, later, on the unvalidated Firehouse Siting Model. The Resource Allocation Model provided the sole basis for the first round of fire-company eliminations and permanent relocations in November 1972. The affected companies (Table 2.1) served high fire incidence, overcrowded, poor minority neighborhoods such as Brownsville and the South Bronx. Both rounds of cuts in 1974 also relied solely on the Resource-Allocation Model and again targeted the neighborhoods in greatest need of fire-control service. Rand Institute and the Fire Department seduced many local minority politicians, such as then Manhattan Borough President Percy Sutton into supporting the cuts by telling them that the ERS fireboxes would make up for the reduced resources by allowing more efficient use of the remaining resources and by "proving" that the resource reduction would not reduce response time significantly. This proof relied solely on constructions of response time by the Resource-Allocation Model. Because of the antipathies between minority communities and the uniformed services, laying off firefighters did not receive much resistance from local politicians who lumped firefighters together with police.

The 1975, 1976, and 1988–89 cuts relied on both the Resource-Allocation and the Firehouse-Siting Models. Again, the great majority of the cut or moved companies lay in poor minority neighborhoods, but a few were in integrated areas in the process of gentrifying. Some of these integrated neighborhoods, unlike the resource-poor neighborhoods before them, had the political clout and the nose for "something rotten" to fight the cuts and to enlist experts to expose the inadequacies of the Rand models and their implementation. Thus, the only fire companies reopened were those closed in the post-1974 rounds of cuts and were primarily in racially integrated areas of economic diversity that promised gentrification.

HUD EXPERIMENTS ON HUMAN POPULATIONS

By 1974, the Rand Institute had achieved close ties with the U.S. Department of Housing and Urban Development (HUD) and received grants for creation and refinement of models such as the Firehouse-Siting Model. In return, the models were turned over to HUD to "sell" to municipalities. Another thinktank, Public Technologies Inc., had developed similar models for emergency service deployment under HUD funding, which were also "sold" to municipalities.[30]

The message from HUD to the cities was "Less is more." Cities learned how to target minority neighborhoods and break civil-service unions behind a shield of equations and graphs which "proved" that emergency service would not suffer from the resource reductions. A large number of cities bought into these models and implemented them: Denver, Wilmington, Hartford, Yonkers, Jersey City, St. Louis, Hoboken, Tacoma, Washington, and Tampa, and others. The City Hall of Jersey City burned down after implementation of the models, as did major portions of its poor neighborhoods.

This HUD approach continued through the Nixon, Ford, and Carter administrations and beyond. Under the Democratic administration of Jimmy Carter, the Assistant Commissioner of HUD for Science and Public Policy was Donna Shalala, who later became the Secretary of Health and Human Services in the Clinton Administration. In the mid-1970s, Dr. Shalala had been the director of the Municipal Assistance Corporation, the New York State entity which oversaw the budget cuts during the New York city fiscal crisis of 1975. She had encouraged Fire Department cuts along with cuts in garbage collection and housing-code enforcement (all interacting to accelerate destruction of low-cost housing) and espoused the idea of the City as a laboratory for innovative sweeping experiment in government and services. According to a 1982 *Report of the President's Commission for the Study of Ethical Problems in Medicine and Biomedical and Behavioral Research*, never in her brief tenure at HUD did Dr. Shalala acknowledge that the public policies which she promulgated and implemented could constitute experiments on human populations:

> The Department of Housing and Urban Development (HUD) is the only other Federal agency conducting research with human subjects that does not have formal

regulations for the protection of human subjects. In HUD's initial response to the Commission's inquiry, Donna Shalala (Assistant Secretary for Policy Development and Research) stated that except for a study co-sponsored with HEW, involving the testing of an aversive additive in paint to deter children from eating paint chips, HUD 'has never sponsored any human-subject or biomedical studies.' Moreover, Dr. Shalala challenged the statement in the National Commission's report that HUD's 'housing-allowance experiment' constituted research with human subjects.[31]

When confronted with criticisms of the inadequate fire-service models being sold to municipalities by HUD, Shalala's response was:

> The Rand work has been recognized by awards from several professional societies. The Office of Policy Development and Research has had the Rand work independently evaluated. These evaluations found the research of high quality and useful for some local government decision-makers. [32]

She also had the Urban Institute perform a routine hatchet job on the criticisms, and because a seemingly technical "answer" was rendered, she decided to put the issue to bed. The models promoted by Shalala continued their mass destruction. Indeed, Alan Siegel, Director of HUD's Division of Community Development and Management Research, wanted no discussion of the quality of the Rand work by policy and decision-makers and wrote to us in 1976: "Concerning the final issue of the models' scientific quality, I believe the proper forum for challenging scientific quality exists in organizations of technical and scientific peers."[33] Thus did HUD dispose of the troublesome question of the potential harm of its prescribed treatments for sick cities.

The Rand/HUD experiment on human subjects makes the famous Tuskegee Institute study on syphilis seem humane and small. The Rand/HUD team would directly and indirectly kill thousands and permanently disable millions of metropolitan residents across the country.

Table 2-1 FIRE COMPANY CLOSINGS, 1972–1991

BOROUGH	NEIGHBORHOOD	NO. OF REMOVED COMPANIES
Manhattan	Lower East Side	4
	Lower West Side	3 (2 restored)
	Times Square	1
	Upper West Side	2
	Harlem	3
Brooklyn	Brownsville	6
	Bedford-Stuyvesant	2
	Crown Heights	1
	Greenpoint	2 (1 restored)
	Park Slope	2 (1 restored)
	Red Hook	1
	Brooklyn Heights	1
Bronx	South Bronx	7 (1 restored)
	City Island	1 (restored)
Queens	Flushing	1
	Richmond Hills*	1
	Rockaway	2
	Stapleton	1
	Tottenville	1 (restored)

Total: 42 areas affected, 34 permanently.
(Only one of the restored companies was in a poor area.)

*This company was closed and reopened twice.

Table 2-2 MODEL ASSUMPTIONS VS. REALITY

ASSUMPTION 1: Unchanging ratios of types of alarms.

REALITY: Rapid changes both citywide and within areas. Physical and social instability leads to rapid changes

MODEL: Resource allocation

ASSUMPTION 2: Predictable alarm rates.

REALITY: Rates highly variable from year to year

MODEL: Resource allocation

ASSUMPTION 3: Service times independent of each other and of state of system.

REALITY: Relocation of units to alien areas increases service times. Exhaustion of firefighters increases service times. Dispatching delays occur during peaks

MODEL: Resource allocation

ASSUMPTION 4: Availability is stable.

REALITY: Massive changes in availability with cuts

MODEL: Both resource allocation and firehouse siting

ASSUMPTION 5: Very low probability of all units busy in area.

REALITY: Even boroughwide unavailability has occurred since April 1975

MODEL: Both resource allocation and firehouse siting

ASSUMPTION 6: All alarms answered from firehouse.

REALITY: Alarms regularly answered from field, especially during peaks in high-alarm area

MODEL: Both resource allocation and firehouse siting

Table 2-3 LOCAL VARIABLES OMITTED FROM THE MODELS

1. Potential for fires to spread between buildings
2. Hydrant pressure and maintenance
3. Design of the streets
4. Parking customs (double parking, parking at hydrants)
5. Presence of special hazards (natural gas tanks, pipelines, etc,)
6. Variable traffic patterns
7. Arson rate
8. Age structure of population: the very old and very young are especially susceptible to fire-injury and death
9. Special seasonal fire characteristics such as brush fires on Staten Island and use of heaters and stoves in areas of many heating violations
10. Access to means of turning in alarms reliably
11. Population density and changes in population density
12. Spatial and temporal patterns of fire occurrence on the neighborhood level. For example: Harlem and the affluent Upper West Side were lumped into a single "hazard region."

WORKLOAD POLICIES CONFOUNDING THE MODELS

1. In busy areas, the nearest fire company was not always the one dispatched to the alarm. A less busy one may have been sent
2. Companies are not available during their two-hour rest after a big fire or after a rapid series of small ones
3. "Interchange" exchanged busy with less busy companies to even out the workload. This resulted in degraded service because of lack of familiarity with the area
4. In mid-1970s, relocation mainly between ghettos

Table 2-4 POLICY CHANGES WHICH INCREASED SIZE OF FIRES OR ALARM RATE, 1972-1976

1. Closing or permanently relocating companies from high-fire areas
2. No-voice contact on ERS boxes gets at most one engine
3. 1972–1974: Less than standard responses to ghetto alarms
4. 1975 manning reduction: 5 to 4 on engines; 6 to 5 on ladders
5. Reliance on firefighters tired from mandatory overtime
6. Understaffing in dispatch centers delays response
7. 1974: reduction by one engine in standard response
8. Dispatchers and battalion chiefs can no longer call automatic higher alarms but are pressured to "special-call" units one by one
9. Cuts in trash collection lead to more trash fires
10. Cuts in building inspections lead to more fire violations
11. Understaffing of fire marshals hampers arson investigation
12. No more inspection for repair of fire damage led to building abandonment
13. Cuts in hydrant inspection and repair led to a high percentage of defective hydrants

Table 2-5 FIREFIGHTING AT TENEMENT AND 1-FAMILY HOME

FACTOR	TENEMENT	1-FAMILY HOME
	5-story, 20-family 35'x75' attached	25'x35' detached
1st engine arriving	3 minutes	4 minutes
Hose stretch	6–10 lengths	3 lengths
Forcible entry	many locks steel door	one lock window or wood door
Time from arrival to water on fire	3–8 minutes*	1–2 minutes
Life hazard	several families	1 family
Escape	cannot jump	can jump to ground
Spread potential	between apartments between buildings	none
Laddering problems	no rear rescue double park or overhead cables prevent front rescue	none
Inhabitants per engine (1975)	34–44,000	17–25,000
Special problems	frequent building collapse	none

*Delays common in multiple-dwelling areas from blocked hydrants, defective hydrants, and delayed forcible entry.

Figure 2-1 THE 59 COMMUNITY DISTRICTS OF NEW YORK

The important neighborhoods which these districts comprise are as follows:

MANHATTAN
1: Lower West Side
3: Lower East Side
4 & 5: Times Square
7: Upper West Side
10: Central Harlem
11: East Harlem

BRONX
1, 2 , 3, 6: South Bronx
10: City Island
4, 5: West Bronx

QUEENS
7: Flushing
8,9,12 junction: Richmond Hills
14: Rockaway
4: East Elmhurst/Corona
1: Astoria

BROOKLYN
1: Greenpoint/Williamsburg
3: Bedford-Stuyvesant
4: Bushwick
6: Red Hook/Park Slope
2: Brooklyn Heights
8: Crown Heights North
16, W. 5: Brownsville

STATEN ISLAND
1: Stapleton/New Brighton
3: Tottenville

3

A PLAGUE ON HOUSES
CONTAGIOUS FIRES

FIRE BECOMES A PARASITE

Testifying in 1976 before the New York State Senate Subcommittee on Police and Fire Protection in New York City, newly retired Deputy Chief George Freidel called the fires "a metastasing cancer on the City." In 1970, Neil Hardy, the Assistant Commissioner of Housing, had viewed housing abandonment as a spreading epidemic: "If it isn't stopped, now sound neighborhoods will become ghost towns." In the 1970s, the language of the civil servants charged with housing preservation borrowed words and phrases from disease medicine and epidemiology. By 1980, op-ed writers also cast their fears in disease and epidemiologic metaphors, although germ and cancer cells were not the triggering mechanism. To these writers and civil servants, fires and abandonments had become contagious, facilitating each other as HIV-infection facilitates tuberculosis.

Fires have always been contagious, but, before 1968, an "immunization program" kept epidemics at bay.[1] Fires became virulently epidemic in 1968. Before then, a large fire ushered in a period of lower-than-average fire incidence in that area because fire-prevention activities by municipal agencies focused there. Still, citywide, the number of structural fires per year grew consistently (figure 3-1). After 1968, fire damage failed to trigger targeted agency action. The damage instead marked the area as neglected and negligible, and fire disease infected the area, eroding the housing stock.

This contagion unfolds as follows: A building in which a structural fire "gets out of hand" because of fire-service reductions is often subsequently abandoned, becoming a focus for vandals, psychopathic arsonists, or serving as a "shooting gallery" for addicts. One abandonment on the block may lead directly to others, if only from the spread of fires from vacant to occupied buildings. More typically, after a nearby burnout, absentee landlords withdraw maintenance in preparation for abandoning their buildings, making them more susceptible to fires. The overcrowding and the age of buildings in poor neighborhoods requires significant attention from municipal agencies and proper maintenance by the landlords to keep fires small in both number and size. In the years after 1968, as fire damage accumulated, fire incidence accelerated accordingly, in a vicious circle.[2]

To epidemiologists, a truly contagious phenomenon, including propagation, occurs when a diseased individual passes the infection, on average, to more than one susceptible. The probability of that happening depends heavily on the density of susceptibles around the diseased. One can easily see how this disease model transfers to neighborhood fires.

The following are characteristics of propagation and epidemics:

1. Epidemics often show an S-shaped pattern of rise in "cases" over time, with a crest and then a precipitous decline.

2. Initial concentration of the phenomenon ("cases") within the areas fostering susceptibility.

3. Clustering of "cases" in time and space at several scales of time and geography (day, week, season, year; building, block, neighborhood, city).

4. The further along in the growth of the epidemic, the less amenable the process to prevention and control.

5. Sociogeographic corridors between areas of high concentration of susceptibles so that one area of high incidence can seed others.

6. Three modes of spread: spatial, hierarchical, and along networks (to be explained below).

7. Increased virulence of "cases" late in the epidemic, during the decline phase. This increased virulence may lead to either hyperendemicity (high but stable incidence) or to a secondary epidemic eventually if prevention and control measures are inadequate.

8. Population-density dependence so that a dense population will have more "cases" per unit population (higher incidence) than a sparse population, and that a critical density of susceptibles is also reached.

9. Large areas with conditions fostering susceptibility, i.e. raising the density of susceptibles.

For professionals and very curious laypersons, details of disease dynamics and of medical geography can be found in several textbooks.[3, 4, 5]

Let us examine the population characteristics of structural fires in New York City between 1968 and 1990 and compare them with our list of markers for contagion and epidemic spread. We shall concentrate our attention on 1972 to 1978, a period of rising, extremely high, and initial crashing structural-fire incidence.

S-SHAPED INCIDENCE PATTERN

Figure 3-1 displays the number of fires per year from 1959 to 1986.[6] The S-shape of this curve's rise resembles that of many disease epidemics such as measles, pre-Salk-vaccine polio, and Asian flu: slow rise, inflexion point, and rapid rise. The epidemic peak, 1974–1977, coincided with the deepest cuts in firefighting resources, with 1976 as the absolute epidemic crest.

The number of fires does not tell the whole story because the size of the fires may have changed over the course of the epidemic. We developed a damage index which took both number and size of fires into account.[7] This damage index (Figure 3-2) tells a slightly different story. Although the number of fires during the post-1977 period quickly declined, the damage declined more slowly.

Note that the damage index improved with the 1969 opening of the ghetto companies required under the FLAME Committee arbitration and began deterioration immediately following the 1972 company relocations and eliminations. The deep dip in 1964 resulted from a massive prevention program with over a million inspections at its core. *Mirabile dictu:* fire service indeed determines fire damage.

Another way of looking at fire damage trends is to look at insurance losses due to fires. Before the 1975 destaffing, each additional loss of property covered by the FAIR Plan increased the amount lost by an average of only $3,638; after destaffing, this average loss rose to $5,915, a rise of 63%. The number of losses also rose, so that the FAIR Plan suffered an excess annual claim payment of about $20 million. The FAIR Plan was created by legislation to assure access to insurance for owners of ghetto property: Fair Access to Insurance Rates. (One of us, Roderick, worked for the Plan and acquired these data.)

Another index, controllability of the fires, looks at fire size independent of number of fires. Figure 3-3 displays the controllability index for 1968 to 1990. Note the severe erosion toward the late 1980's.[8] This index shows how many alarm assignments were dispatched to control the fires. The anomaly of "better controllability" during the height of the epidemic occurred largely because of system saturation during peak periods. Companies could not be dispatched as needed because of non-availability due to extreme clustering of fires in time, which drained large areas of fire companies during the epidemic crest. A miracle occurred: multiple-alarm fires declined in frequency, as whole neighborhoods burned. The official statistics looked great.

Figures 3-1 and 3-2 indicate that the fire dynamic of the post-1968 era satis-
fied the condition of S-shaped pattern of build up to a peak and a crash; and
Figure 3-3, of increased virulence after the epidemic crest.

CONCENTRATION IN SUSCEPTIBLE AREAS

Mapping social and housing measures such as population density, index of extreme
housing overcrowding, percent of the population on public assistance, percent living
in poverty, average number of violations per housing unit, age of the housing, and
other related measures shows satisfaction of condition number 2. These measures
showed concentrations in 1970 in particular neighborhoods, the traditional slums of
New York such as Harlem, East Harlem, the Lower East Side, Brownsville, Bedford-
Stuyvesant, Williamsburg, and the South Bronx.

Mapping of structural fire alarms, hours of engine worktime, serious fires (fires
requiring at least three engines and two ladders for control), relocation time (hours
spent by alien units in the neighborhood firehouses to cover for the neighborhood
units out working at long, serious fires) and other indices of fire activity reveal the
concentration of fires and fire damage in high-population-density neighborhoods of
aged housing in 1970, as part of the initial, pre-cut conditions. Indeed, such maps
formed the background of Moynihan's "benign neglect" memo. As fires increased
after 1972 toward the 1976 crest, this clustering phenomenon intensified.

Shortfall of local service should result in "relocation," the external supply of
fire companies from the other neighborhoods. Clustering of relocation consumption indicates how the clustering of fires in an area renders the available
local-service supply inadequate. Table 3-1 displays for 1972–76 the mean hours
of external worktime and two indices of clustering, dispersion and "patchiness,"
applied to externally supplied worktime. Lloyd's Index of Patchiness contrasts
patches of clusters against the background density.[9] The fall in the Index after
1973 does not mean a decline in clustering of relocation hours but a rise in the
background as the epidemic spread from the epicenters. The rise in dispersion
shows the continued increase in clustering per se.

Engine dispersion declined in 1976. When we looked more closely at what
was happening that year, we found that the Fire Department had strangled the
ghettoes and ceased to send relocation service as needed. Thus, local-service
shortfall was not being totally compensated for by external service, and necessarily the clustering of fires meant clustering of fire damage and loss of homes.

Figure 3-4 maps structural fires on single blocks in Bushwick (Brooklyn) in
September and December 1976. We divided Bushwick into Regions I–VI. In

September, the clustering clearly centered in region III, with one block having 13 fires. Region III had 52 fires in September and region IV, 19. By December, the largest block cluster had moved to region IV (8 fires). Region III still had many fires (33) and region IV, a much smaller area, was up to 22 fires, only one of which was a single fire on a block. The clustering and higher numbers had spread from one region to another. In May 1976, region IV had had 6 fires, only 2 of which were on the same block. As with an epidemic, the rising intensity of case clustering went along with the rise in number of cases.

Fire numbers alone don't tell the whole clustering story. Figure 3-5 shows average engine-house annual worktime in hours from 1972 to 1974 graphed against the Index of Extreme Housing Overcrowding for the community districts of the Bronx.[10] By 1974, the concentration of hours in the South Bronx districts (1, 2, 3, 6) had reached saturation, i.e. the companies could give no more time during periods of peak demand. The flattening of the line at high indices of extreme housing overcrowding reflects this saturation. Notice also that high service demand spread to districts 4 and 5, in the West Bronx, adjacent to the original high-demand districts. In 1972, each of these two districts used about 500 hours of engine worktime on average; by 1974, the average engine was working 750–900 hours.

CLUSTERING OF CASES IN TIME AND GEOGRAPHY

These geographically clustered fires which determine the geographically clustered hours of service clump in time as well as by year, by seasons, by day of week, and by time of day. Certain hours of the day account for a larger proportion of the daily total number of fires. A few hours, a few days, or a couple of months of inadequate service can chart a neighborhood's fate. Because of the greater number and size of fires during winter (due to low indoor humidity and to use of space heaters and holiday lights), dwelling loss and fire deaths are inversely correlated with outdoor temperature: the lower the temperature, the worse the fire losses. The increased drain on fire service in winter is reflected in the greater frequency of higher-alarm fires. Extra alarm assignments per month also inversely correlate with outdoor temperature.

Interaction of clustering in time and space means that blocks, individual neighborhoods, contiguous neighborhoods, and whole boroughs experience peak-activity periods. Clustering of fires geographically and temporally implies that large numbers of homes are damaged in a short time, that new epicenters of spread arise rapidly, and that firefighting resources "dry up" during the times and in the places of greatest need.

AS THE EPIDEMIC INCREASES,
CONTROL IS THWARTED

As clustering intensified, prevention and control efforts were rendered less and less adequate (condition 8). Because control (keeping fires as small as possible) is the most important component of prevention, given the triggering of contagion by large fires, effective prevention declined as clustering intensification led to gross imbalance between supply of and demand for firefighting resources.

CORRIDORS OF SPREAD

The Bushwick maps show the existence of corridors of spread between the regions of a neighborhood such that simple geographic proximity to an epicenter exposes nearby susceptible areas. However, relocation policies of the FDNY established spread between widely separated ghettoes. The FDNY truncated relocation service so that ghettoes served and competed with each other for firefighting resources. Thus, the saturating of resources because of seasonal and time-of-day peak occurrences of fires was borne largely by the ghettoes via FDNY policies dictating which units relocate to which neighborhoods.[11]

HIERARCHICAL, SPATIAL, AND NETWORK SPREAD

The fire phenomenon would have been limited if the company-relocation policies had been left alone. With the subversion of relocation policies, the FDNY introduced what medical geographers calls "network spread" into the picture. By reducing local firefighting resources to levels below those needed during peak periods and relying on relocation to make up for the shortfall, the FDNY changed the system from one of many independent little neighborhood fire departments to a vast citywide interdependent network.[12] High fire incidence spread across the truncated section of the network and spilled over into "good" neighborhoods whose firefighting resources had to be tapped when those of the ghettoes were so grossly inadequate as to pose risk of spread from building to building. The fire control resources of the "good" areas would thereby stretch thin during peak periods and fires would grow large and damaging even in the "good" areas. Thus, widely separated neighborhoods felt the impact, in much the same way that a harp string reverberates along its entire length when plucked at a single point.

Hierarchical spread is the most difficult of the contagion concepts. Neighborhoods vary in susceptibility and domination according to their total populations, population densities, housing conditions, socioeconomic factors, and historic relationships. Hierarchical spread refers to the cascading effect of high fire incidence from the most densely populated, most susceptible area to somewhat less densely populated, slightly less susceptible areas which may lie at a distance from, but have a socioeconomic relationship with, the primary epicenter.[13] Because of the leap frog mode of high-fire-incidence spread between non-adjoining areas and of the characteristics of the areas which came down with "fire disease" during this period, hierarchical spread appears to have occurred. The primary epicenters seeded noncontiguous secondary epicenters.

The S-shape of the rise in number of fires per year mimics the S-shape of disease cases during an epidemic which changes from one of simple spatial spread from a single epicenter to establishment of secondary epicenters and spatial spread from both the primary and the secondary epicenters.[14] The inflexion point (1968), where the initial slow rise in number of fires per year changes to a rapid rise, marks the point of the establishment of hierarchically spread secondary epicenters from which high fire incidence moves out radially increased violence late in the epidemic. In figure 3-1, we can see that as total structural fires "bottomed out" in the late 1980s and early 1990s, the number of serious fires increased. Continued production of visible fire damage and destruction of housing units ensured that fire contagion continued even though fire numbers declined. Figure 3-3 also shows the increased virulence in loss of controllability.

DEPENDENCE ON POPULATION DENSITY

In understanding the relationship between population density and fire incidence, one has to examine two populations: the housing units and the humans. The density of the human population determines the density of susceptible housing units. Large numbers of people per square mile mean that large numbers of people are crammed into the housing, with more cooking, more smoking, more trash-generation, more use of electricity are going on per unit area. When high population density also results in a high proportion of the housing units being extremely overcrowded, the maintenance and services of the buildings require greater effort and resources to keep fire hazards to a minimum. Even neighborhoods far into the fire-and-abandonment cycle, with large numbers of abandoned buildings, usually suffer from extreme housing overcrowding in the remaining occupied buildings, and feature a dangerous mix of occupied and abandoned building fires. Humans thus seem to serve as a vector for the fire disease on the housing stock just as mosquitoes are a vector for malaria.

Figure 3-5 illustrated the relationship between average structural-fire-work-time and the index of extreme housing overcrowding. Table 3-2 illustrates the relationship of population density per unit area to structural fires per unit population.[15] The Index of Extreme Housing Overcrowding represents the percent of housing units with 1.51 persons per room or more.

The two measures of people-packing (by area density and by housing over-crowding) both show associations with simple number of fires and with the combination of number and size of fires reflected in structural-fire worktime. However, the Index of Extreme Housing Overcrowding predicts structural-fire worktime much more powerfully. Density of overcrowding determines the density of housing susceptible to frequent fire ignition and to rapid fire spread.

Why is this so? The Threshold Theorem of disease epidemiology dictates that for a given disease, the density of susceptible individuals in a population must rise above a crucial threshold for sustained contagion to take place.[16] Otherwise, the initial seed case may lead to a few other cases but the chain of contagion will not be sustained simply because there aren't enough susceptible individuals around to catch the disease reliably enough for continuous propagation.

Chicken-pox, for example, usually rampages in epidemic every four or five years because that's how long it takes for enough children who have not had the disease before to reach threshold density. The epidemic itself causes its own demise: it eventually visits enough children so that the density of non-immune children who have never had the disease drops below propagating density; i.e., probability of transmission falls below the critical level.[17]

Another important factor in disease propagation is the density of infectious cases in the population. This density determines the probability that susceptible individuals will be exposed to the disease. A situation of high density of susceptibles and rising density of infectives sets the scene for rapid sweep of the disease through the population. This is precisely what occurred when firefighting resources were withdrawn from the neighborhoods with dense stands of susceptible housing. That withdrawal was the fire equivalent of withdrawing measles-immunization programs from areas with high densities of young children. Adequate fire service is in fact the immunization program for the housing stock in old, densely populated, poor neighborhoods. It keeps the *effective* density of both susceptibles *and* infectives below their critical thresholds for epidemic and for hyperendemicity (stable but high incidence). Adequate fire service keeps fires small (i.e. limits "infective" fire-damage density) and keeps families from having to double and triple up (i.e., it limits number and density of "susceptible" housing units).

HOUSING LOSS, MIGRATION, AND HOMELESSNESS

The fire epidemic crested in the 1975–77 period and ebbed because the density of susceptible housing in the path of the fire wave had fallen below critical threshold. What could burn did burn, leaving behind vast stretches of charred hulks and abandoned shells. The estimates of housing loss in the 1970s range greatly, depending on who makes the estimate and the assumptions on which it is based. The Bureau of the Census developed a data base on housing units in 1970 and in 1980 and mapped the loss between the two decadal censuses. In figure 3-6, the blackened areas are those census tracts losing at least 500 housing units during the 1970s. Each contiguous black area contains many census tracts.[18] According to this map, hundreds of thousands of housing units were lost in these areas of concentrated housing loss, housing stock which had been stable and had served New Yorkers since before 1915.

As shown in the Bushwick maps (fig. 3-4), the rapidity of destruction exceeded the rate inferred by the census map, rapid though that was. Sometimes an individual block would be destroyed in only a few months; a neighborhood would be destroyed in 6–12 months, during its epidemic crest.

The different neighborhoods suffered their respective epidemics at slightly different times. Because of very early concentrated reductions in fire service, the South Bronx experienced an early fire wave (1972–74) whereas a neighborhood like Bushwick, which did not itself lose companies but caught the disease from stretching its fire service to cover other stripped neighborhoods, saw its epidemic crest in 1976–77, even later than the City as a whole.[19]

The clustering of fires and building abandonments meant that housing loss also clustered. Thus, specific neighborhoods and areas within neighborhoods suffered intense social destabilization and destruction of a community-based local economy. Indeed, during the later stages of a local housing-loss epidemic, the much anticipated money-motivated arson would in fact arise in the small commercial establishments—grocery stores, car repair shops, and diners. Arson would also arise in partially occupied buildings, vacant buildings, and occupied buildings on blocks with many burned-out or abandoned shells. Sometimes landlords were trying to cut their losses and get a last payment out of their properties. Other times the mentally unstable turned from killing cats to setting fires because fire became dominant in the environment. Revenge seekers changed from direct assault to setting fires because of the Fire Department's inability to control fires and of likely arson success. Still, even in the midst of one of the worst epidemics, that of Bushwick in Brooklyn, half or fewer of monthly building fires were even suspicious, much less proven arson. The brunt of the housing loss and its consequent social and economic unraveling stemmed from accidental fires.[20]

The loss of housing forced a mass migration. Besides keeping track of the housing loss between 1970 and 1980, the US Census Bureau also kept track of the changes in population by race and of the migrations between census tracts. The text table below shows the change in the population between the two decadal censuses by race. Figure 3-7 displays the migration of the black population from the burned out zones to adjacent neighborhoods. Some areas in the Bronx suffered losses up to 80% of their housing and population.

Many other indicators of migration also point to rapid, massive movement during the fire-and-abandonment epidemics. Figure 3-8 shows the old and new areas of high density of people receiving public assistance in the late 1970s. The West Bronx had not been a poverty area in the 1960's but became the area of highest density of welfare recipients by the late 1970s. Figure 3-9 shows the transfer of public school students within and between school districts in 1974–75 at the height of the South Bronx fire epidemic. Note the streaming of students from the South Bronx districts. Indeed, figure 3-10 plots average engine worktime against school transfers for the Bronx districts and shows an extremely close association.

As the text table below shows, the Blacks and Latinos were not the only ones to migrate. The white middle class pulled up stakes and marched away from many of their traditional enclaves, largely the areas into which the poor were forced to move. The middle class fled to the suburbs. The City lost approximately one-and-a-third million whites, some of them replaced by an influx of legal and illegal immigrants. The West Bronx became the "new South Bronx" where former residents of the South Bronx fled. Because of the greater undercount of Blacks and Latinos in the 1980 Census than in 1970, the number and percent of increase of each is even larger than the following text table shows.

CHANGES IN POPULATION BY RACE 1970–1980

	1970	1980	% change
White	4,972,509	3,668,945	-26.2
Black	1,525,745	1,694,127	+11.0
Hispanic	1,278,630	1,406,024	+10.0

For a short time (1975–78), the vacating of large apartments in the West Bronx, Flatbush, East New York, and other transitional zones allowed the poor families migrating from burned out areas to live in less crowded conditions. However, as the fire epidemic transformed into the fire hyperendemic, and the housing stock continued to erode owing to the Fire Department's inability to control individual fires, housing overcrowding rose again after 1978. The poor had to double and triple up because all of the middle class who could move had done so and no more housing was vacated.[21] Homelessness became an urgent problem only after 1980.

The continued but slower housing stock erosion prevailed through the

1980's. Figure 3-11 a, b, and c compare the patterns of the Index of Extreme Housing Overcrowding in the Bronx for 1970, 1980, and 1990. By 1990, the extent and intensity of extreme housing overcrowding exceeded that of 1970, the initial background condition of the fire-and-abandonment epidemics. The citywide number of extremely overcrowded rental housing units in 1990 (143,000) greatly exceeded that in 1970 (74,000).[22]

This overcrowding carries its own risks. Overcrowding of aged housing makes it fire-prone in many ways: higher densities of smokers, overuse of aged electrical wiring, much more cooking per apartment, more children who experiment with matches and stoves, and greater accumulations of trash. Without additional maintenance, overcrowding leads to more fires, more rapid spread of fires, and to rapid deterioration of buildings even in the absence of fires. Thus, a vicious circle arises of housing destruction, movement into adjacent areas, overcrowding of the new areas, and more fire damage and building deterioration.

Figure 3-12 graphically depicts the relationships between waves of housing destruction in time, outmigration of the middle class, growth of the precariously housed population (those living as secondary tenants with family or friends) and the growth of the overtly homeless population. As long as the outmigration continued, the populations of the precariously housed and the overtly homeless remained low. When housing destruction recurred but the population of emigrants froze (perhaps due to lack of affordable homes within commuting distance or to high mortgage rates). Then the pool of the precariously housed grew and, under the pressure of growing numbers, slopped over into the pool of the overtly homeless.[23]

The poor could not flee a great distance, as the maps on migration show. They often ended up in the path of the very forces which uprooted them in the first place. Families were sometimes burned out two or three times in a few years during the epidemic because they could not move far enough from the spreading centers of decay and always ended up in the path of the encroaching high fire incidence. Because of overcrowding, these families would in effect seed a new area and bring high fire incidence to it, through no individual fault of their own. Of course, each expansion of the radius of housing destruction enlarged the area and population contributing to the numbers of precariously housed (the "hidden homeless") and overtly homeless individuals and families.

SOCIAL OUTCOMES

The fallout from this "bombing" of New York City's ghettoes affects the city still. The public policy of targeting and destroying entire neighborhoods with populations on the order of one-to-two hundred thousand eventually affected the entire metropolitan region with its 24 counties, a radius of more than 50 miles, and a population of 18–20 million people, in round numbers. And the impact of this war on New York City's poor neighborhoods extends far beyond the metropolitan region. Cities closely linked to New York socially and economically have felt the impact by means of secondary contagious phenomena such as infectious diseases, substance abuse, and violence from the New York epicenter.

The effect of the burnout can only be understood by looking at how families and individuals depend on their communities for necessary resources, emotional support, and information in direct proportion to their poverty, lack of education, and ethnic difference from the American majority. Such urban anthropologists as Carol Stack (author of *All Our Kin*)[24] and Ida Susser (author of *Norman Street*)[25] have documented the day-to-day lives of poor families in large cities. Although these families moved frequently, they rarely moved far, remaining within their communities, within walking distance of their extended families and of long-time friends. They often maintained friendships for a lifetime.

These geographically focused social networks in very poor areas form partly through intergenerational links and may or may not be familial. As Stack describes them: "Expectations are so elastic that when one person fails to meet another's needs, disappointment is cushioned. Flexible expectations and the extension of kin relations to non-kin allow for the creation of mutual-aid networks which are not bounded by genealogical distance or genealogical criteria. Much more important for the creation and recruitment to personal networks are the practical requirements that kin and friends live near one another."[26] A young woman may have children by different men and maintain ties with the men's mothers and sisters who are related to her children. Similar strategies of survival are practiced in very poor sectors of Africa, Asia, Latin America and Southern Europe. When one member needs "tiding over" in an emergency, the network pitches in with loans, used clothing, referrals, a temporary place to stay, or whatever else is needed. This is especially important in cities like New York which churn the welfare rolls—periodically cutting families off their benefits and forcing them to re-apply, a process which may leave them without any income for several weeks. The social network (family, friends and "in-laws") may make the difference between retaining an apartment or being evicted during the incomeless period. This also holds true for the working poor who find themselves without jobs for several weeks and whose unemployment benefits do not cover their families' necessities. The buffer, the poor person's equivalent of savings in the bank for a rainy day, is the community network. Thus, social capital compensates for lack of purely economic capital.

Besides actual material resources, vital information is shared along these networks: how to get the children immunized, how to get a job at the local super-market, where to apply for English as a Second Language adult education, and where to get free contraceptives. Research on the networks of new immigrants has shown how vital this informational function can be to families in particularly vulnerable, isolated communities.[27]

And these networks and the weaker connections within a community enforce societal norms and acceptable behavior. Parents in stable communities rely on the extended relationships to reinforce their socialization of their young. When not at home, the children receive supervision from their parents' neighbors, the mem-bers of the local church, the local merchants, and their cousins, uncles, and aunts. Children who misbehave are reprimanded, and word gets back to the parents.

This social control keeps adults in line as well. A church member who beats his wife gets a visit from the elders. Someone seen buying from a drug dealer feels pressure on many fronts. Stable communities keep law and order far more effi-ciently than the police.

Besides the strong, major links of the network, the typical stable community con-tains many minor links which add to its strength and elasticity: people who stand at the same bus stop every workday and chat, the patrons of the local newsstand who see each other everyday, people who meet only when they go to the laundromat. In small ways, these anonymous meeters and greeters keep tabs on each other. If some-one "turns up missing," the others find out what happened and even help out if the missing person has troubles.

The picture of strong community networks, especially in the poor communities, painted by urban anthropologists and scholars of new immigrants departs radically from Roger Starr's notion that community does not exist—his apologia for commu-nity destruction. The mass migrations that arose from the intense housing burnouts destroyed all this. The snowballing migrations resulted in mixing of populations, destruction of the social networks in both poor and middle class areas, and changes in both the geographic pattern of extreme housing overcrowding and the proportion of households living in extremely overcrowded conditions. These changes marked major deteriorations in public health, public order, and the social, political, and eco-nomic functioning of individual neighborhoods and the City as a whole.

THE SLOW DISASTER

A disaster is different from a major event in an individual's life. Disaster victims do suffer the same emotional upheavals as those who are shaken by such major events as death of a loved one, loss of a job, eviction, or divorce; they also have additional stresses and pressures as part of a traumatized community.[28]

The forced migrations caused by and affecting subsequent development of the fire-and-abandonment epidemic of the 1970s were of such a magnitude (as was the urban burnout itself) that they constituted a disaster, "a situation of massive collective stress in which the distress and behavioral disturbance of an individual cannot be understood or managed unless analyzed as elements in the disruption of the equilibrium social system."[29]

Disasters typically produce grief, anxiety, anger, hostility, resentment, marital and family discord, increased substance abuse, and loss of interest in school by children. Such a combination seems particularly fertile for an outbreak of deadly violence which may feed back into further community decay. Loss of interest in school and lack of responsibility by children seem potential precursors, along with family turmoil, of serious delinquency which furthers community decay.[30]

Disaster affects physical health. Long research into contagious diseases from tuberculosis down to the common cold have noted that people under emotional stress come down with these diseases at higher rates. More recent research has revealed mechanisms of connection between the immune system and mental health: stress takes its toll, and alcohol and drugs weaken the activity of both white blood cells and antibodies.

Most importantly, the disorganization from concentrated housing destruction in a disaster yanks away many of the buffers which families and individuals would ordinarily use to recover from a domestic or personal crisis. Several natural and man-made disasters have been studied by community-mental-health researchers like the scientists at the Disaster Bureau of the National Institute of Mental Health. These range from the Buffalo Creek disaster (dam collapse and massive flood) to Love Canal (removal of a community because of toxic chemical contamination). Because the usual community institutions are themselves under stress and are composed of people under stress, the buffering is greatly weakened. Outside help is needed in these cases. Otherwise, the physical and mental sequelae of the disaster are very slow to lift, indeed may never do so, as we have seen in the Bhopal, India chemical-release disaster.

In the previous chapter, we quoted from a 1977 report by the Centers for Disease Control (*The Effect of the Man-Made Environment on Health and Behavior*):

> The importance of the social milieu is such that the dislocation and disruptions of social relations that are produced when one moves a family from a dilapidated dwelling to a modern apartment may have adverse effects upon health and behavior that are not off-set by the clean, comfortable, and convenient new dwelling.... Simple efforts to improve human health and well-being by improving the physical characteristics of the environment or the neighborhood are unlikely to succeed, unless the social and psychological implications of rehousing, removal, or relocation ... are taken into consideration.

How much worse is the outcome when public policy aims for acceleration of urban decay and deterioration of the physical environment!

The resources of the community determine the course of recovery, or non-recovery. In the wake of the Love Canal disaster, the Love Canal Home Owners Association, mostly white and middle class, managed to create organizations devoted to preventing future "Love Canals" and to obtain reparations for Love Canal families. Outside help enabled this transformation from helplessness to exercise of power, although on a personal level many of the families and individuals never transcended their victim status. For the Love Canal Renters Association, mainly African-American and blue-collar-to-poor in economic class, many of the benefits to which they were entitled never materialized. These families were scattered and largely ignored, and they never became an organized power. If the failure of the aided home-owners to overcome their sense of victimization is true of the renters as well, then the renters suffered doubly: they neither transcended victim status personally nor transcended victim status as a community.

Other populations which contributed to our knowledge of post-disaster physical and mental health include Holocaust survivors, communities in Africa battered by famine-forced migrations to relief camps, and civilian populations caught in wars. The picture which emerges from overcrowding, forced migration, and loss of community and of control over family life is unrelievedly bleak: infectious disease, mental illness, breakdown of family ties, substance abuse, and violence.

The New York burnout disaster was caused not by a society and its elite over-burdening natural resources but by a society feeding on itself. The New York City government, HUD, and Rand viewed the lowest classes as separate from the mainstream and, thus, easily sacrificed. But residential and vocational segregation implies a middle-class immunity which, as we shall see, did not hold up in reality. As the condition and behavior of the segregated sectors worsen under the continuing disaster, the alarmed middle and upper classes proceed to distance themselves further and chug the disaster up another notch. This distancing often results in punitive actions and disruptive curtailments of rights and benefits targeting the poor, which accelerate the effects of the previous withdrawals of basic municipal services and social programs.

OPPORTUNISM AND DENIAL

By 1976, most major political players knew that the fire service reductions of 1969–75 devastated poor neighborhoods and destroyed huge numbers of housing units rapidly. The New York State Senate Subcommittee on Fire and Police

Protection in New York City, chaired by John Calandra, held hearings in 1976 and issued a summary booklet, *No False Alarm*. Firefighters, urban scientists, insurance representatives, politicians, and civic association officers testified in detail about the impacts of the fire-service reductions.

At Calandra's hearing, we saw State Senator Carl McCall (now New York State Comptroller), an African-American out of the Harlem machine, take the stand at this hearing against rescinding the cuts for two reasons: home rule by New York City and antipathy to the firefighters' union. And yet McCall's West Harlem district had already begun to burn down.

Mayor Beame ordered a hearing in 1976 specifically on the closing of Engine 212 ("The People's Firehouse") because the largely Polish residents of Greenpoint, Brooklyn held the engine hostage in its firehouse and used an array of political and community-action weapons to force the reopening of the company. Basil Paterson, a prominent black politician also from Harlem, chaired the hearings on behalf of the Institute for Conflict Resolution. One of us (RW) testified before Paterson and later went to see him. He listened intently to the explanation of what the cuts were doing and would do to the minority neighborhoods and believed the explanation. Paterson is a senior black politicians who served as Secretary of State, thus having run for statewide office. What he learns gets into the black inner circle. It seems that the Harlem machine was betting that the emigration of the whites would put them in the driver's seat, even if what they would gain would be power over an ashpile.

We had already, in 1972, seen Manhattan Borough President Percy Sutton, also out of the Harlem machine, praise the change from the reliable electromechanical street fireboxes to the all-electronic voice-contact fireboxes. His explanation that if people describe the fire, the dispatcher can send just enough fire companies to control it, and the coming fire company closings wouldn't be so bad with this greater efficiency, was lifted verbatim from Fire Department propaganda.

From our experience with these and other politicians (Charles Rangel, Robert Abrams, David Dinkins) who represented threatened and destroyed communities and boroughs, we conclude that many banked on certain results of the burning down of whole neighborhoods. Herman Badillo, while still representing the South Bronx in Congress, told Battalion Chief Alfred Benway (who fought fires in the South Bronx) that he wasn't worried about inadequate fire service or service cuts: he'd just get money for new housing.

The BBC and Tass sent reporters to the South Bronx in 1975 to get footage of burned-out buildings, fires, and fire engines whizzing around with lights and sirens on. Numerous political candidates would parade through the South Bronx, Bushwick, Brownsville, and Harlem during the late 1970s to make promises about rebuilding. The local pols would hold community meetings and talk up tiny grass-roots bootstrap efforts as the answer. We remember in particular a community-board meeting in the South Bronx held by Robert Abrams, then Bronx Borough President, who was very enthusiastic about CETA programs and Hostos Community College, but ignored discussion about the closed fire companies and the ERS fireboxes. This meeting was held in 1976, when the South Bronx lay in ruins, and the fires there were becoming larger, eroding away what was left after the epidemic crest had blitzed a high proportion of the housing.

No New York Democrat would step forward and admit that a disaster had begun and progressed. After 1980, very few Republicans concerned themselves because they were betting on gentrification to get them votes. The Democrats had their own bets on how the destabilization and decay would affect voting patterns. They all thought they would end up on top of the ashpile.

Disasters to which responses are inadequate or inappropriate ripple out and amplify, engendering further disaster. A well-known disaster occurred in India when a reservoir was built in an earthquake zone. This triggered a massive quake which the authorities ignored. Their failure to aid the victims and see to sanitation led to an explosion in the rat population and an outbreak of plague. Thousands fled the plague, of whom some were already infected. Before the epidemic was controlled, it had spread across a whole state.[31]

The New York City burnout disaster greatly exceeds this Indian disaster by any measure: time frame, involved population, involved area, number of deaths, number of disease cases, and number of lives derailed. Yet, no one in authority will proclaim it a disaster. Foundations such as the Ford Foundation and the Fund for the City of New York pour money into such misguided programs as neighborhood arson task forces. In the hardest-hit areas, there isn't enough of a community on which to base an effective program, even if it were aimed at the proper target. So the disaster continues its course and draws an ever greater area and population into its meshes as it spreads.

Table 3-1 STATISTICS OF EXTERNAL
WORKTIME DISTRIBUTIONS

YEAR	MEAN(HRS)	DISPERSION	PATCHINESS	%≥100 HRS	%≤5HRS
			Ladders		
1972	13.4	33.6	3.4	0.7	43.1
1973	25.3	83.4	4.3	6.3	31.5
1974	29.4	95.5	4.2	9.8	31.5
1975	39.9	103.1	3.6	12.4	26.3
1976	38.3	111.5	3.9	12.5	20.6
			Engines		
1972	12.7	87.8	3.6	1.8	57.7
1973	25.3	185.6	8.3	6.9	49.1
1974	35.4	242.3	7.8	9.7	48.4
1975	49.1	288.3	6.9	12.4	38.8
1976	46.1	152.7	4.3	12.2	22.0

Table 3-2 BOROUGH POPULATION DENSITIES, PERCENTAGE OF UNITS EXTREMELY OVERCROWDED, AND NUMBER OF FIRES PER UNIT POPULATION

BOROUGH	PD	OC	STRUCTURAL FIRES			RESIDENTIAL FIRES
			Feb	*May*	*Aug*	*1973–1975 mean*
Manhattan	67,808	3.78	8.66	7.57	5.44	7.83
Brooklyn	37,013	3.01	5.84	5.51	3.90	5.68
Bronx	35,721	3.18	6.85	5.92	4.28	8.79
Queens	18,393	1.74	2.36	2.68	2.13	2.49
Staten Island	5,138	1.02	2.53	3.26	2.69	2.93

PD=population per square mile.
OC=percent of extremely overcrowded units
Structural fires = number/10,000 people in 1977
Residential fires = number/1,000 people

POPULATION DENSITIES, OVERCROWDING, AND TWO FIRE-SERVICE INDICES: SIX BROOKLYN COMMUNITY DISTRICTS

CD	PD	OC	TOTAL WORKTIME		TOTAL WORKERS	
			engines	*ladders*	*engines*	*ladders*
16	74.2	23.55	3,086.9	3,263.1	1,570	1,259
3	89.0	20.93	2,573.2	4,113.1	360	2,510
4	75.0	18.08	2,319.7	3,681.5	442	2,868
8	91.5	16.91	2,393.3	3,081.5	162	656
9	67.5	10.62	2,080.4	2,541.7	155	196
17	46.5	7.99	1,735.4	1,839.5	96	109

PD=thousands of people/square mile
OC=percentage overcrowded housing units
Worktime=total hours worktime per average unit 1975–1977
Workers=Incidents serviced by relocation, avenue company, 1975–1977

Figure 3-1 STRUCTURAL FIRES AND SERIOUS FIRES
BY YEAR, NYC, 1959–1991

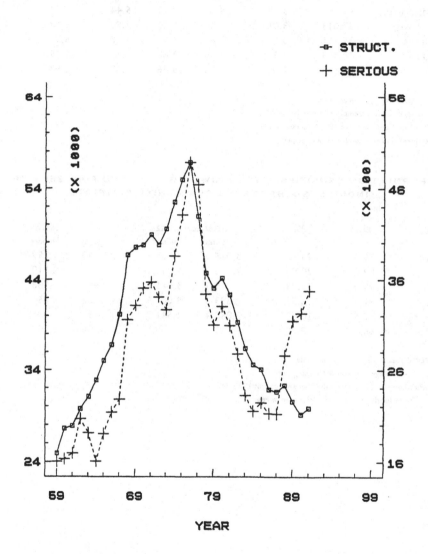

Left vertical axis=structural fires.

Right vertical axis=serious fires.

(Note how the number of serious fires increased after 1987.)

Figure 3-2 FIRE DAMAGE INDEX 1959-1986

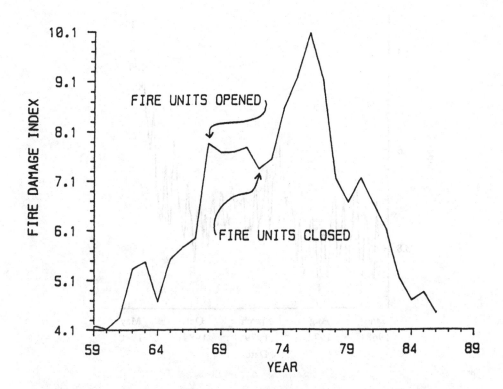

This index is based on hours of firefighting worktime, number of structural fires, and number of serious fires.

Figure 3-3 FIRE CONTROLLABILITY INDEX, 1968–1990

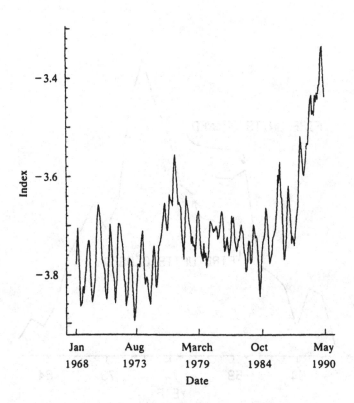

This index is a contrast between number of structural fires and the number of fire companies needed to control them. The less negative the index, the less controllable the fires.

Figure 3-4 STRUCTURAL FIRES BY BLOCK IN BUSHWICK

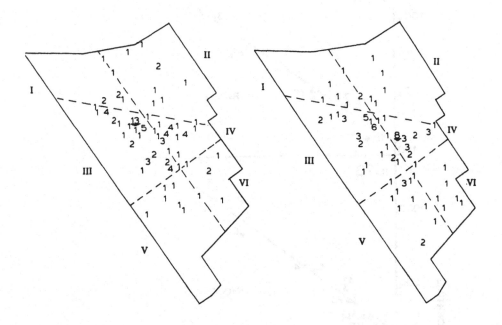

The left-hand map shows the number of structural fires in Bushwick in September 1976. Note the maximum number of thirteen fires on a single block of region III. The right-hand map shows the same phenomenon for December 1976. Notice the shift of the maximum clump into region IV. In each map, the maximum cluster is underlined.

Figure 3-5 AVERAGE BRONX COMMUNITY DISTRICT ENGINE WORKTIME TOTAL FOR 1972-1974 VS 1970 PERCENTAGE OF EXTREMELY OVERCROWDED HOUSING UNITS

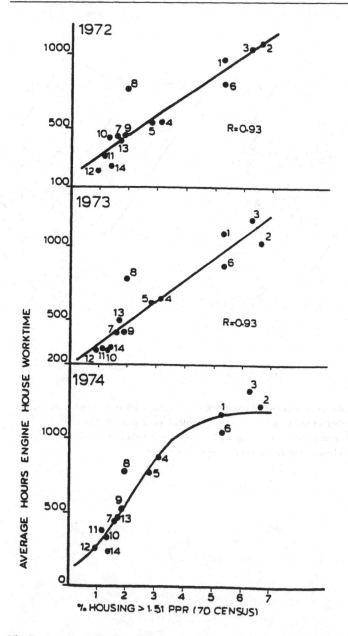

The "topping out" in 1974 represents a resource-limited inability to service total demand, a service shortfall.

Figure 3-6 CENSUS TRACTS WHICH LOST 500 HOUSING UNITS OR MORE, 1970–1980

CHANGE IN HOUSING UNITS: 1970-1980

■ -500 and Over

Each large blackened area is composed of many census tracts.

Figure 3-7 CHANGE IN BLACK POPULATION 1970–1980

The changes of 2500 people refer to census tracts. The stippled and blackened areas are composed of many census tracts.

Figure 3-8 CHANGE IN HIGH DENSITY OF POPULATION ON WELFARE 1967–1977

Figure 3-9 PUBLIC SCHOOL STUDENT TRANSFERS IN 1974-1975

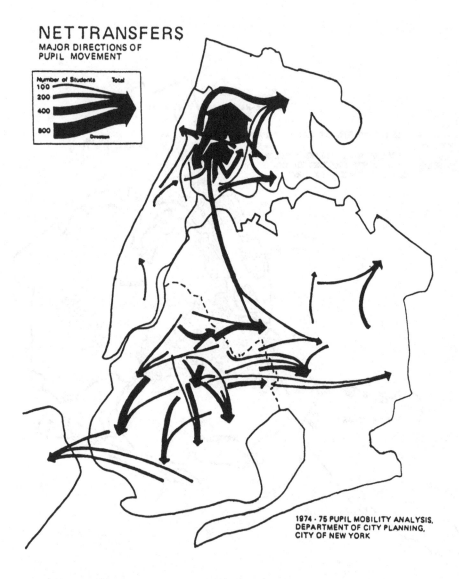

This year was the height of the fire epidemic in the South Bronx. Note the immense shift of students from the South Bronx to the West and Northwest Bronx. Note also the shifts from the Brooklyn fire band which had not yet reached its peak fire activity.

Figure 3-10 ANNUAL PUBLIC SCHOOL TRANSFERS IN THE BRONX VS. AVERAGE HOURS OF DISTRICT ENGINE WORKTIME FOR OCCUPIED STRUCTURAL FIRES: 1972-1978

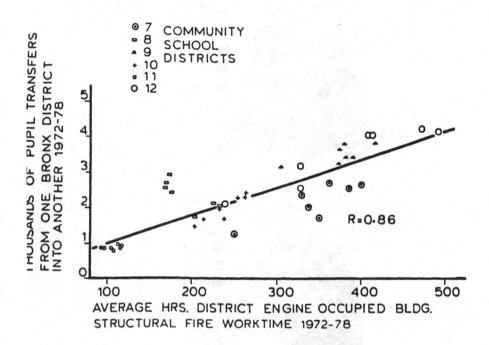

The fires drove the transfers. The statistical correlation was extremely high and the explanatory power of the fires for the transfers extremely high.

Figure 3-11 MAPS OF EXTREMELY OVERCROWDED HOUSING IN THE BRONX HEALTH AREAS: 1970, 1980, AND 1990

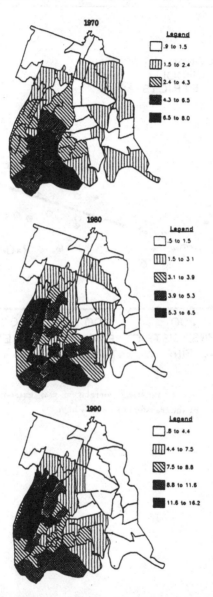

Note the shift to the West Bronx in 1980 of the highest percentage of extreme overcrowding and the subsequent increase in concentration of overcrowded housing units there by 1990. In 1970, the area with the most overcrowding had about 8% of the units extremely overcrowded. The area with the most overcrowding in 1990 had 16.2%, double that of 1970.

Figure 3-12 THE SUCCESSIVE WAVES OF HOUSING DESTRUCTION, EMIGRATION, CESSATION OF EMIGRATION, THE PRECARIOUSLY HOUSED, AND OVERT HOMELESSNESS

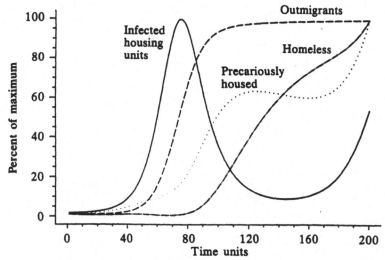

The coupling of contagious urban decay and homelessness.

As housing is destroyed and community conditions decay, those with resources emigrate. Their homes are freed for occupancy by those whose homes are destroyed. When emigration ceases, doubling up and other unstable arrangements lead to a large number of precariously housed residents. When these people fall out of the social network, they become the overtly homeless.

PART TWO

———————◆———————

EPIDEMICS

INTRODUCTION TO PART TWO

EPIDEMICS

Infectious disease depends on both population density and housing overcrowding (as well as job-site overcrowding) for patterns of incidence. Even before the rapid 1970s housing destruction, incidence of such diseases as tuberculosis, syphilis, and gastrointestinal parasitism showed high correlations with the Index of Extreme Housing Overcrowding. The medical system of disease control could not completely overcome the strong influences of population density and housing overcrowding. However, because living and working conditions improved until the early 1970s and because the public-health agencies took upon themselves, at national and local levels, the task of eradicating tuberculosis, measles, and other preventable diseases, incidence declined both in the city as a whole and in the poorest neighborhoods. The commitment to keep pushing the envelope of reform paid off in ever-lower disease mortality rates and annual number of cases from the time of the Great Reform until the Nixon-Lindsay era.

As control of these diseases faltered in the destabilized, even more numerous overcrowded poor areas, epicenters of high case prevalence arose. In 1978, we had predicted that tuberculosis, sexually transmitted diseases, and gastrointestinal microbial and parasitic disease would edge out from under control because of the housing destruction and its fallout. By the mid-80s, these predictions were proving correct. Alongside epicenters of the older diseases, epicenters of AIDS and HIV infection arose in New York City for similar reasons.

Because the epicenters afflicted neighborhoods targeted for destruction, the authorities looked the other way and denied the problem. Only when the diseases began to leak from the targeted populations did strong action arise. By then, containment through reasonable levels of resources had proved impossible. Not only had the diseases crossed class and race lines, they had crossed municipal borders and exhibited regional patterns of incidence, dependent on the case prevalences in the ghetto epicenters. In other words, TB arose on Long Island, in Connecticut, in suburban New York State, and in New Jersey in relation to the TB rates of Central Harlem and the Lower East Side in Manhattan, Morrisania in the Bronx, and Bedford-Stuyvesant in Brooklyn.

These contagious diseases can now reach very high levels of incidence—levels normally seen in such disrupted industrial countries as South Africa—for three reasons: high levels of crowding in homes, workplaces, and public places; instability of residence, worksite, and social sites; and the loss of community structures and the strength to educate, enforce, and nurture. Destabilized communities were marked by large declines in measles immunization rates, high proportions of TB patients who failed to complete their lengthy treatment, and a high percentage of residents cherishing myths about what causes AIDS and how to prevent getting infected. The dire consequences of community unraveling belie Starr's view that American communities can be taken apart and reassembled without adverse effects.

4

TUBERCULOSIS
THE CAPTAIN OF ALL THE MEN OF DEATH

TUBERCULOSIS EPIDEMICS

The captain of all the men of death. The white plague. These names for tuberculosis come from a millennia of universal human terror. Formerly believed to be a European gift to the New World, TB turned up in pre-Columbian Andean and Central American human remains. Even royal Egyptian mummies show evidence of tuberculosis in their bones. Only within the past 60 years did TB lose its status as the leading cause of death in the United States. This ousting took place slowly and surely, not as a sudden medical miracle.

In a previous incarnation as the Tuberculosis League, the American Lung Association focused all its resources and attention on tuberculosis prevention and control. The reports of the local chapters of the League recorded daily life in the cities and country-side of early twentieth Century America—a life of overcrowding in the home and workplace; inadequate ventilation; frequent change of residence; frequent personal catastrophe; addiction to alcohol or drugs; long workweeks; low wages; predation by government, property owners, bosses, and political machines; exposure to respiratory toxicants and irritants; and inadequate nutrition.[1] Industrial Revolution America and Europe incubated TB in the cities and the countryside. In today's de-developing America, we now get a little taste of what afflicted the pre-reform working family.

The TB bacillus, the leprosy bacillus, and their close relatives are hard to eliminate from human populations because they have thick waxy coats. The coatings prevent quick or total antibiotic cures because they prevent drugs from reaching the bacterial cell.[2] The coatings also protect the bacteria from environmental conditions that kill other bacteria, such as rapid desiccation, chemical disinfectants, and temperature and pH extremes. TB-bacillus-laden sputum can remain infectious weeks after being smeared on a surface.[3]

The TB bug adapts readily to human physiological conditions and immune system status. Figure 4-1 displays the natural history of the germ and its life stages. Healthy, unstressed people come away from isolated, casual, light exposures without even being infected. Healthy, unstressed people with good immune systems come away from chronic or heavy acute exposures infected but with the infection controlled by the immune system in a state of dormancy.[4]

For this reason, most human populations have reservoirs of dormant TB infections. The size of these reservoirs, their proportion in the population, and their socioeconomic distribution depend on historic conditions.[5] Although probably concentrated in low-income strata, dormant infections may also appear among the upper classes. Eleanor Roosevelt died of TB from a long dormant infection picked up during her visits to tenements and settlement houses. The drugs she used to control her life-threatening arthritis disarmed her immune system, letting her TB infection reactivate into virulent overt disease.

TB has a life cycle as complex as many invertebrate parasites (see fig. 4-1). Living and working conditions largely determine whether the life cycle progresses from one state to the next and can affect the susceptibility of whole populations to life stage change. Medical treatments can directly influence only two life-stage changes for individuals: 1) infection to disease or dormancy; and 2) disease to cure, dormancy, or death.

Besides overcrowding, poor nutrition, inadequate ventilation and high rates of substance abuse, history teaches that TB breaks out in populations rendered susceptible by instability of residence, mixing of populations, forced migration, breakdown of governmental and social institutions that provide order and protection, major life-threatening events, poor sanitation, high rates of certain other diseases such as measles, and exposure to chemicals and particles which irritate the deep lung. Silicosis, thus, is often accompanied by TB.[6]

In developed countries, the main triggers of tuberculosis outbreaks have been war, long-standing economic depression, and major disasters such as earthquake and flood.[7] In developed countries, during normal peacetime, the disease has declined since the nineteenth century (see figure 4-2). Improvements, in living and working conditions, in the worker's economic and educational status, and in building and planning technologies, have driven new-case and mortality incidence down over time since long before the discovery of anti-tuberculosis drugs.[8] TB was the leading cause of death in the United States until about 1930. Even though both new-case and mortality incidence had been declining since about 1880, one of the motivations of the moneyed classes to support the Great Reform was the spread of TB from the poverty epicenters in the cities and countryside to the middle and upper classes. At that time, even the wealthy caught TB and died of it. Between 1880 and 1995, the great majority of the difference in annual new-TB-case incidence and annual TB-mortality incidence arose from improvements in physical living and working conditions and in socioeconomic level of the population, especially of the poor.[9] In the 1960s, the Surgeon General aimed to eliminate tuberculosis within the borders of the United States.[10]

In New York City, the Health Services Administration convened a Tuberculosis Task Force in 1968 to plan the reduction of TB incidence in New York City. Active disease cases had dwindled into the poverty pockets in which physical and social conditions maintained high prevalence.

The Task Force designed a reduction program with characteristics similar to the program to reduce-mental health institutionalization. Similar to the 1960s plan for de-institutionalization, the first recommendation was to: "provide, on a neighborhood basis, a continuum of high-quality treatment to tuberculous patients, emphasizing ambulatory care and utilizing hospitalization only as required." A program of outpatient clinics and home care was recommended, including coordination with drug and alcoholic community-control programs. As the community-based treatment became available, hospital beds were to be reduced. "An overall reduction of 100 beds per year, for the next five years, should be planned."

The second recommendation called for more intensive-case and contact-finding and treatment.

The Task Force's third recommendation relied on the existence of a strong community: "Develop and formalize community participation in the planning and delivery of tuberculosis control-services."

The Task Force's highest priority came last: "Bring tuberculosis into the mainstream of community medicine by stimulating cooperation of medical schools, voluntary hospitals, and related agencies."[11]

The only Task Force recommendation that was carried out fully was reduction of hospital beds. Funding for community-based programs, community participation, and bringing TB into the community-medicine mainstream remained laughably inadequate.

In 1968, New York Mayor John V. Lindsay looked toward TB elimination, saying in the report, "We can move more swiftly toward the day when tuberculosis truly is a disease of the past." Task Force chairman John Porterfield echoed Lindsay: "Considering the availability of excellent diagnostic, therapeutic, and preventive tools, tuberculosis in New York City remains at an unacceptably high level. Although elimination of tuberculosis as a major public-health problem is extraordinarily difficult in our large urban centers, application of the enclosed recommendations should help accomplish this objective."

Clearly, this Task Force envisioned continued improvement in the physical and socioeconomic conditions of the poorest sectors of the City. Major long-term regression had not occurred since the Great Depression. Yet, Mayor Lindsay, beginning in 1969, applied the policies of "benign neglect" and "planned shrinkage" to reduce the number and power of the poor, policies which had to unleash new TB resurgence.

In the population of the United States, ten to twenty million people carry dormant tuberculosis which causes no problem to themselves or to others, as long as dormancy prevails. These carriers reside mainly in two areas: in large older cities and in poor rural communities. They are not evenly distributed either geographically or across the population. Thus, adverse socioeconomic or environmental changes, either nationally or locally, may trigger localized clusters of disease reactivation and significant increases in localized rates of exposure. A person who caught TB as a child and fought it into dormancy might, as a middle-aged adult, still not be aware of its presence.[12]

The ghettoes of New York had improved to the point in the 1960s and early 1970s where most "new cases" were reactivations in older people, especially foreign and domestic immigrants. This picture of the typical TB case in New York City lulled the New York City Health Department into total inaction during the 1970s when the destruction of low income housing began to lay the groundwork for a new epidemic. Thus, even in 1979, after we wrote to Assistant Commissioner of Health John Marr about the potential for a TB epidemic because of the forced mass migrations and changed patterns of overcrowding, he wrote back the following soothing statement:

> At present the highest case rate for tuberculosis is in the Lower East Side, followed by Central Harlem. The highest rate in the first instance is due to a mix of the Bowery population, the Chinese community (many of them recent immigrants) and the recent large influx of immigrants from Central and South America into large sections of the Lower East Side. Thus, in this instance, it appears that poor people gravitate towards poorer sections of the city which are high-population-density areas, but the indigenous poverty of that area does not necessarily foster new indigenous cases of disease, that is, these people arrive already infected (as opposed to arriving as susceptibles). Similarly, in Central Harlem, the typical 'new case of tuberculosis' is an elderly black male who develops a reactivation of his primary infection which might have been five decades ago. Where that person lived 50 years ago was, in turn, the true source of his infection and not the community where he was living when he developed his reactive disease. And, he rarely infects his neighbors before discovery.

Marr's statement confuses concentration and containment; just because a disease is concentrated in one sector of the population does not mean that it will be contained in that sector under all future conditions. He also erroneously scapegoats immigrants, both domestic and foreign, for degrading the state of public health.

We had written to Marr because of our discovery that the annual number of fires per unit of population, and the average size of fires in a given area, depend on the population density and the percent of overcrowded housing units in that area. Because the fire epidemic would eventually lead to extreme levels of housing overcrowding and localized population densities, we explored how well the public-health system compensated for the influence of population density and housing overcrowding on disease incidence before the 1976 fire epidemic peak. One disease we considered was tuberculosis. Tables 4-1 and 4-2 display population density, housing overcrowding and the incidences of several diseases (TB included) for the five boroughs and for six contiguous neighborhoods of Brooklyn, respectively. The boroughs and neighborhoods of densest population had the highest disease incidences. Boroughs and neighborhoods with a high proportion of overcrowded housing units also had high disease incidence. In other words, we established that the public-health system could not compensate for the rapid transmission of disease caused by the living and working conditions in the crowded areas.[13]

Marr and Lindsay's lack of vision is all the more shameful in comparison to the public-health policy makers of the Great Reform who, years before, understood that housing, working conditions, education, and other broad conditions were determinants of public health. Table 4-3 uses TB cases to compare Reform efforts to the age of "benign neglect" and "planned shrinkage."[14] The Great Reform goal was to make *the public* healthy. They didn't confuse curing individuals with improving public health. They pursued both.

TB AND THE BURN OUT

As is readily seen from Table 4-3, the year 1975 ushered in a period of great instability and signaled the end of control over TB. This timing coincides with the great demographic instability of poor neighborhoods during the fire epidemic, and TB incidence follows the Index of Extreme Housing Overcrowding closely (see figure 4-3). Household transmission occurred more rapidly and surely when overcrowding ensured frequent close personal contact of an active case with many people in a home.

TB cases in pre-school children form a sad but sound index of TB transmission within households. One study by another research team identified the households of child-cases in the Bronx and found that a very high proportion of the households were extremely overcrowded, even having 2 or more persons per room.[15] The US Bureau of the Census defines extremely overcrowded as 1.51 persons per room or more.

TB incidence among children under five was reported by ethnicity for only seven years between 1978 and 1990. Figure 4-4 shows that for these 28 data points (four ethnicities, seven years), incidence among the pre-schoolers corre-lates strongly with total incidence. The correlation demonstrates the potency of household transmission in the overall epidemic. Children were an integral part of this epidemic. By 1990, even white pre-schoolers experienced more TB inci-dence than in the previous years and had been drawn into the epidemic, albeit not as thoroughly as black and Hispanic children. The epidemic reached house-holds in all four ethnic categories.

When the 1990 TB incidence (new cases per 100,000 people) of the 30 desig-nated health districts of New York is mapped (fig. 4-5), the great geographic vari-ability of the disease leaps out at the reader. The very-high-incidence districts coincide with the burned-out areas and the adjacent receiving neighborhoods. These high-incidence districts form two belts: Harlem/West Bronx and Lower East Side/near-Manhattan Brooklyn. Over 80% of the pattern of TB incidence in 1990 can be explained by the 1978 density of cases-per-square-mile of each dis-trict (the initial conditions of the epidemic) and a 1990 housing-related index of poverty, the reciprocal of the average rent, since average rent reflects the domi-nant income level.[16] In other words, the TB incidence in poor areas with high 1978 case densities rose to higher levels by 1990 than it did in other areas.

Table 4-4 lists the 1978 and 1990 incidences of the health districts. To put these into perspective: national TB incidence was about 10.4 cases per 100,000 in 1990. That year, only the Kips Bay/Yorkville health district had a lower inci-dence than the national average, the great majority of districts having incidences of two or more times that of the nation. The table also shows that only Kips Bay/Yorkville improved between 1978 and 1990. All other districts had higher incidence of TB in 1990 than in 1978.

The higher the annual density of new-cases-per-square-mile, the higher the probability of becoming exposed to TB in a given community. In Table 4-5, we show the 1978 and 1990 case densities of the six highest-and six-lowest ranking health districts for 1990 incidence.[17] The case density in the high-ranking dis-tricts was ten to a hundred times that in the low-ranking districts in 1990. In 1978, the disparity was not nearly as extreme but it was enough to determine the course of the epidemic. Residents of Central Harlem in 1990 were about 100 times more likely to be exposed to TB than residents of Kips Bay/Yorkville.

We also found that the density of 25 new-cases-per-square-mile under cir-cumstances of contagious urban decay was the magic number: health districts reaching this density of cases experienced a rapid rise in incidence and case density, evolving into epicenters, districts from which TB would spread into the neighboring districts.[16]

The graph of cases plotted against year (fig.4-6) forms a classic S-shaped curve: slow rise, inflexion point, then rapid rise. Such a curve reflects a mixed hierarchically and spatially diffusing epidemic (see Chapter 3). The slow initial rise comes from spatial diffusion from a primary epicenter. The inflexion point represents the instant when the disease spreads hierarchically and establishes secondary epicenters in vulnerable, densely populated communities at once. The rapid rise reflects spatial diffusion from the primary *and* the secondary epicenters.[16]

High TB incidence diffused across the City from 1978 through 1990 (see fig. 4-7). In 1978, all members of the top quintile (top one-fifth of the 30 districts for incidence) but one were confined to Manhattan. By 1982, both Brooklyn and the Bronx contained members in the top quintile. By 1984, Morrisania (Bronx) and Bedford-Stuyvesant (Brooklyn) had reached the "magic" density of 25 new-cases-per-square-mile or more. The inflexion point of 1982–84 coincides with these signs of hierarchical spread to the vulnerable districts in the Bronx and Brooklyn. From then on, the Bronx and Brooklyn experienced such strong spatial spread of TB that by 1990, no health district in the Bronx and only one in Brooklyn had an incidence at or below the 1978 citywide incidence.[16]

Interaction between household transmission (facilitated by housing over-crowding) and community transmission between households (facilitated by high case density and high susceptible-population density) brought about the spreading epidemic. As the epidemic proceeded after 1978, the number of health districts with incidence above the citywide 1978 incidence increased. Not only did the number of high-incidence districts increase (geographic extent), but the average incidence of these districts also increased (intensity). Extent *and* intensity of the epidemic increased between 1978 and 1990. The driving force behind this spread and intensification was the furiously increased intensity of the main primary epicenter, the top-ranking district, Central Harlem.

Central Harlem during this period was neither the poorest nor the most housing-crowded district, although it contained the single poorest census tract in the City. However, it was and is poor enough, crowded enough, and destabilized enough to be extremely vulnerable. The population densities of Central Harlem and of the Lower East Side (a district which assumed top rank for one year in 1979 and may also be a primary epicenter) exceed those of poorer districts and of districts with greater housing overcrowding in terms of percent of the housing units. This greater population density leads to the greater case-density-per-square-mile and the rapid transmission between households that is necessary for sustained disease propagation.

The major primary epicenter's incidence determined the incidence pattern of the following year during the 1979–90 period. As its incidence rose, it "pulled up" the incidences of the other health districts with similar characteristics. Indeed, the great difference in incidence between the primary epicenter and the rest of the city provided the pressure for disease spread much the same way the difference in height between two connected bodies of water results in flow.

Central Harlem, the major primary epicenter, fulfilled the three require-ments for sustained, intense transmission within and between households: high poverty rate, high percent of extremely overcrowded housing units, and very high population density. The other health district which also fits this description is the Lower East Side. The Lower East Side played a role in the spread of TB into Brooklyn, as the maps of spread show (fig. 4-7).

After elderly Asians, the group with highest rising incidence of TB during the 1980s was black and Hispanic men 25–44 years old. Some of this rise came directly from the rise in infection in this group with human immunodeficiency virus (HIV), the microbe responsible for AIDS (see Chapter 6). Some of the rise came directly from the effect of substance abuse on the immune system. The increase in use of drugs and alcohol translates into increased incidence of immunocompromised individuals. Even in the absence of HIV infection, drugs and alcohol are known to weaken both the cellular (white blood cells) and humoral (antibody) components of the immune system upon which resistance to TB infection and other diseases heavily depend .[18] Drug addicts in the 1960's, for example, would come down with a virulent form of miliary tuberculosis, an invasion of many organs by the TB bacillus.[19]

Some of the rise came from the zipping of infection through pathologically tightened, small, segregated social networks that were precipitated out of the unraveling large, old communities. Overcrowding in any venue causes stress, and its neuropsychological effects debilitate the immune system. Research shows that males react physiologically to overcrowding stress much more than females.[20] Even those young men who remained in households experienced overcrowding and its stress. However, the young men were also usually the first to be kicked out of doubled and tripled up households and rendered homeless. They often slept in crowded shelters, flophouses, and open-air encampments.

We can go down to an even finer scale than the health district to explore the impact of the massive destruction of poor people's housing on patterns of tuber-culosis. Each health district is comprised of 10–12 health areas. New York City has about 340 health areas, of which 63 are in the Bronx. Figure 4-9a maps the geographic distribution of the mean incidence per 100,000 of new cases of TB among men 25–44 years old for 1979–81, the "before" picture, just before housing overcrowding swelled because of the cessation of middle-class emigration and the continued endemic housing destruction by fire. Figure 4-9b maps the same phenomenon for 1982–85, the "after" picture. The huge increase in incidence followed the housing overcrowding both into the newly extremely overcrowded West Bronx and into the increasingly overcrowded remnant of housing in the Hunt's Point area of the South Bronx. This map makes clear how an epidemic stalked the path of community burn-out.

ERADICATION STRATEGY

There is no question that TB cases must be given full curative treatment because individuals must be cured. There is no question that infected contacts of active cases must be found and receive prophylactic treatment because for each infection, the risk of active disease eventually arising is high (probability over 10% in a lifetime). These are medical requirements for individual cases and infections. But curing of individual cases and infections differs vastly from control of the disease in populations.

All major declines in TB mortality and morbidity occurred long before the invention and use of anti-TB drugs. Population-level prevention and control has only one proven pathway: wholesome living and working conditions.

Anti-TB drugs prevent the bacteria from reproducing. When the bacteria divide, the daughter cells must plug the gap in the wax coat caused by cell division before becoming refractive to the drugs. The drugs kill off the daughter cells, but cannot reach dormant, non-reproducing cells. Treatments require 6-12 months to "cure" TB while these dormant cells gradually die off. The tuberculosis and leprosy bacilli can live a very long time in a dormant state, and a "cure" really leads to a low number of live bacteria remaining in the body. Some rare cases are not cured even after "full" treatment but recede into long-term dormancy with the potential for reactivation even decades later.

One of the early anti-TB drugs, streptomycin, fell into disuse as the more potent post-World War II armory became available: isoniazid, ethambutol, pyrazinamide, and, most recently, rifampicin. Isoniazid, in combination with one or more of the others, is the drug of choice. Rifampicin comes into use most often when the diseased or infected person harbors a strain of TB resistant to the three more frequently prescribed drugs. Several secondary ancillary drugs may also be prescribed, but only along with these primary anti-TB weapons.[21]

Isoniazid and rifampicin poison the liver and have caused fatal liver failure in TB patients.[22] Even when liver toxicity doesn't cause marked changes in liver function, these drugs are so toxic that they make people sick with their side effects. The debilitating side effects often motivate diseased or infected people to stop taking the drugs before the population of bacteria declines sufficiently to represent a "cure." Repeated brief exposures of the bacteria to the drugs weeds out the drug-susceptible strains and fosters growth of drug-resistant strains. Thus, the very toxicity of the drugs ironically fosters drug resistance indirectly. When the strain of TB bacillus resists all available drugs, the only intervention possible harkens back to the late nineteenth early twentieth Century: surgical removal of infected tissue.[23]

Why wouldn't anti-TB drugs be the answer to an epidemic such as New York City's? Anti-TB drugs require very stable social conditions, even if directly observed therapy (DOT) is used on *every* reported case. First, the cases have to be found. In the conditions of widespread disrupted residency that pervades poor neighborhoods, unreported cases may comprise a significant proportion of the true total. Using the correlation between 1990 TB incidence and the product of index of extreme housing overcrowding times the poverty index times years in epidemic, we found the health areas of under-reported and over-reported cases. The areas of over-reported cases were those with large census undercounts, i.e., true incidence was lower than officially calculated because true population was higher. We then estimated the number of cases which should have been reported from the grossly under-reported areas and found that about 23% of the cases were unreported. This percent of underreporting is within the range estimated off-the-cuff by the Director of New York State TB Control during a conversation at a New York Academy of Medicine TB Conference in 1991: 20–40%. It is very close to the 22% estimated by the Los Angeles Department of Health from the number of cases reported only at death.[24]

Likewise, infected contacts must be found, an expensive and laborious task in times of upheaval. Of course, the harder it is to find cases, the longer the time during which transmission of infection can occur and the more infected contacts. The more crowded and unstable the living and working arrangements, the larger the number of contacts. The more frequent the changes in residency, the more people exposed.

With increased funding from the Public Health Service (to the tune of $40 million per year beginning in 1992), the New York City Health Department hired many more case managers to go to the homes of reported TB cases and directly observe the taking of the drugs daily, locked up recalcitrant reported

cases who refuse to take the drugs, and followed up case-contacts more inten-
sively with a larger staff and computerization. These are the major components
of the beefed-up TB prevention and control program. There is nothing in the
control program about the determinants of TB susceptibility, transmission, or
reactivation: the socioeconomic and environmental factors.

Because in the first two years, the beefed-up program of medical intervention, with its squadron of case-finders and workers, its Directly Observed
Therapy, and its forceable confinement of recalcitrant cases, led to large
declines in *reported* new cases, the TB establishment quickly claimed that it
worked. The claim meant that the threat of TB to the middle class was cosmeti-
cally removed without ameliorating the living and working conditions of the
poor. It allowed middle-class people to believe that TB could be controlled even
if vast numbers still lived in substandard, grossly overcrowded housing, go
homeless entirely, or work 60 hour weeks in illegal overcrowded, dangerous
sweatshops. It allowed them to believe that they could be made safe by risking
the livers and lives of the poor with the anti-TB drugs. No one mentioned that
even the middle-class working and living conditions—overcrowded "tight"
workplaces, pressure-stressed work relations, the threat of so-called "downsiz-
ing" and isolation-stressed home relationships—leave workers from data-entry
clerks all the way up to upper management more generally susceptible to TB.

Nor have public-health officials admitted that the massive medical intervention does
not work all the time, even when it is being applied with might. In fact, during
February and early March 1995, the weekly reports of new TB cases from the CDC
revealed an outbreak so that for several weeks, more cumulative TB cases were being
reported than had been reported during the analogous weeks of 1994.

We shall not know if this control program worked until about 50 years have passed
and revealed the extent of the dormant infections acquired now, during the beefed-up
program. The emergence of multiple-drug-resistant tuberculosis (MDR-TB) may also
be an outcome of this drug-centered program. The more people who are treated with
the drugs, even with DOT, the higher the probability that drug resistance will arise. If
no part of the program minimizes the number of reactivations, the number of infections which immediately go to disease, and the number of susceptibles, then the population taking the drugs becomes very large. Only good working and living conditions
can minimize eventual anti-TB drug recipients and lower the risk of emergence of
MDR-TB.

But when data don't support the medical interventionists, they, like Dr. Marr
in 1979, blame the immigrants. In making statements about the proportion of
TB cases which occur in the foreign-born, public-health officials, like the director of the New York City Bureau of Tuberculosis Control, mislead the public

into thinking, first, that all infections among the foreign-born were brought in and not acquired in the US, and second, that the flare-up of active disease, wherever the infection was acquired, has nothing to do with the American urban socio-economic structure only with immigrant status. Harping on the proportion of new cases which arise in the foreign-born mythologizes the total rise in cases in New York City and other large American cities.

But conditions fostering both reactivation and transmission prevail widely here. We know that transmission occurred from the rise in cases among pre-school children and from the case/contact studies. We know it from the maps of spread. We know it from the relationship between new-case incidence and the socioeconomic factors of housing overcrowding, population density, and poverty. Only a cynical decision to mislead the public and to reinforce the worst xenophobic bigotry can explain attributing the epidemic to immigrants.

Housing overcrowding, localized population density, and poverty worsened horribly after municipal service cuts created massive housing destruction in New York City's traditional ghettoes. It was this destruction of physical and social community that led directly to increased TB reactivation and transmission and to epidemics of substance abuse and AIDS/HIV.

Table 4-1 POPULATION DENSITY, PERCENTAGE OF EXTREME OVERCROWDING, AND INCIDENCE OF TUBERCULOSIS BY BOROUGH

BOROUGH	POPULATION DENSITY	EOC	TB INCIDENCE
	people/sq mi		*(new cases/100,000)*
Richmond	5,138	1.02	13.2
Queens	18,393	1.74(0.86-3.12)	21.2
Brooklyn	37,013	3.01(0.83-6.60)	27.9
Bronx	35,721	3.18(1.41-5.84)	29.0
Manhattan	67,808	3.78(2.08-5.47)	52.3

Population Density: 1975

EOC (Percent Extremely Overcrowded Housing): 1970

TB new cases/100,000: annual average 1973–1975

Table 4-2 PERCENTAGE OF EXTREME OVERCROWDING AND TB INCIDENCE BY BROOKLYN HEALTH DISTRICT

HEALTH DISTRICT	EOC	TB INCIDENCE
G	0.83	8.8
I	1.24	8.6
H	1.34	15.3
F	1.61	19.0
J	1.72	19.2
A	4.28	25.3
B	4.41	27.7
D	4.48	43.5
E	5.10	40.3
C	6.60	66.8

EOC = extreme overcrowding

TB Incidence = number of cases per 100,000

Table 4-3 DECLINE OF TB IN NYC

YEAR	CASES	INCIDENCE	DEATHS	MORTALITY RATE
1840/1845				473*
1870				433*
1900			9630	280 (210)*
1901–1905			9400	248.3
1906–1910			10120	226.3
1911–1915			10160	201.2
1916–1920			9104	165.7
1921–1925		179 (1925)	5691	92.2
1926–1930		180 (1930)	5244	78.2 (54*)
1931–1935		131 (1935)	4566	64.3
1936–1940		121 (1940)	4025	54.7
1941–1945	7,062	91.9	3585	47.2
1946–1948	7,676	98.7	3161	40.6
1949–1951	77,127 (1950)	97.6 (1950)	2345	29.6
1952–1955	6,857	87.2	1275	16.2
1956–1960	4,699 (1960)	60.4 (1960)	876	11.3
1961	4,360	56.0	738	9.5
1962	4,437	57.0	740	9.5
1963	4,891	62.9	683	8.8
1964	4,207	53.7	581	7.4
1965	4,242	53.3	592	7.4
1966	3,663	45.6	537	6.7
1967	3,542	43.6	525	6.5
1968	3,224	39.7	485	6.0
1969	2,951	36.4	418	5.2
1970	2,590	32.6	386	4.9
1971	2,572	32.6	316	4.0
1972	2,275	28.8	335	4.2
1973	2,101	26.6	259	3.2
1971	2,022	25.6	215	2.7
1975	2,151	27.2	208	2.6
1976	2,156	27.3	187	2.4
1977	1,605	21.1	175	2.3
1978	1,307	17.2	181	2.3
1979	1,530	20.1	121	1.5
1980	1,514	19.9	143	2.0
1981	1,582	22.4	155	2.2
1982	1,594	21.7	168	2.4
1983	1,651	23.4	151	2.1
1984	1,629	23.0	168	2.4
1985	1,843	26.0	155	2.2
1986	2,223	31.4	186	2.6
1987	2,197	31.1	219	3.1
1988	2,317	32.8	247	3.5
1989	2,545	36.0	233	3.3
1990	3,520	49.8	250	3.5

* Age-adjusted mortality rates. All others are crude rates.

Table 4-4 TB CASES PER 100,000 PEOPLE BY HEALTH DISTRICT

HEALTH DISTRICT	INCIDENCE		DIFFERENCE
	1978	*1990*	
Manhattan			
Central Harlem	52.2	233.4	181.2
East Harlem	14.2	124.2	110
Kips Bay/Yorkville	12.3	7.4	-4.9
Lower East Side	45.8	133.1	87.3
Lower West Side	36	62	26
Riverside	31.5	64.7	33.2
Washington Heights	33.8	71.6	37.8
Bronx			
Fordham/Riverdale	14.2	35	20.8
Morrisania	19	112.8	93.8
Mott Haven	12.9	83.8	70.9
Pelham Bay	7.5	29	21.5
Tremont	19.2	82.5	63.3
Westchester	6.9	24	17.1
Brooklyn			
Bay Ridge	5.3	10.3	5
Bedford	30.4	112.7	82.3
Brownsville	25.5	59.5	34
Bushwick	15.5	85	69.5
Flatbush	11.4	36.7	25.3
Fort Greene	43.1	84.3	41.2
Gravesend	5.7	19.2	13.5
Red Hook/Gowanus	13.5	39.4	25.9
Sunset Park	10.7	27.4	16.7
Williamsburgh/Greenpoint	9.8	65	55.2
Queens			
Astoria/Long Island City	15.3	52	36.7
Corona	20.4	38.2	17.8
Flushing	5.6	15.9	10.3
Jamaica East	15.4	46.7	31.3
Jamaica West	8.9	24.7	15.8
Maspeth/Forest Hills	9.8	14.9	5.1
Richmond (Staten Island)	5.8	12	6.2

Table 4-5 TB CASES PER SQUARE-MILE BY HEALTH DISTRICT

HEALTH DISTRICT	1978	1982	1986	1990
Top five districts in 1990 for incidence				
Central Harlem	43	66	82	144
Lower East Side	29	34	56	89
East Harlem	13	18	48	81
Morrisania	15	18	31	45
Bedford	19	21	35	55
Bottom five districts in 1990 for incidence				
Gravesend	2	5	5	7
Flushing	1	2	1	2
Maspeth-Forest Hills	2	2	2	4
Richmond (SI)	<0.5	1	1	1
Bay Ridge	2	3	3	4
Kips Bay/Yorkville	6	5	7	4

Figure 4-1 THE LIFE CYCLE OF TUBERCULOSIS

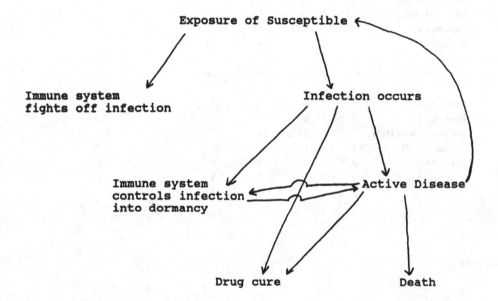

Figure 4-2 EXAMPLE OF THE DECLINE OF TB IN WESTERN CITIES: NEW YORK CITY, 1900–1990

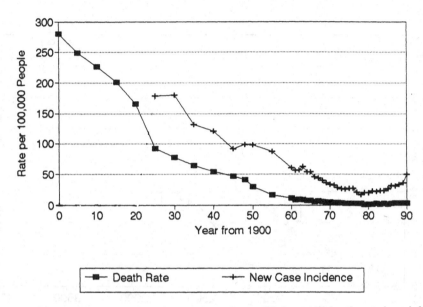

Note that the decline in both mortality and in new-case rate began well before anti-TB drugs began to be used after World War II.

Figure 4-3 CITYWIDE PERCENT OF
EXTREMELY OVERCROWDED

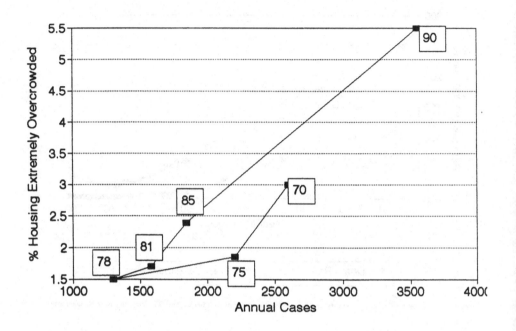

Housing vs. Annual Number New Cases of TB.

The numbers in the boxes are the calendar years. As crowding increased, so did the number of TB cases. When it declined, TB cases declined.

Figure 4-4 INCIDENCE OF TB AMONG CHILDREN
UNDER 5 VS. TOTAL INCIDENCE BY RACE

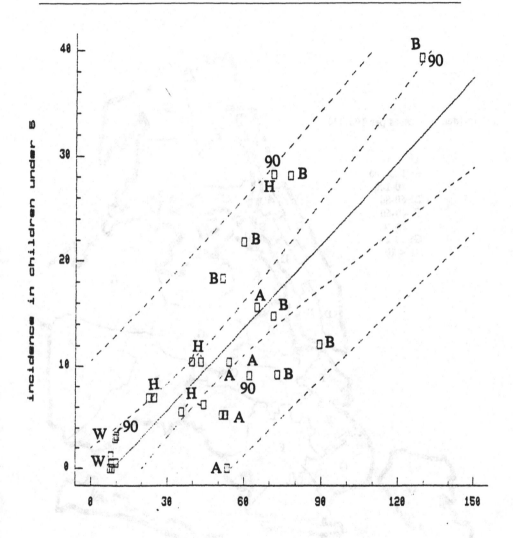

W = white   B = black   A = Asian   H = Hispanic

TB among pre-schoolers indicates home transmission. Note even white children had their highest incidence in 1990, as did black and Hispanic children. Even white children were drawn into the epidemic by 1990.

Figure 4-5 GEOGRAPHY OF TB INCIDENCE IN 1990

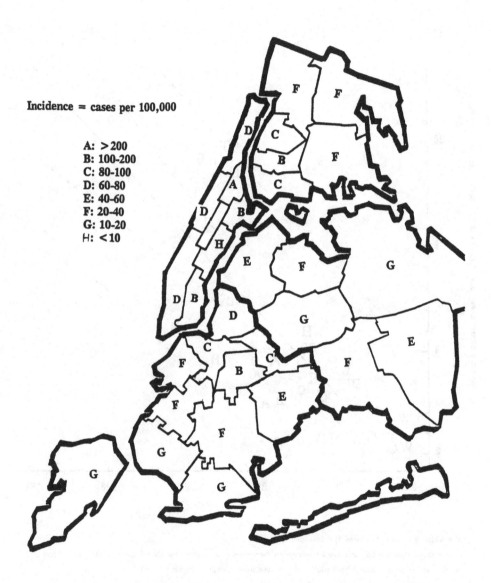

Incidence = cases per 100,000

A: >200
B: 100-200
C: 80-100
D: 60-80
E: 40-60
F: 20-40
G: 10-20
H: <10

Note the two bands of high incidence: the Harlem-South Bronx band and the Lower East Side–near-Manhattan Brooklyn band (Fort Greene, Williamsburg, Bedford-Stuyvesant, Crown Heights, Bushwick, and N. Brownsville)

Figure 4-6 THREE-YEAR RUNNING AVERAGE OF NEW TB CASES VS YEAR

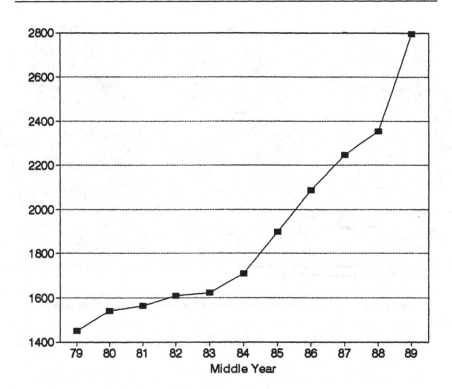

Note the slow rise until 1983. Then the rise is rapid. This is the classic S-curve of an epidemic with mixed hierarchical and spatial diffusion. The rapid rise occurs after the secondary epicenters are established.

Figure 4-7 THE SPREAD OF HIGH TB
INCIDENCE OVER TIME

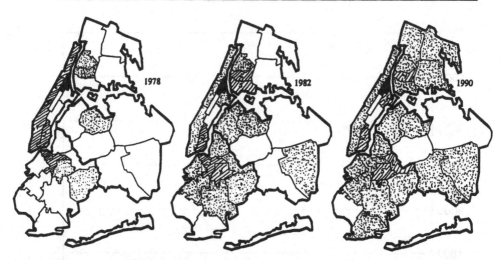

Note. Black = top district; striping = remaining quintile districts 2–6 as numbered; stippling = "over 1978" district. Staten Island (Borough of Richmond) has been omitted and is not in the top quintile or the "over 1978" group.

—Maps of the top quintile and of the additional districts with incidences above the 1978 citywide incidence.

By 1990, all districts in the Bronx had incidences above the 1978 citywide level, and all districts in Brooklyn but one also had high incidence.

Figure 4-8 INCIDENCE VS RANK OF THE TOP 15 HEALTH DISTRICTS.

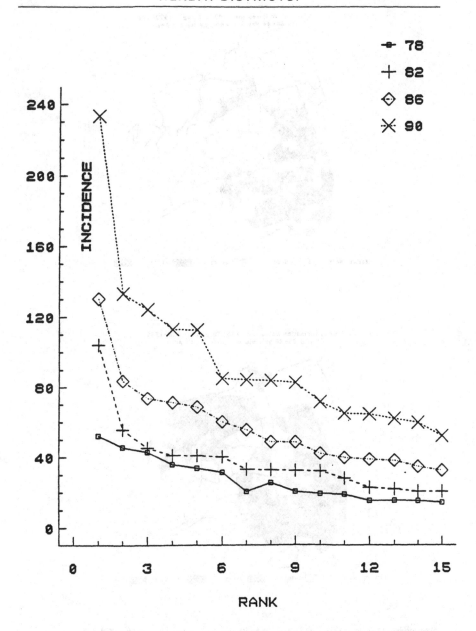

Note how in 1978, the top-ranked district lay along the same line as the others. By 1982, the top-ranked district is much higher than the others. By 1990, districts with ranks 2-5 had also pushed above the others so that the line is no longer smooth.

Figure 4-9 GEOGRAPHIC DISTRIBUTION OF TB IN THE BRONX

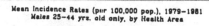

Mean Incidence Rates (per 100,000 pop.), 1979–1981
Males 25–44 yrs. old only, by Health Area

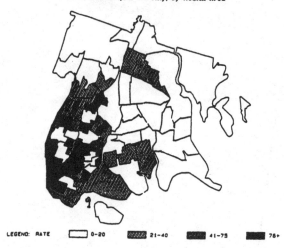

LEGEND: RATE   ☐ 0–20   ▨ 21–40   ▨ 41–75   ■ 76+

Mean Incidence Rates (per 100,000 pop.), 1982–1985
Males 25–44 yrs. old only, by Health Area

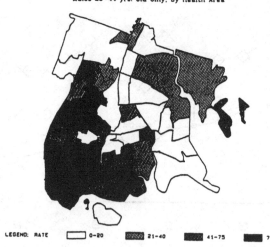

LEGEND: RATE   ☐ 0–20   ▨ 21–40   ▨ 41–75   ■ 76+

Mean incidence rates for males 25–44 years old by health area. Top map (a): mean rates for 1979–1981.

Bottom map (b): mean rates for 1982–1985.

Note how the disease massively consolidated in the newly overcrowded West Bronx.

5

SUBSTANCE ABUSE

AMERICA AND "SUBSTANCES"

Americans obsess about race, sex, money, and "substances." Images of use and abuse of tobacco, alcohol, heroin, cocaine, LSD, and, recently, virtual reality pervade American popular culture. Older cultures—whether European, Asian, or African—accepted use of alcohol and other mood-altering drugs. They knew that these chemicals can become problematic and developed communal methods of containment. The United States is one of the few countries where the use of psychoactive substances slips easily into massive epidemics of addiction and violence.

Most addictive substances, even caffeine, elicit some level of disapproval in most American communities. The challenge, thus, is to indulge in forbidden pleasures without succumbing to addiction or without getting caught. This challenge is especially true for illegal drugs and applies inconsistently to alcohol and tobacco. Morality plays about failing the challenge range from the hit movie *Lost Weekend* which won Ray Milland an Oscar, to *Down These Mean Streets* by Piri Thomas, the whiny, druggy ghetto autobiography much touted in the 1960s.

Substance abuse is largely linked to one's status and identity in America and these are usually determined by race and money. Although identity is classically associated with neighborhood or town, in America, it is often not conferred by the physical dwelling place because Americans move so frequently. Thus, large sectors of the population feel that they do not belong and that they are less than human in the eyes of "real Americans," an experience of psychic pain that is a prescription for substance use, especially among men. While women make up about two-thirds of diagnosed cases of depression, men make up about two-thirds of alcoholics,[1] and the male proportion of illegal-drug users is even larger. For details on the relationship between substance use and the psychic pain of dislocation and alienation, see the appropriate chapters in *Substance Abuse: A Comprehensive Textbook* (specifically, the 1991 edition).

Here we narrow our focus to alcohol, because of its impact on public health and public order and to heroin and cocaine because of their recent importance in New York and other deteriorating cities. Heroin and cocaine are at the heart of the massive drug trade at all scales of geography, from the international traffic down to the seller on the block.

ALCOHOL: LEGAL, LETHAL, AND ADDICTIVE

With the advent of sophisticated economic analysis in the mid-1970s, the research on the health, safety, and economic costs of alcoholism to American society has revealed its pervasiveness and intensity. The popular press regularly reports on the vast annual cost of alcohol (billions of dollars) when its impacts —health care, property loss and damage, loss of life—are summed up, on the high proportion of traffic accidents in which at least one driver had a blood-alcohol-level above the legal limit, and on the number of violence-induced injuries connected with alcohol. We will not go into the details of these facts and figures here. Rather, we shall touch on the following topics as they relate to the burning down of New York City neighborhoods:

1) the relationship between disaster and alcoholism,

2) the changing geography and incidence of cirrhosis, indicative of the changing geography and incidence of alcoholism.

3) alcoholism and violence, both domestic and in the larger community, and

4) employment and substance use (discussed in the section on drugs). The analysis applies to alcohol as well.

In the section on illegal drugs, we shall also discuss the phenomenon of cross-addiction.

In chapter 3, we described the burning down of New York neighborhoods as a man-made disaster and noted several studies that show the individual and community psychological outcomes of man-made disasters to be worse than those of natural disasters because of the victim's recognition of the failure by those responsible for the event to value them as worthy humans.[2] This betrayal in the case of "planned shrinkage" occurs on a continuing basis in public policy, an ongoing violation of the individual and communal humanity of target populations.

Recourse to alcohol after a serious individual-life event is not uncommon.

Recourse to alcohol and heavy dependence on it have been noted in groups of people after such serious community-life events as massive layoffs, toxic contamination of neighborhoods, and loss of homes due to disaster.[3] "Planned shrinkage" acted as such a disaster in New York City and appears to have triggered elevated use of alcohol.

If we accept incidence of cirrhosis and cirrhosis mortality as indices of incidence and prevalence of alcoholism, changes in the rate and geographic pattern of cirrhosis deaths over time should indicate trends in alcoholism in affected and unaffected areas. A lot of booze has to flow through a liver before it becomes fatally cirrhotic. Indeed, most alcoholics do not die of alcoholism, but of other effects like the alcoholic impairment of the immune system which leaves them open to a variety of infectious diseases and the injuries, both accidental and violent, to which people under the influence are prone. Not all alcohol-related deaths occur in drinkers; drinkers also cause death in others. But still, cirrhosis-mortality patterns can serve as a crude indicator of other alcohol-related deterioration in individual, family, and community function.

We have taken the Bronx cirrhosis-death rates as an example in Figure 5-1 because the Bronx is composed of 63 health areas, rather than the larger number in the other heavily affected boroughs. Please note the change in intensity scales on the two parts of Figure 5-1: the most intense range in the cirrhosis-incidence map for 1970–73 is 38 to 76, but for 1978–82, it is 51 to 97. The ranges of incidence each represent one-fifth of the health areas (a quintile).[4]

Before the burnout, high cirrhosis death incidence formed a stable spine in the center of the western "lobe" of the South Bronx. A set of independent variables consisting of housing overcrowding, socioeconomic-status rank, population, and incidence of low-weight births could explain 28% of the cirrhosis-mortality-incidence variability among the Bronx health areas.[5]

After the burnout, high cirrhosis-death incidence marked nearly all the health areas of the Southwest and West Bronx. Many more people were dying annually from cirrhosis than before the burnout. The same set of independent variables could explain 57% of the cirrhosis-mortality incidence variability among the Bronx health areas.[5] This means that cirrhosis-mortality incidence, the index of alcoholism, became much more heavily influenced by poverty, overcrowding, and lack of connectedness.

Similar changes in incidence and geography occurred in Manhattan, Brooklyn, and Queens: cirrhosis-mortality rates increased and shifted in their geography to include both the old burned-out areas and the areas which received the refugees.

Freeman and McCord, in their classic study of mortality rates in Harlem, found that cardiovascular-disease deaths accounted for 23.5% of the excess deaths in men, and cirrhosis 17.9%. In post-burnout Harlem, cirrhosis ranked second as a cause of excess deaths in men. Indeed, homicide, cirrhosis, and drug deaths accounted for over 40% of Harlem's excess deaths. Black men in post-burnout Harlem are less likely to reach age 65 than men in Bangladesh, and alcoholism plays a large role in this pattern.[6]

The congressman who represents Harlem, Charles Rangel, accepted contributions from the tobacco and alcoholic-beverage industries for years and headed off any efforts at health-promotion campaigns in his district which advocated decreased consumption of his contributors' products. When higher taxes on cigarettes and alcoholic drinks were proposed in the mid-1980s, Rangel would defend tobacco and alcohol as the poor man's recreation. Well-financed ad campaigns specifically target low-income communities like Harlem. Many of these ads feature gangsta youth and glorify hostility and violence. These alcoholic drink ads target mostly those too young to buy booze legally, and numerous "sting" operations by police and health departments across the country which have youngsters going into stores and buying beer, ale, and other booze have shown that the great majority of retailers sell to the underage without even asking a question.[9] The upshot is that large numbers of under-21s buy the fashionable 40-ounce St. Ives and Colt malt liquor bottles.

The Harlem churches began painting over the huge cigarette and liquor ads concentrated near schools and churches and to denounce Rangel as a protector of his constituents' killers. It was only after this popular resistance that Rangel changed his position about poor people's right to this recreation—the right essentially to cancer and cirrhosis.

As a deadener of inhibitions, alcohol has always been a factor in promiscuity, violence, and spur-of-the-moment crimes of robbery and vandalism.[7] A community experiencing a rise in alcohol abuse as indicated by both the citywide temporal trend and the Bronx maps is also one experiencing more brawls, stabbings, broken store windows and vandalized park benches, spilling of garbage cans, muffed robberies ending in injury or death of the victim, and domestic violence. The papers published in the social- and medical-science literature—the same ones which inspire the media stories on the costs of alcohol— provide both statistics and case histories on the role of alcohol in these events.

Public drinking may become the rule and involve large groups of men who become rowdy and abusive. The police are generally reluctant to intervene because alcohol is not an illegal drug. But the combination of property destruction, violence, and gross disorder is one from which people with resources will flee. The failure to control the disorder of alcoholism, especially to prevent alcoholism, leads to further community destabilization, marked by the flight of the remaining middle class. This further destabilization renders more people susceptible to needing alcohol.[8]

Even if this belligerent alcoholism were the only outfall of the housing and community destruction caused by planned shrinkage, it is enough to mean further disruption of family and community life.

HEROIN AND COCAINE

Just as disaster leads to elevated rates of alcoholism, particular kinds of disaster lead to elevated rates of heroin and cocaine use. Viet-Nam veterans, for example, had high rates of heroin addiction and required a disproportionate number of treatment slots, compared with their representation in the general population. When Robert Lifton surveyed these veterans in the late 1970s, he found that most of them suffered from post-traumatic syndrome dysfunctions (PTSD).[9] Besides the flashbacks which are the most dramatic symptom, PTSD features an ongoing dread and fear, depression, guilt, anger, inability to concentrate and to learn easily, hyperirritability, uncontrollable reactions, and disrupted sleep. Of course, these men and women went through an extended time of danger and of immense uncertainty. They never knew when or where their lives would be at immediate risk. They saw companions wounded and killed and knew that they, too, could go that route at any time.

Mindy Fullilove, a professor of community medicine in the Columbia School of Public Health, organized a project on female addicts-in-treatment in Harlem. She gave each of about 70 women a standard diagnostic psychiatric test and found that a very high proportion fit the profile for PTSD. Additionally, she found that drug addiction correlated highly with having been abused more than once as a child.[10] The women she studied were children at the time of the burnout. If the aftermath of community burnout is a high proportion of adults with PTSD, their children are at high risk of repeated abuse and will also have PTSD. Heroin and cocaine will fill the same needs for these adults and for their children when they reach ages 12–20 as for the Viet-Nam veterans.

Alcohol and hard drugs serve many purposes for those suffering from PTSD, not least of which is slow suicide. The withdrawal of fire service left burned out communities defenseless and insecure and churned out wounded spirits as surely as the Viet-Nam War did.

Incidence of drug addiction has been correlated with certain chronic social ills: a weakened family well embedded in a community; housing overcrowding and very high population density, so that large numbers of unsupervised youth congregate; no older mentor or family member with the responsibility of caring for the youth; and great uncertainty hanging over the family with respect to income or residence.[11] These ills resemble each other in that they all signal lack of structure and security. Before the burnout, when the communities were far more structured, families were poor but not abject and not simply straws on the tide of urban waves of destruction. Poverty did not automatically translate into instability and lack of support and supervision for the young.

Figure 5-2 shows the pre-burnout and post-burnout patterns of drug-overdose-death incidence for the health areas of the Bronx, analogous to Figure 5-1. As with cirrhosis deaths, the pre-burnout high incidence areas occupy the central spine of the western "lobe" of the South Bronx. These areas, however, lost 50–80% of their housing during the burnout. The overdose deaths shifted to the east and west of that central spine and into the eastern "lobe" of the South Bronx as well. High overdose incidence affected a much larger number of health areas after the burnout. The change in scale between the two parts of figure 5-2 does not indicate a decline in drug abuse, but a change from heroin, which easily causes overdose, to cocaine and crack, which cause overdose much less easily. The important data in the two maps is the change in the geography of the index of drug use. The newly overcrowded, newly disrupted, newly impoverished neighborhoods which received the refugees became further disturbed by high rates of drug use and drug traffic.[12] Our material was presented at a state-wide drug prevention and control conference in 1986 with the backing of Dan Beauchamp, then special alcohol and drug consultant to the governor and lieutenant-governor. It was, however, never factored into state drug policy, which never shifted from the ineffective and narrow focus on individual present and potential users and addicts.

Our maps clearly show that drug use and abuse rocketed in the path of the burnout and became spread out over so many large areas that the usual educational and treatment programs would require vast resources to cover these enlarged areas sufficiently to make any difference at all. "Planned shrinkage" seems to have smeared drugs all over the Bronx, Upper Manhattan, the Lower East Side and East Village, the poverty corridor and transitional neighborhoods of Brooklyn, and the immigrant neighborhoods of Queens. Even Staten Island did not escape; it grew a drug problem on its north shore which received the spillover of refugees from Brooklyn and Lower Manhattan.

Throughout this period, Governor Cuomo and public-health authorities recognized demand, not supply as the main problem in the drug epidemic. Going after supply merely shifts attention to other countries, the supplier countries, and diverts attention from the American side of the equation. But, unlike Cuomo, to truly face the demand for drugs, we would have to look beyond the individual to the large-scale patterns of demand: specifically, poor minority youth constitute a hugely disproportionate sector of drug buyers, users, abusers, and addicts,[15] and geographic analysis places them in either the destroyed communities or the communities receiving the refugees. These are also the communities with youth unemployment rates in the 30–60% range and with underemployment rates of the employed even higher. (By "underemployed," we mean a combination of less than living wages and dead-end, menial jobs with high risk of occupational injury or illness.)

The other social ill highly correlated with drug addiction is high community rates of unemployment among the youth. The double-headed hydra of lack of economic opportunity and lack of community social networks leaves the youth of these hard-hit areas without a structure on which to mold their time and effort. One of the great attractions of the drug-selling scene is that the organization provides hierarchical structure and opportunity for advancement. If you work hard, show initiative, and take risks, you will get some kind of immediate reward. You will have a schedule on which you can depend, co-workers to share tasks and experiences with, a dependable boss, and a whole organization behind you. You will be a part of something bigger than yourself. You may even meet "businessmen" from Colombia, Nigeria, Myanmar, Thailand, or the Middle East. Not bad for a young man passed over by the mainstream economy and mainstream society.[13]

Advancement of this kind, however, usually does not come to addicts, but to sellers who don't sample the wares. Addicts usually do not rise beyond the level of street seller. Indeed, most addicts are buyers and not involved in the business. But for these addicts, too, drugs offer a structure for their lives. They actually feel better taking the drugs. The reality of the unbuffered poverty and its constant threats to shelter and daily bread is more pain, fear, and worry than many of us can take. Drugs give temporary relief from these feelings and make the addict rise to the challenge of somehow assembling enough money for necessities and the next fix. Drugs are holding many addicts together, even though only temporarily and at a great cost to the body and soul. Elliot Currie describes this benefit of drugs, one which few health or law enforcement officials ever acknowledge.[14] To acknowledge it would be to point to the segregation, discrimination, and deliberate grinding down of poor minority communities.

Terry Williams in *The Cocaine Kids* describes the alternative economic and social structure of New York's cocaine industry from the Colombian cartels to the Dominican middlemen down to the black and Puerto Rican street sellers.[16] The drug industry is the strongest, most functional organization in many disrupted neighborhoods and a major employer of the youth. It offers discipline, solidarity, chance of advancement, better wages, an outlet for strategic creativity and marketing talent, and respect.

Recruiting young men into the drug trade is easy in disorganized neighborhoods because there is nothing else going on. Large groups of unemployed youths hang around with nothing to do. There is no prospect of anything else, and the young men face being pushed out of the family home when it becomes overcrowded. The non-productive young males are the first to be "fledged" when families double up or when an adult daughter with children has to return home, either because of a breakup or because of loss of her own apartment. If the young man is bringing good money into the house, he may not be evicted even if doubling-up occurs.

On the other hand, Currie described programs in which ex-addicts and ex-offenders were given meaningful jobs. These jobs were located in the communities of residence and involved community service and improvement. Recidivism and re-addiction were low, much lower than for similar individuals who were returned to their communities without such opportunities. Some of the lucky ones in these programs moved up the ladder, went to school, and became professionals.[17]

The sentencing for drug offenses now made mandatory by recent laws funneled young black and Latino male drug-users and sellers into state prison in New York. Since 1980, over 80% of the prisoners in these upstate facilities have come from only seven New York City neighborhoods, the most disrupted, broken communities.[18] Looking at the individual and at drug supply will not address the forces which this amazing statistic demonstrates as underlying the drug problem in New York City and State.

Elliot Currie's 1993 book *Reckoning* explored the American illegal-drug picture and dynamics. The pattern and process has remained essentially the same as when first observed by social scientists in the 1950s: segregation, constricted opportunity structure, and weakened families all interact to raise the susceptibility of black and Latino youths to drugs. The major changes between the 1950s and now feature predation on minority communities by public policy, reinforcement of workplace discrimination by recent Supreme Court decisions, and deepening of the general employment crisis.[19] This last factor includes de-industrialization on a national level, movement of the remaining factories to areas which discourage union organizing and workplace integration, and shipment of industrial work to countries with very low wage scals and unhealthy, dangerous working conditions.

The simultaneous shredding of community social networks and decline of good jobs in the older industrial cities essentially denies employment to urban minority Americans, especially the young with no previous employment records. Community social networks once channeled information of all kinds, including job availability. Even when jobs are available, awareness of them and knowledge of how to apply for them now flow along very short channels and never get to many young people who would have been part of a larger network if "planned shrinkage" had not shredded the communities.

Due to the large proportion of young minority males entering prison, a criminal social network has ended up substituting for broken community networks. Besides having bonded in prison with members of that network, they are released with a prison record and have an even more constricted set of opportunities than before their arrests. They have nowhere to go for opportunities but the drug scene.[20]

Reckoning describes how even users who don't sell drugs can structure their lives around drugs. They have street business. They have to raise the money for their buys; they have to find safe places to use their buys. They have to get food and shelter. These are busy people who survive from hour to hour. They feel capable of meeting tough challenges. Drugs give them a sense of worth because they get so much done. Drugs make them feel better.[21]

DRUG POLICY

Politicians from Andrew Cuomo to Rudy Giuliani who turned City Hall into a prosecutor's office have narrowed their drug policy, especially in connection with the homeless, to individual treatment. The Giuliani-era policy is that the homeless are not to receive shelter, food, or medical care unless they are either drug-free or in treatment. Besides the fact that there aren't enough treatment slots of any kind to fulfill the demands of the poor addicts who voluntarily sign up for treatment, let alone the homeless involuntarily ordered into treatment as a condition of getting a bed for the night, the treatment of individuals has never been proven to affect the incidence of drug use, abuse, or addiction. Treatment is like the anti-TB drugs: at best, individuals may be "cured," but the population processes dominate the incidence patterns.[22]

At worst, like the anti-TB drugs, treatment may not work in all cases. Indeed, less is proven about drug-treatment effectiveness than about the effectiveness of antibiotics. "Treatment" covers a range of interventions from supply of a substitute drug like methadone to individual counseling to group therapy. Some programs also get clients into jobs, social groups, and houses of worship. Some programs do very little, nothing beyond checking the client's urine weekly and telling the client to stay clean for another week. Programs show a wide range of recidivism rates. This is another reason why reliance on treatment backfires.[23] Currie noted that a good part of the recidivism is inevitable if the client returns to his or her neighborhood with its narrow opportunity structure, its overcrowding and disorder, its disease, and its continued victimization by public policy and private interests.[24]

S. South in 1982 found that communities experiencing high rates of in- or out-migration (but especially in-migration) had high rates of deviant activity like drug use, alcoholism, violence, and property crimes. Community control over behavior is weakened by the chaos of rapid migration; breakdown of community control lessens the ability of weakened families and individuals to control themselves.

The traumas which lead to one addiction leave the individual and group open to others. Cross addiction is common. Cigarettes and alcohol often go together. In 1981, C. P. Kane[25] found that a high proportion of the alcoholics who signed up for treatment in the Bronx had the added complication of drug use. Polyaddiction means that various combinations of behavior appear in the affected groups and individuals: alcohol, drugs, sexual hyperactivity, violence, and destruction or disruption of community function.

When Charles Rangel contrasted legal and illegal drugs and stymied needle exchange programs designed to prevent AIDS spread among drug addicts, claiming they encouraged hard drug use but ignoring the addictiveness of tobacco and alcohol, the contexts of their increased use in Harlem, and their relationship to hard drugs, he set up a false dichotomy.

True prevention must go beyond treatment to minimize the losses, traumas and abuse which bring on the need for pain killers, for relief from reality, and for a vacation from the self, even loss of self. The individual does not exist in a vacuum, but in family and in community. Stability of residence is not just staying in a physical home. It fosters the connectedness which underlies individual and family strength, function, and satisfaction.[26]

Yet our only systemic response has been to look to authorities such as police power to keep the excesses within limits. The irony is that, after the rise of the drug trade, New York experienced massive police corruption in nearly all precincts covering ghetto neighborhoods. Police officers would steal the drugs seized during raids and sell them in the suburbs. Others would buy "wholesale" and sell in the suburbs as a kind of suburban annex to the inner-city organizations. A large contingent would take a regular cut from the sellers' profits, a kind of city tax.

During the early 1990s in the 30th Precinct (Manhattan, West 135th–155th St.), dozens of officers would steal drugs directly from the street pushers and sell them. The pushers would continue to sell openly. This bizarre situation occurred in the midst of a highly publicized war on all levels of the drug trade. The former policy of going after the top levels and leaving the street pushers alone had been repudiated in favor of an all-out assault on the whole machine. Officers would arrest a few uncooperative street pushers and appear to be doing their jobs. The theft of the drugs and subsequent sales were hidden from public view, but everyone was puzzled that there seemed to be as much open drug traffic and as many addicts nodding out in public as before the "declaration of war." There seemed to be as much petty crime associated with addicts getting their fix money. The corruption went on for a long time before an arrest in Rockland County of an officer selling dope there broke the whole mess open. Long after the "Dirty Thirty" was supposedly cleaned up, the district was still awash in open drug dealing.[27] It appears that the only way the police hierarchy can keep the patrol officers from deep involvement in the drug trade is to instruct them to ignore the street-level action. Another benefit of ignoring open selling is stability and minimizing of bloody turf wars. Each time an operation is closed and its territory opened up, all the rivals come out armed to the teeth to stake claims on the new areas. The sound of gunfire becomes habitual in these wars. Lots of people are killed, including mothers and small children in playgrounds caught in the crossfire. A big public outcry ensues, and the police look bad. The police brass appear to have decided that a stable territorial division is better than a high level of overt violence.

But this open dealing makes drugs easily accessible to susceptible youth. It also leads to general neighborhood deterioration, including decisions by landlords not to invest in proper building maintenance and operation and by potential buyers of apartments not to buy there. Who would want to live on a block with 16–18 hours a day of drug dealing? Thus, the already floundering neighborhood continues to spiral downward, due to public-policy decisions.

The decision to trade no hassling for "peace" may not work. If an important function of the drug scene is challenge, an outlet for talent, and a way for young men to earn respect, then the temptation for one or another organization to increase its market share will be too great. The truce, at best, will be only temporary

Figure 5-1 AVERAGE CIRRHOSIS DEATHS PER 100,000 FOR BRONX HEALTH AREAS

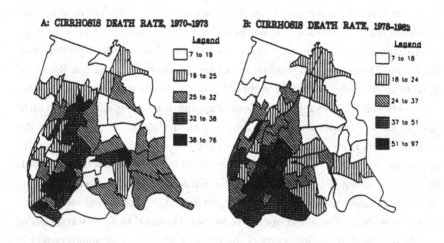

A. Map of average annual rates, 1970–1973.
B. Map of average annual rates, 1978–1982.

Figure 5-2 AVERAGE ANNUAL DRUG-OVERDOSE
DEATHS BY BRONX HEALTH AREA

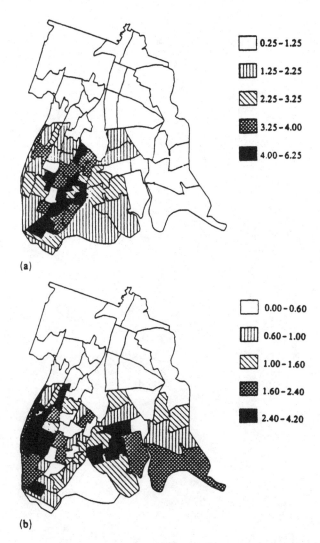

Bronx Health Area map of annual number of drug-related deaths by quintiles:
(a) 1970-73, (b) 1978-82. (Note that the shaded scale is not the same in the two parts.)

6

AIDS
INCURABLE AND FATAL

HIV AND AIDS:
BASIC SCIENCE AND TRANSMISSION[1]

The new drug combinations which contain protease inhibitors can prolong the asymptomatic period of HIV infection and even life itself. However, they do not cure, and have been found to allow retention of the infection in particular cells. Thus even now, the terror which AIDS (acquired immunodeficiency syndrome) holds over us flows from its incurability and fatality. Although a few infections have reversed themselves and another few infections have remained dormant for very long periods (over a decade), the nearly invariable course of infection ends in full-blown disease within 5–8 years of initial infection of a healthy person and death within 2–3 years of overt disease without the new protease-inhibitor treatment. The life spans under the new treatment are not yet known. A person who is infected while in poor health has a shorter time of latent infection. Pediatric infections, usually of infants born to infected women, end in disease and death in a much shorter time than even adults who are infected while in poor health.

Unlike tuberculosis overt disease isn't necessary for HIV-infection transmission. Thus, an ignorant or denying person may be or pretend to be unaware of being infected and may transmit the disease. Initial infection has only minor signs in most people: sore throat, swollen lymph glands, fever. They pass after a few days, like a minor respiratory infection, and the infected person returns to seeming good health. Even the HIV-seroconversion blood tests in general use cannot pick up the infection in its earliest stages. About six months must elapse between the initial infection and reliable detectability of the anti-HIV antibodies in the blood. Opportunities for transmission abound.

The disease is caused by a virus ("retrovirus") which attacks the immune system, especially the white blood cells which remove and kill invading microbes. Without a normal battery of these white blood cells and their attendant antibodies, microbes propagate in the body and cause serious disease. Microbes which usually cause no problems and are normally present in the lungs, mouth, and digestive tract can become pathogenic if nothing controls their numbers. AIDS sufferers generally don't die directly of AIDS but of an onslaught of other diseases and infections, including virally-induced cancers.

HIV is transmitted when blood, breast milk, semen, or vaginal lubricating mucus from an infected person enter the body fluids of an uninfected person. Mucus membranes such as the lining of the genitals, the anus, and the mouth can provide a conduit into the bloodstream. Heterosexual vaginal sex and gay or straight oral or anal sex are common transmission routes. Mixing of blood is the other major avenue of transmission. Intravenous-drug users sharing needles and people receiving blood transfusions from poorly screened sources run high risks of infection. All blood in the U.S. is now screened. HIV can also be transmitted from women to their babies during birth and from infected nursing mothers to their infants in breast milk.

HIV/AIDS is one of several so-called "emergent" diseases which arose in the very recent past (less than 30 years ago). They received that label because humans had not been recorded as hosts for the microbe before. A number of these diseases, including HIV/AIDS, Lyme disease, hanta, Ebola, Green Monkey virus, and human granulocytic Ehrlichiosis, are thought to have been transferred from animal hosts to humans. Other "emergent" diseases arose from mutants of older strains which have infected humans for centuries and include new forms of cholera, malaria, gonorrhea, and tuberculosis. Most of these mutants represent the microbe's reaction to the evolutionary pressure of antibiotics and are more virulent, antibiotic-resistant forms of older human pathogens.

HIV/AIDS is one of several diseases which have evolved ways of evading both the body's defenses and curative medicines. Typically, the microbe or parasite can rapidly change its outer protein or composite coating. The genes may be already programmed for rapid coating change or for rapid mutation which leads to coating change.

One of the primary defenses against microbes and parasites is the battery of antibodies which the body creates when confronted by alien proteins or polysaccharides ("antigens"). The antibody is finely sculptured to lock onto the microbial antigen, to "recognize" that antigen and only that antigen. Major changes in the antigen cause failure of the antibody to lock onto it. This stops the body's immune response from recognizing the infection and proceeding. HIV/AIDS is a mutation machine. Once in the body, it mutates rapidly so that an infected person harbors a plethora of different substrains. This is one reason that, to date, no successful vaccines to immunize humans against this fatal disease or any truly curative drugs have been developed. The drugs in use can prolong life but the virus still finds refuge in such cells as nerves and lymphocytes and eventually may mutate.

Other diseases with rapid mutation or programming for rapid coat change are malaria and African sleeping sickness. Diseases which have become more mutation-prone from widespread use of antibiotics include tuberculosis, cholera, gonorrhea, and pneumonia from certain bacteria (pneumococcids). The multiple-drug-resistant tuberculosis has led to several fatal outbreaks recently because it is more virulent than the normal strain and can be cured only by lung resection.

Many diseases are propagated by vectors, transmissive factors without which the disease could not be contagious. For example, malaria and yellow fever are transmitted by mosquitoes. Although most epidemiologists think of vectors as biological species which transport and transmit disease microbes, Paul Ewald, a proponent of Darwinian epidemiology, has developed the concept of social vectors, mechanisms arising out of the structure and function of social organization which lead to disease transmission. Furthermore, just as insect vectors influence the virulence of the disease microbe, Ewald finds that social vectors do also.[2]

As we have said above, the HIV virus mutates continually after infection. Each infected individual contains a spectrum of different substrains, although usually closely related to the original infecting strain. The modes of transmission will influence which substrain actually gets transmitted. Some are more fit for homosexual transmission (anal), some for heterosexual (vaginal), and some for direct bloodstream injection. Sociogeographic isolation of human groups practicing different modes of transmission give rise to the major strains of HIV. These strains differ in their virulence. What is believed to be the original African heterosexually transmitted strain (HIV-2) is much less virulent than HIV-1, the major strain which dominates the North American epidemic. HIV-1 further divided into several other strains, designated by letters A-G, which differ in geographic area, major mode of transmission, and virulence. What the people afflicted by the various strains have in common, with the exception of those infected through medical devices or treatments ("stick" accidents, blood transfusions, and organic transplants), is marginalized status: sexual orientation, poverty, ethnicity, and, in some societies, gender. In Southeast Asia, girls from poor families are sold to be prostitutes in Thailand, whereas the boys are kept home.

THE AMERICAN AIDS EPIDEMIC

Ah, the index case, the famous INDEX CASE! What reams have been devoted to this peripatetic mortal portal through which HIV entered America! He was a gay man, a flight attendant who traveled continuously, and sexually hyperactive. He probably became infected with HIV in Paris, where many populations mix, including frequent visitors to Africa and African immigrants to France.

On his return, he hopscotched around the major cities of the country but spent much time in California, New York, and Chicago. His frequent changes of sex partners in these places left several latent infections in a short time. These infections became the bases for the first wave of the AIDS epidemic in North America, the male homosexual wave.[3]

Gay communities in the United States resemble African-American communities in being segregated and suffering from heavy discrimination. The discrimination against gay individuals and couples in the larger society leads to establishment of gay ghettoes which, like black ghettoes, suffer community-level discrimination and violence. They respond by turning inward. The severe pressure then causes intense, tight social interaction within the gay community and a tendency of gay men to invest heavily emotionally in the sexual aspect of their identities, similarly to the investment of black males in racial and sexual aspects of identity.

The first cases in the first wave of the AIDS epidemic appeared in San Francisco and New York around 1980. By 1983, cases began appearing in large numbers in the population of intravenous-drug users who, as mentioned in the previous chapter, are disproportionately Latino and black. In those three short years, AIDS deaths among gay males skyrocketed. Because the post-burnout population of intravenous drug users, like other poor communities, is fragmented into many small, tight core-groups, the AIDS epidemic lurched through it, taking a relatively long time to enter a given core group, but sweeping through it rapidly because of the tight relations within each group and the loose connections between the groups.[4]

As we detailed in the previous chapter, many more drug users were added to the user population because of the wave of housing destruction and its fall out. The increased population (and density of users in the affected neighborhoods) not only increased the number of exposed people but brought them to a density which ensured a self-propagating epidemic. Thus, the increased AIDS cases from 1984 onward reflect an increasing proportion contributed by intravenous-drug users, most from the burned-out zones or the adjacent receiving areas.[5]

Drug-related HIV transmission also reflects increased cocaine and crack use. These drugs require no injection. In fact, when the connection between needles and HIV transmission became general knowledge, many users substituted cocaine for heroin. The majority of entrants into drug use opted for cocaine or crack to avoid the needle risk, because of the lower risk of overdose death, and because of the very low initial price asked by sellers of new users. Cocaine and crack, however, also raise the libido. Unprotected sex occurs frequently among the users. In addition, female addicts, especially crack addicts, prostitute themselves for very little money, just enough for the next fix. The high number of partners a cocaine or crack user may have in a short time greatly raises the probability of HIV transmission.

Via drug-related transmission, HIV entered its third phase: heterosexual transmission. One major source of heterosexually transmitted HIV infection arose from the widespread prostitution of addicts. Many prostitute patrons would have unprotected sex with infected prostitutes and then have unprotected sex with their unsuspecting wives or longterm lovers. Mary Fisher, who addressed the 1992 Republican Convention to plead for a compassionate AIDS plank in the platform, had been infected by her addict husband. The fastest rising rates of AIDS during the early 1990's were among heterosexual women, although this group had begun the decade with rates much lower than those of gay males or IVDUs (intravenous-drug users). These early heterosexual transmissions tended to be between adults over 25 years of age.

Now, the fastest growing rates of heterosexual transmission are among the young, especially young black and Latin women. Recent (early 1996) reports by the CDC show that infection rates have leveled off for the various sectors of the population over 25 years of age but have kept rising with no indication of slowing among 15–25-year-olds.[6]

Contrary to conventional wisdom, the amazing feature of the HIV/AIDS epidemic is that it is a single epidemic. Although the groups represented among AIDS cases may shift in sexual orientation, race, class, age, and sex, the trend over time is a single smooth curve. These populations overlap. Some gays are addicts. Bi-sexuals have both homosexual and heterosexual contacts. Some prostitutes are addicts. Some "good family men" inject drugs or visit prostitutes. The progress of the disease through American society illustrates the ultimate unity of that society.

In his book *The Slow Plague*, Peter Gould, the guru of medical geography in the US, produced the first detailed maps of the successive spread of AIDS across the face of the country.[7] The relentless march of death rode on the backs of a succession of interlocked subpopulations. Gould's maps show how the international cities on each coast with large gay populations were seeded first. In a second step, the disease spread to other large cities at a distance (hierarchical spread) and out into the suburbs (spatial diffusion). In time, the hierarchical process carried AIDS from the large cities of over a million people to middle-sized cities of one-hundred thousand to a million. From them, it spread both hierarchically and spatially.

Now, over fifteen years into the epidemic, very few places, whether urban or rural, have no AIDS case or HIV infection. In only fifteen years, an estimated one-to-two million people in the United States have been infected. To date, AIDS has racked up over 200,000 deaths in this country alone.

HIV/AIDS IN NEW YORK CITY

Let us turn to our compact research borough, The Bronx, to examine the geography of AIDS and what it tells us about the context of the epidemic in New York City. Figure 6-1 shows AIDS deaths and death rates through 1988. We see two different geographies: the very high death rates per 100,000 in the burned out zone (south-central) and the high number of deaths resulting in high death rates in the areas adjacent which received refugees.[8] Compare these figures with those of drug deaths in the previous chapter. High numbers of AIDS cases coincide in geography with high numbers of drug deaths. Clearly, the two have a relationship. These data are confirmed by Schoenbaum's testing for HIV positivity of ER patients and pregnant women in the South-Central Bronx: as much as 20% of the emergency-room patients and 5% of the pregnant women attending prenatal clinic were HIV-positive in the mid-to-late 1980s.[9] High rates of AIDS spread from the South-Central burned-out zone to the destabilized adjacent areas. Because of the long incubation time, we must be careful in interpreting the maps and Schoenbaum's data: in these years, both population and HIV infection patterns changed greatly. The pictures we see, especially AIDS deaths, reflect the interaction of forced migrations and increase in drug use and sexual activity of many years.

Chapter 5 described the relationship between the shredding of communities, the new face of unbuffered poverty, housing overcrowding, and the increased incidence of substance abuse. When the large interlocked social networks of the pre-burnout communities fractured into small slivers, the pattern of disease transmission, particularly of sexually transmitted diseases, changed greatly. Transmission between individuals and between communities in the pre-burnout era had lower probability for several reasons: 1) interaction was less concentrated and spread out socially even while it was more geographically focused; 2) intact networks maintained better behavioral control; 3) networks supported their members in need; and 4) alternative anti-social structures affected only a small fringe which was left powerless. When fragmentation gave rise to many smaller networks of intensely interacting individuals, the very intensity of the interactions and the alternative behaviors fostered by fragmentation determined rapid transmission of any sexually transmitted disease (STD) which penetrated a given group. Very high rates of infection in these small groups determined a high probability of eventual disease spillover into other groups if even a very small number of inter-group interactions occurred. Because of the residential instability attendant on the housing famine, the individuals composing the small hyper-interactive groups vary over relatively short periods of time, and individuals switch from one group to another, a pattern assuring transmission between groups.[10]

These dynamics underlay the AIDS epidemic entering the subpopulation of young black and Latin heterosexuals. However, even without the rise in incidence of substance use and abuse, this shift between the gay-male population and minority heterosexuals would eventually have occurred. Non-European cultures often have less rigid definitions of sexual identity and orientation than those of the dominant Anglo-Saxon strain in America. The idea that risk from homosexual activity poses no risk to heterosexuals ignores the existence of bisexuals, of homosexuals with a facade which includes a marriage, and of such cultural concepts as machismo which implies a rather febrile pan-sexualism. Human sexuality is much more plastic than most of us want to admit. At best, sexual identity is a cultural construct; more likely, it's a fairy tale we tell ourselves.

Back in 1978, as part of our expert-witness testimony on the move of Engine 234 from the center of black North Crown Heights to serve whiter South Crown Heights and East Flastbush, we looked at patterns of the conventional venereal diseases gonorrhea and syphilis. Table 6-1 repeats some data from tables in the tuberculosis chapter, namely the population densities and housing overcrowding indices, and adds incidences of gonorrhea and syphilis for the five boroughs and for a smaller scale, the health districts of Brooklyn. Housing overcrowding and population density each correlate significantly with venereal disease incidence, but the former more strongly than the latter. The only anomalies seen in this pattern reflect differences in the age structure of the neighborhoods. Even overcrowded neighborhoods may have low venereal-disease incidence if a very high proportion of the population is elderly. On the other hand, neighborhoods with both high frequency of overcrowded housing units and high proportions of the population under 25 years old had very high incidence of venereal disease. These data are from pre-burnout years.[11] Even under the best circumstances, housing overcrowding overcame the efforts of the public-health system. After burnout, epidemics of syphilis and gonorrhea flared in the wake of the social disruption and increased housing overcrowding.

Incidences of venereal disease indicate frequencies in the population of unprotected sex and multiple sex partners. Because of short incubation periods for gonorrhea and syphilis, these disease incidences reflect either rapid changes of partner or more than one partner, rather than slow serial monogamy. Because of the long incubation period of AIDS, its incidence reflects all forms of departure from strict monogamy practiced by the various subpopulations: rapid change, multiple partners, and slow serial monogamy. Conventional venereal disease, however, signals behavior conducive to HIV transmission. Overcrowding must be taken as a contextual factor for sexual transmission of HIV as well as for the drug-related modes of transmission.

Staff clinicians at Bronx Lebanon Hospital kept track of the HIV status of the expectant mothers using the prenatal-care clinic. They found 5% were positive for HIV infection in the mid-to-late 1980s.[12] Similarly high rates of infection have been reported from prenatal clinics in other ghetto areas such as Harlem. We believe that the women who don't use available prenatal care may have even higher rates of infection because of their greater disconnection from and possible aversion to the mainstream social network. In contrast, rates reported from sentinel hospitals in white suburban areas typically do not exceed 0.5% With the prenatal clinic and the AIDS-deaths data as indices, we can conclude that the destruction of low-income housing, through a variety of direct and indirect mechanisms, fueled the AIDS epidemic in New York City, concentrated it heavily in the poor minority areas, led to a much larger epidemic than would have otherwise occurred, and marked a generation as surely as did Pharoah's and Herod's murders of babies.

If substance abuse and sex without condoms transmit HIV infection, AIDS deaths should depend on the same social and environmental factors as cirrhosis deaths and low-weight births which indicate the respective behaviors of HIV transmission. We measure poverty and its living conditions with the Index of Extreme Housing Overcrowding and socioeconomic rank. Our measurement of community disintegration is annual number of low-weight births per thousand live births. Together these indices of poverty and community disintegration explain a high proportion of the health-area patterns of the two indices of transmission behavior and of AIDS deaths in the Bronx: 57% of cirrhosis deaths (annual average 1978–82), 79% of the intentional deaths in 1980, and 67% of the AIDS deaths (cumulative 1980–85).[13] The AIDS deaths in the Bronx are classed as mainly drug-related and/or heterosexual. The *Atlas of AIDS* describes the southwest corner of the Bronx as "the primary focus of this second epidemic which spills out into the neighboring black ghetto of Harlem." The poverty belt of Brooklyn is noted as a secondary focus of drug-related heterosexual AIDS.[14]

TRAVELING WAVES AND FEEDBACK

The physical and social conditions following the burnout jacked up the rates of substance use and addiction and thereby ratcheted the AIDS epidemic into high gear much more rapidly than would otherwise have happened. As the next chapter will describe, violent crime also bloomed, partly as a fallout from the drug increase. Violence itself contributed to social and physical destabilization in the post-burnout period, a vicious-circle effect of destabilization to more violence to more destabilization. We speculate that AIDS and TB may also have contributed to destabilization. People with resources or with family to help may have gotten as far away as possible from their neighborhood's danger, disease, and disorder .

In our earlier discussion of the fire epidemic, we described how an epidemic can be viewed as a traveling wave passing through a community. HIV/AIDS can also be viewed this way. The speed and intensity of the wave depends largely on the structure of the community. If the connections between the individuals and families are stable and strong, the number and density of susceptible individuals will be low; the wave will move slowly and be no more than a surface ripple. If the community has "melted down" socially and is fragmented into isolated small groups, the number and density of susceptible individuals will be high. The wave will travel rapidly and deeply through the fragmented community.[15]

Many years of research on traditional STD's like syphilis and gonorrhea support the conclusion that the stability, size, and connection strength of social networks determine the incidence of disease and probability of high incidence. Core groups composed of a small number of individuals who move around or who migrate between two or more places are particularly vulnerable to a traveling wave of infection.[16]

A highly developed formal mathematical treatment has also examined the size and structure of social networks with respect to STD and AIDS dynamics.[17] If the density of susceptibles goes below the level needed to propagate the disease through the population (threshold level), the wave simply won't travel. It will dash itself harmlessly against the rock of community.

However, in broken communities, AIDS took hold and claimed many victims. The population suffering from AIDS added to the feeling of degeneration which open drug-taking and drug-dealing conferred, on top of the physical decay of the empty, charred hulks of buildings, since poor AIDS sufferers are much more visible than middle class and wealthy ones. Data on length of hospital stays of AIDS cases in areas of differing income levels indicate that poor AIDS sufferers were much sicker and required longer hospital stays. For causes of admission other than AIDS, the poor were discharged after much shorter stays compared to the middle and wealthy classes. The anomaly of AIDS hospital-stay length means that the poor were admitted at a much later stage and were much sicker.[18]

We aren't positing that in and of themselves, high concentrations of AIDS sufferers trigger migrations, but we do think that the AIDS epidemic is another straw on the camel's back, further breaking down communities destroyed by the city's burnout. AIDS is another factor that the overworked, shrinking community organizations in these areas must heed and service. Indeed, Upper Manhattan has a separate Task Force on AIDS to the meetings of which hospitals, clinics, and community groups send representatives. Because people cannot be ignored in their life-and-death struggles with AIDS, the remnants of community extend whatever help is possible. This drains attention and energy from traditional gadfly political activities needed to ensure hard services and maintenance of the infrastructure. So the vicious circle takes another turn, as it churns out more homeless, more AIDS cases, more addicts, more children born to children—all of whom demand help.

HIV AND TB[19]

HIV and TB infections have a special relationship. Both of these infections drain the immune system as the body fights to keep from succumbing to overt disease. HIV infection increases the probability of TB infection if exposure occurs. The doubly infected person often experiences a rapid, virulent onset of active tuberculosis disease with difficult diagnosis because many HIV-infected people do not show normal antibody reactions and give a false-negative skin test. As of early 1996, the new diagnostic methods relying on TB DNA had just been approved for general use by the FDA. HIV-infected people also have a higher frequency of non-pulmonary and miliary tuberculosis. Miliary TB, invasion of several organ systems by the TB bacillus, is especially difficult to cure even with the anti-TB drugs.

HIV-infected people also come down with mycobacterial diseases from other species, such as avian mycobacteria. This susceptibility further complicates diagnosis. Some of these other mycobacteria respond better to anti-leprosy drugs than to anti-TB drugs.

People with TB infection appear more susceptible to HIV infection and succumb to full-blown AIDS more rapidly than others. The two diseases facilitate each other.

Double infection by TB and HIV is now highly concentrated in the black and Latino male age group 25–44. With rising HIV-infection rates among the under-25-year-old youth, this picture may become even grimmer, as the age range of this so-called risk group widens.

We must restate an important fact here. HIV did not cause the TB epidemic, although it undoubtedly contributed to it. That epidemic began before HIV had penetrated poor communities and fed on the burnout and post-burnout housing overcrowding, mixing of populations, and disruption of community. Likewise, TB did not cause the AIDS epidemic but facilitated it.

CHILD VICTIMS OF THE AIDS EPIDEMIC

HIV-infection rates on the rise among the youth presage a continued rise in HIV-infected newborns. The infection usually progresses to AIDS more rapidly in children than in adults. HIV and AIDS in children present additional complications to those in adults. Children need to play with other children, and we are all familiar with the phenomenon of colds, flu, and other diseases zipping through nursery schools, playgroups, and kindergartens. Those in charge have to develop complex, ironclad prevention programs to keep the HIV-infected children from harm.

Concentrated presence of HIV/AIDS children in certain areas may dispirit the neighborhood residents much more than similarly afflicted adults. Deaths of children from incurable disease are heavy blows to a community.

The other child victims of the AIDS epidemic are the orphans. Both parents may be lost to the disease or one may be imprisoned on drug-related convictions and the other dead of AIDS. The grandparents or an aunt sometimes steps in and raises the orphans, often in circumstances of great poverty. Why shouldn't the same problems arise in a New York ghetto as were seen in villages of the Rakai District in Uganda, a high-AIDS-incidence area: Children orphaned by AIDS and raised in circumstances of extreme unbuffered poverty characteristic of disrupted communities are especially prone to crime and reliance on deviant peer groups. The Rakai District was the theater of the war between Tanzania and Uganda.[20]

BEYOND CONDOMS AND NEEDLE EXCHANGES

The medical establishment offers "harm reduction" as the ultimate means of preventing HIV infection. Needle-exchange programs have been shown to reduce transmission among IVDUs. Condon use could greatly reduce transmission and, among older gay males, certainly did. However, comdoms are not consistently used in all sexually active sectors.

Indeed, even the progress in behavioral change made in the gay community is not being completely sustained. A higher proportion of younger gay males participate in risky, unprotected sex than the older generation which experienced the shock of the first wave of AIDS as adults. Part of the continued rise of HIV-infection rates among the young may come from behavioral relapse.[21]

However, the preponderance of the rise in infection rates rests on risky heterosexual activity. When AIDS became a major source of mortality in Africa, it was transmitted mainly by heterosexual relations, long chains of couplings. After faithful wives began dying in large numbers because of their husbands' infidelities, relief organizations and public-health agencies told the women to make their husbands wear condoms. Because of the powerlessness of the wives, this did not work, and the women divided into two camps: those who persisted in unprotected sex with their husbands and those who retreated into celibacy to protect themselves.

Now American women face the same dilemma, especially those in high-incidence areas. The strategy of non-profit organizations and public-health agencies here echos the African failure.

Because most drug-related HIV transmission now does not involve needles and because drugs destroy large number of lives in many other ways, our prevention vision must go beyond needle exchanges. Because condom use is not happening consistently enough even among those educated about sexual HIV transmission and how to prevent it mechanically, our prevention vision must go beyond condom distribution. We must rebuild communities so that substances or compulsive promiscuity are no longer needed (or indeed tolerated) to relieve pain. Both economic opportunities and socially functional neighborhoods are the best AIDS-prevention programs.

The deaths of the young, orphaning of children, and sense of danger hanging over all sexual relationships followed from Roger Starr's denial of community and form the true legacy of "planned shrinkage."

Table 6-1 POPULATION DENSITIES, HOUSING OVERCROWDING, AND SEXUALLY TRANSMITTED DISEASES

A. by borough

BOROUGH	POPULATION DENSITY,	IEO	GONORRHEA	SYPHILIS
Richmond	5138	1.02	221.9	21.0
Queens	18393	1.74 (0.86–3.12)	261.9	33.4
Brooklyn	37013	3.01 (0.83–6.6)	485.5	70.7
Bronx	35721	3.18 (1.41–5.84)	540.1	83.0
Manhattan	67808	3.78 (2.08–5.47)	1028.2	198.9

B. by Brooklyn health district

DISTRICT	IEO	GONORRHEA	SYPHILIS
G	0.83	127.9	18.6
I	1.24	105.1	16.9
H	1.34	139.7	25.7
F	1.61	365.4	58.7
J	1.72	115.0	21.0
A	4.28	764.3	116.8
B	4.41	319.5	59.2
D	4.48	902.0	122.6
E	5.10	738.2	104.0
C	6.60	1430.1	164.1

Pop. Dens=population density (people per square-mile)

IEO=index of extreme housing overcrowding (percent of housing units with 1.51 persons per room or more)

Gonorrhea, syphilis=incidence of the disease (new cases per 100,000 people)

Figure 6-1 THE BRONX HEALTH AREAS

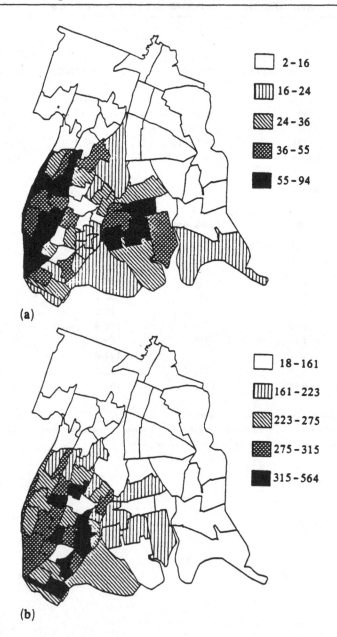

(a)

(b)

a: Cumulative number of AIDS deaths through 1988

b: Rate per 100,000 of cumulative AIDS deaths through 1988

7

EPIDEMICS GALORE

CLUSTERING, CONTAGION, AND INFECTION

Several cases of a disease or other health impairment may arise in a small area within a short time. If the disease is measles, flu, or any other caused by a microbe, the pattern of clustering develops primarily as a result of infectious-disease transmission. The pattern of index case (first one in the area), primary cases (contacts of the index case), and secondary cases (contacts of the primary cases) is a jigsaw puzzle which epidemiologists can assemble with well-established tools.

However, not all contagious health impairments arise from infectious disease. Substance abuse follows the pattern of index, primary, and secondary cases (a branching process), but involves no microbe, having a behavioral-spread mechanism.

Some clusters of disease develop not out of contagious phenomena, but from shared environmental exposures. Gerard Rushton's elegant analysis of birth defects in Des Moines could not, as of January 1996, identify the toxic exposures responsible for the geographic pattern of birth defects, but ruled out chance and other causes.[1] The rise in cases of and deaths from asthma in the urban ghettos may result from environmental exposures such as automobile exhaust, nitrogen oxides from cooking on gas stoves in overly-insulated buildings, and cockroach feces and exoskeletons.[2]

Most disease patterns cannot be neatly classed under one of the three headings of infectious disease, spread of a behavior, or environmental exposure. Environmental exposures affect the immune system and modulate rates of infectious disease. Environmental and socioeconomic conditions also contribute to susceptibility for contagious behavioral conditions. Infectious disease may modulate susceptibility to environmental health effects.

In previous chapters, we discussed a purely contagious infectious disease (TB), an infectious disease heavily dependent on behavior (AIDS), and a contagious behavioral pattern greatly influenced by socioeconomic structure and function (substance abuse or addiction). These three health impairments far from exhaust the list of those greatly intensified and spread by the burnout. In this chapter, we discuss a variety of other public-health impacts of the burnout.

LIFE EXPECTANCY OF THE ELDERLY

In 1990, McCord and Freeman had noted the specific causes of excess mortality in Harlem.[3] The top-ranked cause was cardiovascular disease, a spectrum of conditions which affect the middle-aged and elderly most. We found a decided change in life expectancy trend in 1980 for elderly blacks in New York City, as opposed to elderly whites. Figures 7-1 and 7-2 show life expectancy of blacks and whites at age 60 and age 70 respectively, 1950–80. Something terrible obviously happened to the elderly blacks but not the whites. Cardiovascular disease reflects stress, exposure to carbon monoxide (mainly from vehicle exhaust, bad furnaces, and cigarettes), and family and community malfunction, so that the senior citizen cannot get help and medical care when needed. Other stresses may include raising one's children's children.

INFANT MORTALITY AND LOW-WEIGHT BIRTHS

At the other end of the age spectrum is infant-mortality rate and rate of low-weight births. Although higher than that of whites, the infant-mortality incidence of non-whites in New York had been falling at a faster rate and was closing the gap in the late 1960s and early 1970s. By the mid-to-late 1970s, the fall had slowed decidedly and the gap began to widen again. Geographically, infant-mortality rate resembled our maps of cirrhosis, AIDS deaths, and drug DOA's.

Infant mortality is closely connected with low birthweight. Newborns weighing less than 2500 grams (5.5 lbs) show lower survival and are considered low-weight births; those weighing less than 1500 grams are considered extremely low-weight births and usually suffer from a multitude of developmental deficits if they survive. Several studies in recent years have followed groups of children, pairing cases and controls.[4] The results of these studies consistently reveal the human and economic costs of low-weight births. These children require vast medical, educational, and social-service resources. Many never lead independent lives.

Changes in incidence of low-weight births per 1000 live births over the Bronx health areas closely resemble the changes in substance-abuse incidence and incidence of violent death. Indeed, regression analyses showed that SES (socioeconomic status rank,) proportion of housing units with 1.51 persons per room or more, and number of low-weight births per 10,000 live births together predicted incidence of intentional death. The incidence of low-weight births is taken as an index of the unraveling of the social networks and of families and of the disconnection of the resulting fragments from the mainstream. In well-functioning families, family members check to be sure that a pregnant relative goes to the doctor, follows the doctor's advice, and lives in a healthy way. The community also keeps watch over her, especially the other women. Health information from the public-health authorities, from clinics, and from educational institutions (agencies of mainstream society) flows to pregnant women both directly and indirectly through community channels. The fact that incidence of low-weight births is one of the three independent factors which together predict incidence of violent death supports the interpretation that low-weight births indicate social unraveling, as do the maps and the temporal changes in incidence.[5] Figure 7-3 shows that the incidence of low-weight births per ten thousand live births shifted geographically in a way similar to substance abuse and violence, and worsened from 1970 to 1980 and from 1980 to 1990.

We should also consider low-weight birth densities per square mile. The boroughwide measures of central tendency all showed large increases in 1990 over those of 1970 and 1980:

	1970	1980	1990
average	3404	3346	3794
median	2951	3198	3294
mode	2802	2751	3018
geometric mean	2229	2185	2558

The borough as a whole thus struggled under increased burden from these births; poor, disrupted communities and the isolated families within them faced huge increased demands from the sheer densities of these extremely needy newborns.

A high percent of the women giving birth to low-weight babies receive late prenatal care or none at all. So the theory arose of reducing low-weight births by making prenatal care more available. This greater availability did little to influence incidence of low-weight births partly because many of the women did not take advantage of the health care. Similarly, offering immunization for preschool children did not bring the proportion of children immune to measles to acceptable levels (see below). The problem is not merely medical.

Another medical "solution" led to vast spending on intensive-care neonatal units in ghetto hospitals. Many black elected officials like the Mayor of Detroit snuggled up to these high-tech baubles. The babies saved in these units would never have needed them if public policies hadn't turned American cities into Dresdens and kept them that way for decades. The babies saved in these units then proceed to absorb vast sums as society copes with their developmental deficits. The decision-makers would never think of putting resources into the root problem because cutting the ribbon on a new neonatal intensive care unit garners much more political mileage than providing adequate fire service.

More recently, premature birth and resulting low weight has been associated with infections of the mother's reproductive tract, including venereal diseases. The medicos then decided that doses of antibiotics would take care of the problem and carefully proved that women at risk who were treated had a lower frequency of premature births and larger babies. So the recommendation to treat with antibiotics rang through the medical journals.[6]

Like treatment for TB, this will cure individual cases but make little or no difference in the population processes determined by living conditions and social structure. Like treatment for TB, the potential for antibiotic resistance to arise is high. Like treatment for TB, this medicalization of a socioeconomic problem simply window-dresses continued oppression.

We view high incidences of low weight births and infant mortality in two ways: as public-health and community tragedies and as indices of the connectedness of reproductive-aged women to community and family support, particularly bonds between generations of women. In organized communities and families, a pregnant woman gets advice, protection, help, little presents, and, when necessary, correction for behavior which may endanger the health of the baby or of herself. The changes in support and social control offered by the family/community combination show their power in the changed incidences of low-weight births and infant mortality.

Carol Stack described how poor women would increase their connectedness in the community and essentially enlarge their kinship claims by having children with several different men. The families of the children's fathers became family to the mother who could then rely on a wider circle for help in time of need. The networks of each father could be tapped, a very large number of people.[7]

In fragmented communities with their residential instability, these very large numbers of kin cannot be organized. The families have only truncated networks.

As one panelist in a Harlem focus group said, "We used to know everyone, even just to say good morning to. Now we don't. People are strangers."

VIOLENCE

Violence also signifies deep disconnection to the point of dehumanization. In her essay on the Eichmann trial, Hannah Arendt called violence the last recourse of the powerless and the descent into the ultimate powerlessness. Homicide and violent non-lethal crimes such as armed robbery and mugging are forms of community-level violence. Child abuse, wife-beating, and injuring of parents and grandparents ("elder abuse") are forms of household-level violence which may end in death. Suicide is violence against the self.

The Burnout affected all forms of violence. Figure 7-4 shows annual number of murders in New York City from 1945 to 1987. During the same years when TB control crumbled, when venereal diseases went wild, and when improvements in mortality rates of non-white infants slowed greatly, the murder rate soared. When we lump together murder and suicide, we get the number of intentional deaths, an index of violence. Murders greatly exceed suicides.

The Bronx geography of violence showed similar changes to those seen in previous chapters for drug deaths, cirrhosis deaths, tuberculosis, and, in this chapter, low birthweight rates. Average rates of intentional death for the entire borough changed greatly:

Ca. 1970	Ca. 1980	Ca. 1990
32.42	49.43	53.26

These are rates per 100,000 people, averaged over a few years bracketing the decadal year, to get away from any quirks and glitches likely from use of a single year. Some of this violence involved the drug trade, both battles over turf at different levels of organization and actions by users or addicts either to get money for buying or because of drug-related psychosis. Dual diagnosis (addiction and mental illness) rates also soared.

DIFFERENTIATION AND BEHAVIORAL CODING

During the 1970s, the Burnout transformed the black and Latino populations in many neighborhoods into isolated, fragmented core groups. The broad-based sociogeographic networks, with their strong connections to the mainstream, political machines shattered. Only remnants, the well-heeled sector, remained connected to the mainstream machine. More about this particular sector later in the chapter on the present situation.

The young in the small isolated core groups had few socializing influences and few supervisors. Robert Sampson, a respected criminologist, noted:

> The concentration of family disruption in black communities, especially in housing projects, underscores an important policy issue. Specifically, there are good theoretical reasons to expect that the concentration of family disruption in poor urban environments is a potential disaster so far as crime is concerned. I have argued that marital and family disruption may decrease informal social controls at the community level. The basic thesis is that two-parent households increase supervision and guardianship not only for their own children and household property, but also for public activities in the community. A century of criminological research demonstrates that most delinquents have delinquent friends and commit delinquent acts in groups. The territorial concentration of young males who lack familial social controls thus facilitates a peer-control system that supports group offending by simplifying the search for accomplices. Indeed, a central fact underlying Shaw and McKay's classic research was that most gangs developed from unsupervised, spontaneous play-groups. Residents of stable-family communities are better able to control such peer-group activities as street-corner congregation (e.g., hanging out) that set the context for delinquency, especially gang-related. Hence, awareness and supervision of peer group and gang activity does not simply depend on one child's family, but on a network of collective family control. [8]

The discrimination and segregation, as well as the simple inequality, turned white-dominated society and culture into enemy territory. In their rejection of dominant culture and in their fragmentation, the black and Latino youth became disconnected. These youths adopted a behavioral code totally against the dominant orderliness and scheme of things, a code which they could implement because of the shredding of community networks.

Denton and Massey noted that ghetto youths who tried hard to excel in their school work were accused of acting white by their peers. [9] Staying in school, working at scholastics, going to church, dressing conservatively and neatly, obeying parents and teachers, and nurturing ambition for a mainstream career constitute "acting white."

"Acting non-white" must be different. In general, this antithetical behavioral code includes dropping out of school, ignoring or openly disrespecting parents and teachers, dressing provocatively and expensively but slovenly, speaking provocatively and obscenely, using one or a combination of the addictive substances, indulging in promiscuous sex, and practicing violence. [10] This code of behavior reinforces the disconnection from the dominant society and allows the

myth to prevail among the youth that they control the disconnection and reject
The other, not that they are the rejected.

We have commented already on the importance of population density. In
areas of very high population density with large proportions of the population
under 25 years of age, there may be 10,000 to 40,000 people per square-mile
between 12 and 25 years old. If even 40% subscribe to the alternative-behavior
code, a serious challenge to public health, public order, and the future of community life rears itself. In disrupted communities, this challenge may over-
whelm the weakened normative forces.

In Chapter 4, we noted the importance of density of new cases of tuberculosis in
sustaining the epidemic. The "magic number" was 25 new cases per square-mile per
year. When contagion depends on behavior and imitation, the density of the alternative behavioral-code practitioners also determines the sustaining and spread of the
component conditions (violence, substance abuse, promiscuity, illiteracy, etc.).

We find many of the 62 contiguous health areas of the Bronx with extraordinary
annual densities of intentional deaths around 1970, 1980, and 1990. When we look
at the descriptive statistics, we find that densities of intentional deaths per square-
mile increased between 1970 and 1990:

	1970	1980	1990
average	27.78	23.86	27.38
median	19.15	19.48	23.22
mode	15.00	17.69	22.15
geometric mean	14.36	15.42	17.38

These numbers are the unweighted average, median, mode, and geometric mean
over the Bronx health areas of the annual average densities of violent deaths for several years around 1970, 1980, and 1990.

Although the average declined in 1980, it rose back up for 1990. Because the data
are not normally distributed (not a bell-shaped curve), the average cannot represent
the central tendency. The other measures of central tendency listed here represent
the whole group of health areas better. They all show increases. Although in the 1970
period, one health area had the incredible density of 110 intentional deaths per
square-mile, the largest number of areas had zero to five. Housing overcrowding
explains a high percent of the variation in intentional deaths per square mile in each
of the three periods: 60.45% for 1970, 44.6% for 1980, and 53.7% for 1990.

The following factors together explain 75.2% of the variation in the difference between 1970 and 1990 intentional death densities: 1970–90, difference
in population, 1970 population, and the 1970–90 difference in housing over-

crowding. Thus, the major factors are population and disruption of patterns of population and housing overcrowding, both probably indices of community disruption, fragmentation, and decline.[11]

A more complete index of violence is its impact, i.e. the number of intentional deaths per square-mile in the health area times the population of the health area. In order to have a more manageable index, we then divided by 100,000. We mapped the quintiles of this index for 1970, 1980, and 1990 (Figure 7-5). When we looked at the factors which explain the geographic patterns in 1970, 1980, and 1990, we found that they had changed. In 1970, socioeconomic status rank, drug deaths, and cirrhosis deaths explained 71.8% of the variability of violent death impact index over the health areas. In 1980, the determinants were 1980 socioeconomic status rank, 1980 cirrhosis deaths, and the change in index of extreme housing overcrowding between 1970 and 1980 (66.1% of the variability). By 1990, the determinants had become 1990 cirrhosis deaths and the 1970–90 changes in the extreme housing overcrowding index and in cirrhosis deaths (70.1% of the variability).[11]

The changes in the factors dramatically illustrate dynamics of the housing famine and the breakdown in social control. By 1990, the Bronx was in serious economic trouble, its health areas having slipped steeply in rank, but the intentional-death rates of the health areas responded less to the purely economic slide than to the particular exacerbators of the effects of poverty: housing and community destruction. It is also likely that SES drops out of the picture because by 1990, SES was determined by historic-housing loss and community disorganization. SES being co-linear with and dependent on these terms, the computer program drops it out of the regression equation.

When high numbers of susceptibles live in a community which has been broken or successfully targeted for destruction, not only is the structure for limiting the types of contagious behavior greatly weakened but the behavior will consist of acting out (expressing in exaggerated ways the hidden feelings of family, friends, and self) *and* reaction-formation (the oppressed behaving like their oppressor). The kind of behavioral code which zips through the core groups of youth will be both destructive and self-destructive.

The behavioral code essentially consists of information transmitted within and between groups. Because of the disrupted community structure, each code must compete with many similar codes. In other words, the noise-to-signal ratio is high. In order to "come through over the wires," the signal must continually get louder. Each group transmits its signal more loudly to be distinguished from the others. In this context, the components of the code must become more anti-social, more violent, more promiscuous, riskier, and more destructive. The competition for distinction in this arena destroys the arena itself, like turning up the volume of a microphone so high that feedback over-whelms the intended sounds.[12]

Thus, "planned shrinkage" brewed that volatile mix of incredible housing overcrowding and social disruption which flared into substance abuse and inten-tional deaths through the behavioral code spawned by the isolation and discon-nection. In the Bronx alone, hundreds died and hundreds killed, all victims of this bizarre experiment.

In *Messengers of God*, Elie Wiesel expounds upon Cain's murder of his brother Abel as an unfathomable mystery. The Talmud and subsequent rabbinical commentary attempted to explain the motivations of all three actors in the drama —the two brothers and God—in order to preserve faith in divine justice and love.[13] Those who study violence among the young of disrupted communities find little mystery because this story is ever old and ever up-to-date.

The parents were forced to migrate from a place where they had been well-regarded, comfortable, and embedded in relationships, where they named and were named. In the new home, they were unknown, barely surviving "by the sweat of their brow," and unable to supervise their children. When the children tried to estab-lish themselves as adults in the new place, the creative Cain was treated unfairly and rejected. What mystery is there, that murder occurs when a young, unsocialized man from an uprooted family is cut off from all aspirations of creativity, when his image of divine creativity is murdered?

As if the one story weren't enough, Genesis continues into Noah and the Flood. Noah's family survived a major disaster brought about by a conscious decision by The Powers That Be to destroy. The anger which prompted the mass destruction also led to the total forgetting of Noah and the Ark. Even after the Ark reached dry ground, Noah and his sons trembled in fear that their sacrifice would be rejected and that they too would be killed. No wonder Noah became an alcoholic!

The relationship between forced migration and disaster, on one hand, and sub-stance abuse and violence, on the other, has been understood for thousands of years. Only denial keeps us from achieving this ancient wisdom. Part of this denial is rooted in our fear that we will empathize and suffer with the disaster survivors and that we will realize how we too could be victimized.

Needleman et al. [14] found that, for a group of about 200 Pittsburgh public-school students, the body's burden of the toxic heavy metal lead had an association with various measures of antisocial and aggressive behavior in males, specifically African-American males. This study is methodologically suspect. For example, the beginning study population was 41% white, but the final one was only 30% white. The causes and consequences of this change in racial composition were inade-quately discussed in the paper, although the paper obsessed about race.

We find the authors' explanation that lead is responsible for violence not credible on other counts as well. Our Bronx study revealed dynamics of violence in time and space which reflect the destruction of poor neighborhoods and the subsequent urban decay contagion. The epidemic of violence in New York followed a pattern similar to tuberculosis, AIDS, low-weight births, and substance abuse. Indeed, the Bronx analysis correlated violent deaths with socioeconomic status changes, drug and cirrhosis deaths, and housing overcrowding. The results of these stepwise regressions explain the fluctuations in intentional deaths far more convincingly than lead body-burden could.

Needleman et al. also committed a form of racism: they attributed criminality to individual's race and sex, African-American males, based on a book by Wilson and Herrnstein, *Criminality and Human Nature*. Both the book and the Needleman et al. paper ignore neighborhood conditions and change in conditions, although now even the CDC asks that researchers first rule out neighborhood effects before attributing inequalities in health to race.[15] If only case/control studies and no population-level studies are conducted and reported in health science journals, this poisonous form of racism will simply continue.

The violence is best explained as a repeated social re-enactment of Cain killing Abel and as part of the behavioral code of the fragmented groups setting up alternative structures to the mainstream in the wake of the disaster. Escalation of violence cannot be explained by the lead body-burden theory. It can be explained both as an expression of the increasing helplessness, deprivation, and isolation, and as a consequence of its own dynamic. Escalation occurs when a group's given level of violence is matched by the other little groups and can no longer serve to differentiate between groups. The noise-to-signal ratio becomes too large. The signal cannot be heard. Eventually, the strength of the signal becomes so great as to damage the channel, i.e. the people flee the violence in the neighborhood and re-fragment the community into even smaller, more isolated slivers.[16]

A SPOTTY OUTCOME: MEASLES

Community fragmentation cut many families and individuals out of the "information loop," the flow of vital information about economic opportunities, educational opportunities, and disease-prevention opportunities. The rates of immunization against preventable childhood diseases plummeted in most major cities to the point where the CDC sponsored a special high-priority immunization campaign.

One such preventable disease is measles. Measles is caused by a virus, can lead to death, and has relegated large numbers of children in the past to the "iron lung." Measles is not a minor itchy rash and fever, but a serious disease.

New York City experienced an epidemic of measles among young children. This is different from outbreak among college students whose vaccinations have worn out. Some vaccinations wear out after about 15–20 years. Typically, these post-adolescent outbreaks are mostly light cases because the immune system has been previously primed . Epidemics among young children occur because they were never immunized at all. These cases vary in seriousness according to the underlying health of the individual child. Indeed, measles killed children during the epidemic of 1986–92. Children died of a preventable disease because immunization coverage dipped below what would keep the density of susceptibles below epidemic threshold. In the densely populated poor neighborhoods, even 2% of the children going unimmunized can achieve this crucial level of susceptibility. If a neighborhood has 25% of its population under 18 and 10% under 6 years of age, the population density of children under 6 would range between five and ten thousand per square mile (overall population densities being 50–100,000 per-square mile). Two percent unimmunized yields densities between 100 and 200 per square mile of susceptible young children. In the epidemics of 1986 and 1990, the majority of cases occurred among young children, not among previously immunized post-adolescents:

NUMBER OF CASES BY AGE RANGE (% OF CASES)

AGE RANGE	1986	1990
<1	194 (21)	319 (29)
1-4	463 (50)	447 (41)
5-9	123 (13)	78 (7)
10-14	73 (8)	60 (5)
>15 + unknown	77 (8.5)	204 (19)

On a citywide basis, cases of measles showed a peak-and-plummet cycle typical of childhood diseases:

YEAR	1986	1987	1988	1989	1990
CASES	930	469	57	135	1,108

A 4–5 year peak-to-peak interval reflects the time needed to accumulate the threshold density of susceptibles. The problem with this dynamic of typical childhood disease is that in a properly immunized population, it shouldn't happen. It doesn't happen.

Where did these cases occur? Figure 7-6 displays the ZIP-Code zones with 15 or more cases in 1990. These zones accounted for a disproportionate number

of cases. Two of the worst burned-out areas, Bushwick and Brownsville, contributed 51 and 43 cases, respectively. In Brooklyn, the affected zones were the
burned-out ones and those receiving the refugees. The same picture emerges in
the Bronx. In Manhattan, Southeast Harlem, the very worst and earliest burned-
out zone showed elevated case numbers. Measles flares into epidemic under
conditions of crowding and disorder such as refugee camps.

From our research into patterns of TB, AIDS, conventional STDs, measles,
morality, and widened substance abuse as well as the issues discussed in this
chapter, we conclude that the public policy on which the fire-service and other
housing-preservation service cuts rested led to contagious epidemics of disease,
clusters of chronic physical conditions, shortened life expectancy, contagious
violence and criminal activity, addictions, and a self-proliferating process of
urban decay which further fueled these public-health and public-order epidemics.

Figure 7-1 LIFE EXPECTANCY OF 60-YEAR-OLDS, BLACK AND WHITE, 1950–1980, NEW YORK CITY

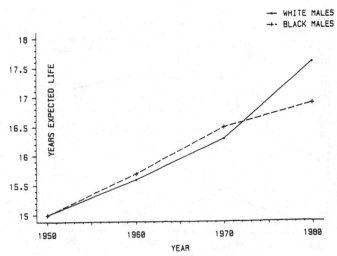

a. Life expectancy for black and white males at age 60, New York City 1950–1980.

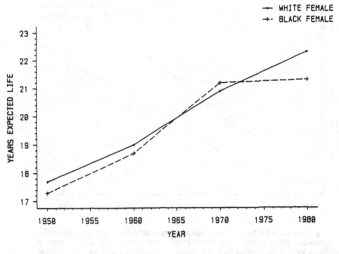

Same as *a* for females, age 60.

a. males   b. females

Figure 7-2 LIFE EXPECTANCY OF 70-YEAR-OLDS, BLACK AND WHITE, 1950–1980, NEW YORK CITY

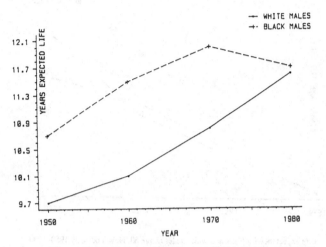

c. Life expectancy for black and white males at age 70, New York City, 1950–1980.

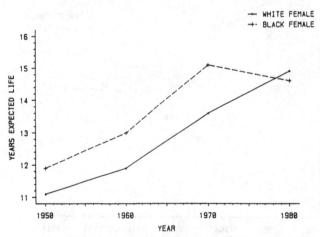

d. Same as *c* for females. Note substantial or relative declines in expectancies for blacks between 1970 and 1980, while those for whites continued to increase. This seems to constitute a kind of case-control study for community disintegration, since most of those whites whose communities disintegrated under the pressure of forced migration from burning neighborhoods between 1970 and 1980 moved out of the city.

c. males   d. females

Figure 7-3 NUMBER OF LOW-WEIGHT BIRTHS PER 10,000 BIRTHS, BRONX HEALTH AREAS: 1970, 1980, 1990

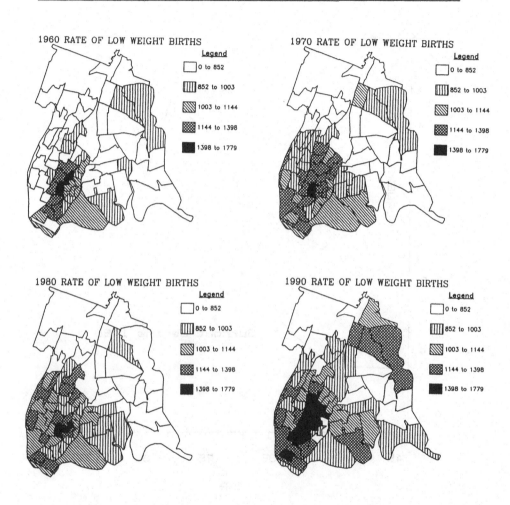

Note the shift from the compact southcentral area in 1970. Also note the change in scales of the top quintile: the areas of highest incidence in 1980 and 1990 had higher incidence than those of the preceding decade. The problem became worse, as well as geographically shifted.

Figure 7-4 NEW YORK CITY HOMICIDES, 1945-1987

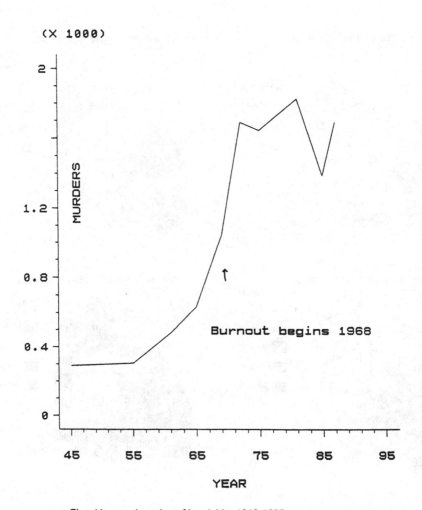

Citywide annual number of homicides 1945–1987.

Figure 7-5 IMPACT OF INTENTIONAL DEATHS BY HEALTH AREA, BRONX: 1970, 1980, 1990

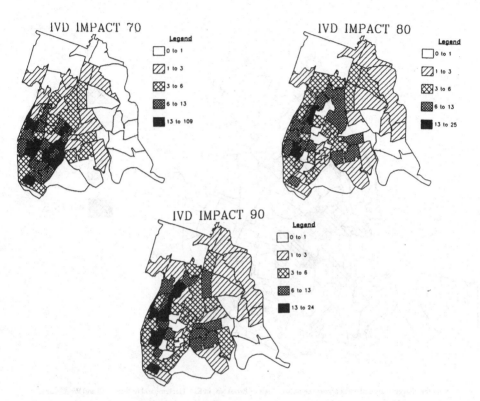

The impact is the intentional deaths per square-mile population/100,000. It is, essentially, the probability of health-area residents being affected directly by violent death.

Figure 7-6 NUMBER OF 1990 MEASLES CASES, REPORTED BY ZIP CODE, NEW YORK CITY

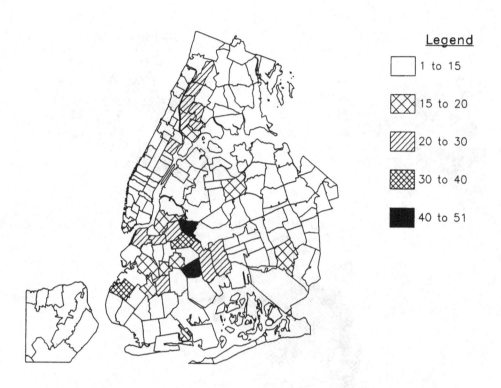

Legend

☐ 1 to 15

⊠ 15 to 20

▨ 20 to 30

▩ 30 to 40

■ 40 to 51

Note the concentration of cases across the poverty belt of Brooklyn, in East Harlem, and in the South and West Bronx.

◆

BEYOND NEW YORK CITY AND POLICY

INTRODUCTION TO PART THREE

BEYOND NEW YORK CITY AND POLICY

The public-health and public-order epidemics described in Part Two did not respect political boundaries; they spread beyond city limits into the suburbs. In this part of the book, we describe the socioeconomic links between the suburban counties and the city. County-level disease incidence is partly determined by the incidence rates in the city and the linkages between county and city. Thus, the policy-triggered-and-sustained disaster that targeted poor neighborhoods ended up eroding the public health and public order of even the wealthiest counties in the New York City metropolitan region.

When we looked beyond the New York City metro region at other metro regions, we found that these also show tight linkages between city and suburban county. Which diseases are "regionalized" from a city into its suburbs depends on the tightness of the linkages and the socioeconomic structure of the particular metro region. We conclude that the American combination of segregation and discrimination against segregated populations does not work so well that the nontarget populations don't feel the effects.

In this part of the book, we also examine the flow of disease and disorder between metropolitan regions. In our research, we found that Miami and Los Angeles are the epicenters from which violent crime spread hierachically to other major metro regions; New York and San Francisco are the epicenters from which AIDS spread hierarchically to other major metro regions. The AIDS incidence in a metro region depends on its contact with New York and San Francisco and its local incidence of violent crime (an index of the degree of social-network weakness and instability). Thus, the disaster of New York impacted national public health.

The magnitude of the impact of the New York disaster makes remedial policies of vital concern at the metro region and national levels. We also develop remedial social and economic policies for the New York metro region which are vitally needed to deflate the epicenters in the city that affect the metro region-al, and national, public health and public order.

Finally, we summarize the post-epidemic years in New York City (from 1993 on) with respect to public policies and the changes in public health and order. In contrast to our recommendations in Chapter 9, the new public policies rely on policing and on medical interventions ("disease policing"). There has been a coincident improvement in public health, but even diseases such as low-weight births that were not targeted by these policies have declined in incidence. We attribute these improvements to the re-establishment of community social networks in the absence of rapid, massive housing destruction.

8

METROPOLITAN REGION AND NATION

SUBURBS GROW

After World War II, national and state policies fostered the "American dream," the little house in the suburbs with the car parked next to it. Federal mortgage programs, federal and local road building, local land use planning, and partnership programs between local government and chambers of commerce provided the infrastructure for the suburban subdivisions springing up like weed patches. In 1992, N. Denton and D. Massey[1] documented the ways that these programs fostered segregation and housing discrimination. Many large cities, including New York, began slowly losing middle-class and highly paid working-class populations in the 1950s.

The pace of emigration from cities to suburbs accelerated markedly in the 1970s as explicit federal programs supporting suburbanization expanded and were supplemented by extra-legal policies of "benign neglect" in the Nixon Administration and thereafter. Block-grant programs starved the central cities and threw money at wealthy suburbs. Contracts for governmental purchase of goods and services went increasingly to suburban and Southern firms. Because of the crumbling of cities physically and socially from benign neglect, planned shrinkage, and the diversion of resources to less needy and less populated areas, living and working environments in cities deteriorated severely during the 1970s. Contagious urban decay produced an explosive rate of emigration from older rustbelt cities. Indeed, the Northeast and Midwest, traditional areas of high unionization and left-wing politics, lost population between 1970 and 1980, but the South and West grew and grew, to the point of overextending water supplies.

MUTATION, COMMUTATION

Even after these suburban and long-distance migrations, the economic heart of the country continues to be the large cities. The highest concentrations of employment are still in places like Manhattan, Chicago, Washington, and Los Angeles.[2] Large numbers of workers live in suburban counties beyond the city limits, and journey every workday from miles out and back again. This is commuting: a heavily subsidized process that wrecks air and water quality, and is harmful to wildlife populations, landscape integrity, and soil conditions. It also, as we shall see, plays a role in spreading city-based epidemics.

In and around each major city, the worker tides establish the "commuting field," a gradient of the percents of workers who live in a given place and work in the city. The gradient diminishes with distance from the centers of employment in the city, usually called the Central Business District (CBD).

The US Bureau of the Census constructs a residence/work place matrix based on the decadal census: counties of residence are the rows, and counties of work are the columns. Each cell is the number or percent of workers who reside in a given county and work in that or another county within the Bureau's designated Standard Metropolitan Statistical Area (SMSA). The designation of the SMSA counties depends on this journey-to-work matrix. Table 8-1 is an abbreviated journey-to-work matrix of New York City's SMSA—about 25 counties, including the five boroughs: the number of resident workers in each county and the number who worked in Manhattan in 1980 and 1990. People come from Ocean County and Hunterdon in New Jersey and from Fairfield and Litchfield in Connecticut to work in Manhattan—all with county centers 50 or more miles from the center of Manhattan. People travel from Baltimore to work in Washington, D.C., from San Diego to work in Los Angeles, and from Kenosha to work in Chicago. Table 8-2 reveals the *average* commuting roundtrip taken by workers in and around nine major cities, calculated on the assumption that the distance between the center of a county and of the city constitutes the average commuting distance for residents of that county who work in the city. The Census has the actual data on commuting distance but releases these only by the four regions and nationally.

We became interested in the journey-to-work matrix when our friend and colleague Peter Gould plotted the AIDS incidences of several counties in the New York SMSA against their distances from 42 St. and Fifth Ave. He obtained an exponentially declining curve. He did the same for counties around Washington, D.C. and got a similar curve. Obviously, the entire population around these central cities was united in a single system. We plotted the AIDS incidence of several wealthy counties around Manhattan against the percent of resident workers with jobs in Manhattan and obtained a linear relationship with a high correlation (92–4 %) (Fig. 8-1).[3]

Occam's Razor refers to the dictum of medieval philosopher William of Occam which underlies scientific explanation: "Do not multiply entities needlessly" (i.e., adopt the simplest theory which explains all the data). We thought we had found the sharpest of Occam's razors, a pattern and explanation so simple even a health commissioner could understand it. Indeed, when we presented it to a group of representatives of four New York SMSA health departments, three of them county commissioners, they understood the pattern and its implications immediately. The commissioner in Westchester said very simply, "I can't present this to my county executive," and proceeded to try to prevent publication with accusations ("This looks racist") and fear ("How am I supposed to respond to the media when they hold microphones in my face after this is published?"). The commissioners both in the New York and Washington SMSAs (a later presentation) realized that this discovery could put an end to their absolute fiefdoms because it would force cooperation among health departments and creation of a regional entity to address regional public-health dynamics.

COMMUTING, POVERTY RATE AND EPIDEMIC SPREAD

It turned out that our Occam's Razor simplified too much. When we put all 24 counties of the NYC SMSA into the regression, out jumped the heart of the region, the poor counties which formed an extended epicenter (figure 8-2).[4] As can be seen from the graph in figure 8-2, several counties' AIDS incidences were much above those predicted by the relationship derived from the eight wealthy counties of Occam's Razor.

Our commuting field matrix is 24 × 24 counties, each cell containing the proportion of workers who live in a given county and commute to another county. Thus, the sum of the rows is all workers who live in the county (100%). This matrix represents what mathematicians call a Markov process and shows the probabilities for transition from county i to county j at any step in the chain of repeated transitions. In this matrix, an infection can reach any county from any other county after a number of steps. A definite number of infections can be distributed at time 0 in any manner across the counties and will, after sufficiently numerous steps, be redistributed in an equilibrium distribution, just as a given amount of water in a pipe system will reach an equilibrium across the system in a sufficient time. Because the commuting pattern is repeated over 200 times a year, equilibrium distribution emerges rapidly.

Let us assume a disease acts as follows: an infected individual travels from county i to county j, infects one person, and leaves the system (constant number of infections). The equilibrium distribution of these Markov infections within the SMSA indicates general regional diffusion and spread.

When we used the Markov equilibrium value as the independent variable in the correlation with AIDS incidence, the relationship was linear and had a high correlation (82%). But when we factored in poverty and density of the commuting measure per square mile of county area, the correlation rose to very high levels (94%). Tuberculosis showed essentially the same relationship of incidence to the composite index of commuting density and poverty rate. (See figure 8-3.) The Washington SMSA behaved similarly.[4]

THE DYNAMICS OF METRO REGIONS

With two SMSAs showing a single system of AIDS diffusion (and of TB diffusion also) from the inner city to the suburban counties, the next step was consideration of SMSAs and more public-health problems. The eight metropolitan regions that we studied varied greatly: those of moderately large cities (St. Louis, Detroit, San Francisco, Boston, Washington), large cities with over a million people (Chicago, Philadelphia), and, of course, New York. We could not include Los Angeles because only four immense counties constitute its entire SMSA, too small a number to manipulate statistically. Even some of the regions with seven counties pushed the limit of statistics' ability to differentiate between true pattern and chance.[5]

Besides considering eight different SMSAs, we expanded the number of inner-city markers from two (AIDS and TB) to four by adding violent crime and low-weight births. Countless deficit studies confirmed a pattern of high inner-city incidence of these and similar public-health and public-order problems and low suburban incidence. Thus, we labeled them inner-city markers. This label proved misleading.

When we correlated AIDS incidence with commuter index for the San Francisco SMSA, the initial result was a respectable, statistically significant correlation. When we plotted the variables against each other on a graph, however, we could see immediately that the single highest data point, San Francisco itself, was the forcer of the correlation and statistical significance. We thus designated a marker as being regionalized over an entire SMSA if the correlation remained statistically significant even when the inner-city data point was omitted. Table 8-3 shows the results of these correlations with the inner city omitted.[6]

This table features several important characteristics: differences between SMSAs with respect to which markers are regionalized; differences between SMSAs with respect to the strength of regionalization as indicated by the percent of incidence associated with the commuting index (the R-squared) and the low probability level; and the fact that each SMSA showed regionalization of at least one of the four markers. This last observation means that metro regions form single socioeconomic systems, extended conurbations of intense linkages which transport and diffuse the problems of the inner cities out to the suburban counties, even to distant and wealthy ones.

The New York SMSA deserves more comment because of certain important differences from the other SMSAs. All four inner-city markers are regionalized across the SMSA and provide evidence of a single, extremely linked entity containing nearly 20 million people. At least three of the four markers (AIDS, TB, and violent crime) yield regression lines parallel to each other in the graph of log of marker incidence vs. composite index (figure 8-4). Essentially, the three markers show the same relationship to the composite index of linkage (commuter density per square mile) and vulnerability (poverty rate). We interpret this consonance to mean that the extent and severity of the New York City urban decay and its public health and public order consequences are such powerful determinants as to overcome the localized different responses to the markers. In other words, a huge steamroller passes through and flattens everything. The extent of flattening depends only on linkage to the city and the county poverty rate, with no significant effect of local history, social structure, county geography and land use, local development programs, etc. New York City essentially has a population of 18 million and a radius of over 50 miles, a remarkable but never acknowledged fact . The Mayor, City Council, and the City's permanent government to a remarkable extent decide the fates of the citizens of Suffolk County, Passaic County, the cities of Bridgeport and New Haven, the city of Newark, Putnam and Dutchess Counties, and the afore-mentioned Ocean and Hunterdon Counties.

On the other hand, San Francisco had only one regionalized marker, tuberculosis, even though San Francisco has a very high AIDS incidence. The incidence in the whole SMSA is elevated, compared with most other metro regions. However, local county conditions appear to overcome the effects of the concentration in the city. There may be "leakage" from the city, but it isn't so strong as to overcome the effects of local conditions. Urban decay isn't diffusing out of San Francisco. The only disease showing regionalization is one which is usually acquired through personal contact and airborne contagion; you get it simply by breathing. High density of people in buildings is connected with patterns of TB.

Indeed, the pattern of housing overcrowding across the San Francisco SMSA correlates strongly with the pattern of TB incidence. San Francisco does not have large burned-out areas or neighborhoods with stand after stand of abandoned buildings. Even the earthquake of 1989 failed to produce widespread urban decay. The particular way San Francisco eased out the poor did not (and does not) feature physical destruction of the neighborhoods. We believe that this difference from New York and several other cities has saved the entire San Francisco SMSA (about 3 million people) from the steamroller effect we see in New York.

So the spectrum has two extremes: New York, which tried to uproot its poor by destroying their housing, and San Francisco, which kept its poor contained in an economic corral and made sure nothing really got out of hand with respect to urban decay, public health, or public order. In between the two extremes lie the other cities. Some, like Detroit, St. Louis, and Washington, approach the New York SMSA end of the spectrum for decay. Others like Chicago and Boston are a little ragged around the edges but holding onto essentials. These in-between cities and regions merit a few observations.

Four cities have populations of about 600,000: Boston, Washington, Detroit, and St. Louis, the last three suffering severely from urban decay. Indeed, these are trashed-out little cities full of vacant lots, rubble, and burned-out abandoned hulks. Although the St. Louis SMSA achieved statistical significance only for AIDS, violent crime had a definite trend, and the two other markers were "trendy" (probability less than 0.2). The St. Louis SMSA has only nine counties, a number which makes the statistical test rather crude for seeing relationships well. St. Louis appears to resemble New York more closely in its across-the-board regionalization or trend to regionalization than the other cities of its size. Most remarkably, the population and industrial base of St. Louis County, to the west of the city, dwarfs what remains in the city, and the fact that this regionalization occurs nevertheless bears testimony to the extent and severity of urban decay in the city. The tail is wagging the dog.

Both the Detroit and Washington DC SMSAs show regionalization of two markers and a trend toward regionalization of a third. Surprisingly, Detroit is the only SMSA of the eight without regionalization or trend for tuberculosis. Table 8-4 displays important demographic and geographic data for these metro regions.[6] Detroit has a low proportion of extreme housing overcrowding in general and the longest average roundtrip commute of all the SMSAs. The workforce is spread out far from the city center. The markers with a behavioral component (AIDS, violence, and low-weight births) are all regionalized or trend toward regionalization in the Detroit SMSA.

The Chicago SMSA has only seven counties. Although violent crime and low-weight birth are not regionalized, AIDS appears weakly trendy, with the commuting index explaining nearly a third of the pattern. Philadelphia also shows regionalization for one marker and a trend toward it for another. The SMSAs of both these large cities appear less devastated and less tightly linked than New York's. The smaller city of Boston also enjoys these advantages. The SMSAs show vastly different structures, but each functions as a single system.

When all the data on commuting, poverty, and marker incidence from all eight SMSAs are pooled, a picture of large American cities and their regions emerges (Table 8-5).[5] All markers correlate significantly with commuting, poverty rate, and effect of region and city. If we use the statistical F-ratio as an indicator of strength of influence, we see how structure influences the different markers. Commuting pattern influences AIDS incidence much more than poverty rate or effect of city and region. Commuting and poverty rate have about equal influence on TB incidence, a much greater than effect of city and region. Poverty rate affects incidences of violence and low-weight births much more than commuting; the effect of city and region is a fairly small influence for these two markers. Indeed, when the averages, standard deviations, and extremes are compared across regions for the four markers, the averages of low-weight births and of violent crime incidence occupy a far narrower band than that of TB incidence and especially that of AIDS incidence (Figure 8-5).[5] Log of low-weight-birth-incidence average ranges from about 8.5 to 8.9 and that of violent crime from 5.2 to 6.0. Those of TB (3.3–4.4) and AIDS (2.5–4.5) are much broader. (Remember that the log indicates order of magnitude: one, ten, one hundred, etc.)

The population of the eight metro regions represents 54 out of the 250 million people in the country. The great strength of the associations (probability level nearly zero) indicates that adding more regions may not change these relationships, although we intend to do so as part of our future research. The markers of urban decay diffuse from the inner city through the suburban counties in proportion to the contacts (index of commuting) and local susceptibility (poverty rate). Even rich counties face an incidence of these markers determined by the incidence of the inner city. Essentially, the American system of apartheid (that combination of segregation and targeting of the segregated population) has turned around and bitten the middle and upper classes.

THE NATIONAL PICTURE

It was with some difficulty that we took this diffusion concept up to the national level. Acquiring data which could possibly indicate linkage *both* within and between the major SMSAs would tax the ingenuity of Odysseus and the persistence of Isaiah. Airline-passenger data, acquired by Gould, indicates linkage between metro regions but not within metro regions. Migration data show linkages between and within metro regions, but the temporal scale is on the order of one-half to one decade. Data on commerce don't usually track domestic trade within and between metro regions. The scarcity of data on this vital aspect of the domestic economy demonstrates an ignorance of vital processes.

Pursuing migration flow proved productive, as Pennsylvania State University, Gould's institution, gave us migration data from the Census Bureau for the SMSAs of the 25 most populous American cities so that we could create a matrix of migration similar to the journey-to-work Matrix.[7] We did not look at county-to-county migration but migration within and between the 25 metro regions. As with the daily commuting data, a stochastic matrix was created, and equilibrium distribution obtained. The equilibrium distribution revealed that New York, Los Angeles, and Chicago account for 43% of the total equilibrium distribution, the New York SMSA alone 22%. When log population is correlated with log equilibrium distribution, the two factors correlate strongly (R-squared=81%). When log population is regressed against Log of the reciprocal of the sum of all mean first-passage times, R-squared is even higher at 86%. Thus, the large metro regions dominate the migration process and probability of contact.

The mean first-passage times (the mean number of steps it takes to get from one region to another) are short: the Miami SMSA is only 33 "steps" from the New York SMSA, for example. The farthest SMSA from that of New York is only 71 "steps". With this matrix, we can see the strength of contact between individual SMSAs and all the SMSAs together as a system, the socioeconomic distances. Los Angeles is 57 steps to Portland Oregon and 60 steps to San Francisco, for example. The network is well-defined and well-linked.

This linkage means that an infection rising above a threshold incidence in any American city should fan out into the other metro regions. It should spread hierarchically according to the linkages between the regions, the populations of the regions, and the density of susceptibles within the regions. Usually, this last vulnerability factor depends on the overall poverty rate, the concentrations of the poor, and the size and social stability of the social networks of the poor.

To explore this hypothesis of linkage and local structure, we used AIDS incidence as we did the infection and violent crime (an index of weak social networks) and the poverty rate, as the independent socioeconomic variables. We analyzed these data with stepwise, or hierarchical, regression which creates a parsimonious model (one with the fewest influential independent variables).

Our dependent variables are the log of the number of AIDS cases through

April 1991 and of the number reported between April 1991 and June 1995. Our independent variables are the logs of the rows of the matrix which yield indices of contact with New York and San Francisco and logs of several socio-economic factors. Most of the independent variables drop out of the regression. Well over 90% of the variance of the dependent variables depends on the logs of the contact index with New York and San Francisco and the SMSAs incidence of violent crime. None of the other independent variables were significantly associated with either period's pattern of AIDS cases. The relationships of the two periods are parallel, but displaced vertically (figure 8-6).

Although on the regional scale, poverty rate provided an adequate index of the vulnerability of the counties to exposure from the social contact with the city (indicated by commuting density), on the national scale, violent crime provides this index. We interpret this change of vulnerability index to mean that on the national scale, social disruption and loss of social controls subsume poverty and present the contours of the "new poverty" more fully than does the percent of households or individuals who earn less than a given annual income.

From the study on the structure of eight metro regions, we saw that violent crime was rather uniformly distributed across them. This makes sense because violence is an old pathology, not a newly spreading epidemic like AIDS. However, if we regress the log of number of violent crimes in 1991 against the same independent variables as was done for AIDS in the hierarchical regression, we see that 90% of the variance of the dependent variable is explained by the log of the metro-region population and the log of the reciprocal of the mean first-passage time from Miami to each metro region (fig. 8-7). Miami is the major port of entry for immigration from the Carribean and the Atlantic side of Central and South America and for cocaine from Colombia and Peru.

If we remove log population from the regression and insert log of the reciprocal of mean first-passage time to Los Angeles, the correlation is only slightly less than from the previous model (85% vs. 88%). Los Angeles is a major epicenter of youth-gang activity and Miami of cocaine trade and very low-wage labor.

IMPLICATIONS

These models describe how American metro regions interact hierarchically and how a national system of linkages between these metro regions ensures that the formation of epicenters within them for disease or behavioral problems leads rapidly to spread between the regions, incubation within the poor and socially-frayed inner city neighborhoods, and diffusion out to the other neighborhoods and the suburbs of the SMSA.

The very finding that AIDS and violent crimes spread hierarchically through the major conurbations of America implies that a communications network has developed nationally (possibly internationally) among these metro regions. Each marginalized, shredded community within the large cities will communicate with other urban areas along this hierarchy, this large-scale sociogeographic structure. The communication network implies that the opportunity structures of the individual marginalized communities, both separately and collectively, may determine the public health and public order of the nation.

Thus, the question arises of how closely linked and well attuned these metro regions are in their public-health and public-order status. In what way do external perturbations (public policy, private interests, economic cycling, disastrous weather, etc.) vibrate through this large-scale network? The body of ecosystem studies by Holling on the stability and resilience of natural communities prompted a codicil by Ives to measure linkage tightness and the propensity of a natural community to magnify effects of a perturbation as they travel through the linkages.[8] Physical scientists call such magnification "stochastic resonance" for good reason. In dynamic systems ranging from molecules in a fluid to the interwoven food webs of an ecological community, the whole system and its parts "wobble" within a given realm of stable structure. An imposed perturbation can do one of two things: make it temporarily "wobble" faster or farther but still within the stable realm, or push the "wobble" beyond the limit of stability and into a different realm where the system's structure and function assume a different configuration. Resilience is the ability of a system to "take a hit" and remain in the same realm, the same stable configuration. It is a function of the nature and density of the linkages *and* of whether the system has already taken so many "hits" as to be already near the limit of stability.

Table 8-6 takes the mathematically-minded through the steps of the calculation of the amplification factor. If lambda approaches unity, external perturbations will cause instabilities in the mix of pathologies affecting all the metro regions in the hierarchical structure. Lambda is calculated from the correlations of the many, many inner-city markers and factors such as SMSA commuting pattern, poverty rates, contagious diseases, behavioral problems, housing, etc. It is an over-all index of linkage between factors and pathologies.

If we apply the Markov migration process four successive times to the initial distribution of 60% AIDS cases in the NYC SMSA and 40% in the San Francisco SMSA, the resulting lambda (0.9793) yields an amplification factor of 48.41, nearly 50. This factor suggests that perturbations of the system result in greatly enhanced impacts because of tight linkages and large existing instabilities. The New York City SMSA itself has an amplification of 145.3 (almost 150), three times that of the 25-region system; the Washington SMSA has one of about 120, also much higher than that of the 25-region system. Philadelphia, however, has one nearly the same as the 25-region amplification factor. These three SMSAs were analyzed for amplification factor because they have enough counties to satisfy unambiguously the statistical requirements of sample size for this analysis.[7]

A spider web consists of both loose and tight strands. Plucking a loose nonstructural strand makes a small web sector ripple slightly for a brief instant. Plucking a tight structural strand makes the entire web vibrate for a long time. Our country has become a web with tight strands, the metro regions, vulnerable to extensive, intense vibration. This analogy understates our country's dire situation because it does not include the contagious processes transmitted through the linkages. Amplification means transmission *and* intensification consequent on the perturbation.

Technologies of communication, commerce, and transportation have conferred on the macro-scale some of the contagious properties of the meso-scale. Just as the "city" grew from a five-mile radius in 1800 to a fifty-mile radius in 1980, the functional city may have grown to encompass several metro regions; the functional SMSA may include the major metro regions and a huge proportion of the American population. The implications of "one nation under God" have never before been so deep and sweeping. If the Chicago Southside has a violent crime wave, intentional deaths will rise in Boston's Roxbury and the Bronx's Tremont neighborhoods. If the social fabric of St. Louis unravels, proportion of low-weight births in Bedford-Stuyvesant, Gary, Indiana, and Houston rise. If Miami sneezes, Chicago and Los Angeles have to blow their noses. *It is a global village, indeed!*

The New York City metro region dominates the hierarchy of metro regions. A disease or pathological behavior pattern which arises in a smaller metro region flows into New York City's poor neighborhoods along the travel routes, is incubated there to high incidence beyond the epidemic threshold, and then spreads both spatially to the rest of the metro region and hierarchically to the other metro regions of the nation. The conditions in New York's poor neighborhoods dictate the health and order of the nation's urban population (three-fourths of the total). The denial of adequate fire service and other housing-preservation municipal services to these poor neighborhoods under the planned shrinkage policy threatens both national public health and national security.

Table 8-1 MANHATTAN COMMUTING FIELD 1980, 1990

COUNTY OF RESIDENCE	TOTAL WORKERS 1980	TOTAL WORKERS 1990	WORK IN MANHATTAN 1980	WORK IN MANHATTAN 1990	MILES TO MANHATTAN
Ocean	109,411	178,966	2,446	2,870	75
Fairfield	350,638	423,064	18,621	24,285	62
Hunterdon	37,776	57,721	448	937	55
Monmouth	196,317	274,238	13,008	19,050	55
Orange	97,816	141,664	4,407	7,032	50
Sussex	47,347	66,593	1,331	1,474	0
Middlesex	257,181	353,628	14,165	24,030	50
Suffolk	476,042	652,989	32,617	38,505	42
Somerset	91,701	134,390	2,978	5,064	40
Putnam	30,882	44,216	2,440	3,418	38
Passaic	179,689	220,595	5,995	7,796	37
Morris	183,653	231,093	7,941	9,385	36
Westchester	360,378	437,753	64,097	80,628	30
Union	209,790	247,205	10,724	14,414	28
Rockland	103,312	133,757	15,501	17,369	24
Nassau	571,036	650,947	10,224	97,205	20
Bergen	384,469	429,102	54,532	60,013	20
Essex	302,096	356,562	16,989	25,750	18
Richmond	130,332	174,090	48,001	54,292	18
Kings	699,337	907,010	301,614	343,762	10
Queens	727,515	918,063	321,890	34,401	9
Hudson	210,480	262,745	30,722	52,292	7
Bronx	342,195	429,777	162,837	170,318	5
NY	600,375	754,148	508,905	635,761	0

Table 8-2 AVERAGE COMMUTING ROUNDTRIP
IN MILES FOR 9 SMSAs

SMSA	AVERAGE COMMUTING ROUNDTRIP (MILES)
Houston	21.6
New York City	23
Philadelphia	23
Washington, D.C.	24
Atlanta	29.3
Chicago	29.9
San Francisco	33.9
Los Angeles	34.1
Detroit	40.8

The commuting considered here is to, from, and within the central city. It does not include to, from, or within the suburban counties.

Table 8-3 SIGNIFICANCE AND PERCENT R² OF REGRESSIONS WITHOUT THE TRAVEL CENTER

CITY	AIDS	TB	VIOLENT CRIME	LOB	N
Boston	.04 (54.7)	.04 (52.9)	.71 (2.5)	.28 (18.9)	8
New York	.0 (76.3)	.0 (69.8)	.0001 (62.5)	.0001 (62.6)	23
Philadelphia	.02 (44.3	.11 (24.0	.659 (2.0)	.66 (2.0)	12
Washington	.0 (90.8)	.001 (70.8)	.085 (29.3)	.23 (15.2)	11
Chicago	.19 (31.6)	.04 (60.2)	.37 (16.2)	.72 (2.8)	7
Detroit	.004 (84.0)	.49 (10.1)	.01 (79.6)	.08 (49.1)	7
St. Louis	.02 (77.3)	.17 (25.3)	.07 (40.4)	.18 (23.7)	9*
San Francisco	.84 (0.7)	.017 (58.2)	.47 (7.8)	.33 (13.4)	9

Note: p, (r-sq). the number of counties, n, is given in the last column.

For St. Louis only the 7 counties with nonzero AIDS rates were used in the regression for AIDS.

TABLE 8-4 DEMOGRAPHIC DATA ON FIVE SELECTED METRO REGIONS

PARAMETER	REGION				
	NYC	DC	Philadelphia	Detroit	San Francisco
area (sq.-mi.)	7,627	6,574	5,619	5,176	7,369
pop (000)	17,953	3,923	5,899	4,665	6,253
pop/sq mi	2,354	597	1,104	901	849
commuters*	2,017,731	710,067	747,278	842,670	555,917
commuters/sq.-mi.	71,819	11,565	5,531	6,075	11,904
TB R^2 #1	69.4%	79.7%	16.9%	34.6%	30.8%
TB R^2 #2	68.1%	44.4%	46.5%	27.5%	38.8%

*commuters=number of people working in the City. For NYC, this means Manhattan.
commuters/sq mi=number of workers per square mile of City, not metro region. For NYC, this means Manhattan.

TB #1=percent of county incidence pattern of TB over the metro region explained by pattern of county extreme housing overcrowding.

TB #2=percent of county incidence pattern over metro region explained by county poverty rate.

Table 8-5

ANALYSIS OF VARIANCE FOR LOG (1Eζ*AIDS/POP) SELECT AIDS>0 TYPE III SUMS OF SQUARES

source of variation	sum of squares	d.f.	mean square	f-ratio	sig. level
Covariates					
Log Mu80/area	29.170295	1	29.170295	278.347	0.0000
Log Perpov	5.916323	1	5.916323	56.454	0.0000
Main Effects					
A: City	49.423758	7	7.0605368	67.373	0.0000
Residual	8.4886759	81	0.1047985		
Total (corrected)	116.89783	90			

3 missing values have been excluded.
All F-ratios are based on the residual mean-square error.

ANALYSIS OF VARIANCE FOR LOG (1Eζ*TBPOP)—TYPE III SUMS OF SQUARES

source of variation	sum of squares	d.f.	mean square	f-ratio	sig. level
Covariates					
Log Mu80/area	9.0724932	1	9.0724932	61.610	0.0000
Log Perpov	9.3180516	1	9.3180516	63.277	0.0000
Main Effects					
A: City	12.185532	7	1.7407904	11.821	0.0000
Residual	12.369593	84	0.1472571		
Total (corrected)	55.897944	93			

0 missing values have been excluded
All F-ratios are based on the residual mean square error.

Table 8-5 CONTINUED

ANALYSIS OF VARIANCE FOR LOG (1Eς*LOB88/BR88)—TYPE III SUMS OF SQUARES

source of variation	sum of squares	d.f.	mean square	f-ratio	sig. level
Covariates					
Log Mu80/area	0.7304998	1	0.7304998	55.367	0.0000
Log Perpov	1.8888121	1	1.8888121	143.158	0.0000
Main Effects					
A: City	0.9442201	7	0.1348886	10.224	0.0000
Residual	1.1082863	84	0.0131939		
Total (corrected)	6.2072431	93			

0 missing values have been excluded

All F-ratios are based on the residual mean square error.

ANALYSIS OF VARIANCE FOR LOG (1Eς*VC8ς/POP)—TYPE III SUMS OF SQUARES

source of variation	sum of squares	d.f.	mean square	f-ratio	sig. level
Covariates					
Log Mu80/area	10.157519	1	10.157519	70.444	0.0000
Log Perpov	18.520113	1	18.520113	128.440	0.0000
Main Effects					
A: City	6.0519455	7	0.8645636	5.996	0.0000
Residual	12.112211	84	0.1441930		
Total (corrected)	68.646376	93			

0 missing values have been excluded.

All F-ratios are based on the residual mean square error.

Table 8-6 CALCULATION OF AMPLIFICATION FACTOR

1. Take many indicative variables such as infectious-disease incidences, violent-crime incidence, substance-abuse death rates, population density, housing-overcrowding percentage, socioeconomic status, probability of contact between metro regions, etc.

Perform regressions between them all so that a matrix of regression coefficients is created with a zero diagonal: matrix B.

2. Calculate a vector (U) containing effects of nonlinearities in the interactions between the variables and the effects of external factors such as changes in public policy, economic structure, demography, etc.

$$X(t) = BX(t) + U(t), \text{ where t is a point in time after } t=0.$$
$$u_1(t) = b_{1,0}(t) + E_i(t, X(T)).$$

3. Perform Principal Component Analysis to obtain the eigenstructure of B. Q=the matrix of eigenvalues diagonalizing B.

$$QY(t) = X(t)$$
$$QW(t) = U(t)$$

4. For the eigenvectors Y_k of B, $lambda_k$ denotes eigenvalues.
$$Y_k(t) = lambda_{kyk}(t) + w_k(t).$$

5. Mean E[f] of time-dependent variable f(t) is defined:
$$E[f] = 1/T \mid f(t)dt, \text{ over time interval 0 to T.}$$
$$\text{variance } V[f] \text{ is } E[(f-E[f])^2].$$

Term-by-term variance of components of the eigenvectors of B yields:
$$V[1-lambda1)Y1(t)] = V[w1(t)], \text{ so that}$$
$$V[y1] = V[w_i]/1-lambda_i)^2.$$

$$\text{Thus, } \sigma(y_i)/\sigma(w_i) = 1/\mid 1-lambda_i \mid.$$

The variance of the relationships between the original variables of pathologies, income, crowding, probability of contact, etc. is driven by the variance in the external forces as amplified by the term $1/\mid 1-lambda_i \mid$. Ergo, as lambda approaches 1, the impact of external forces on the system of outcome variables increases greatly.

Figure 8-1 CUMULATIVE AIDS CASES PER 100,000 PEOPLE THROUGH 1990 FOR THE TEN MOST AFFLUENT COUNTIES OF THE NYC SMSA AS A FUNCTION OF THE 1990 PERCENT OF THEIR WORKFORCE COMMUTING INTO MANHATTAN

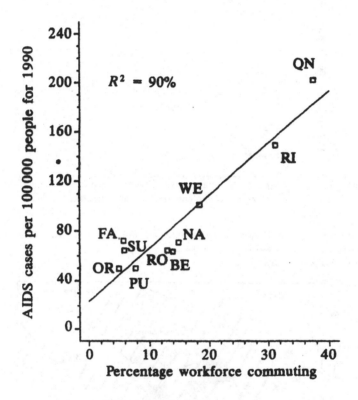

The counties are Queens (QN), Richmond (RI), Westchester (WE), Nassau (NA, Rockland (RO), Putnam (PU), Suffolk (SU) and Orange (OR) in New York State, Bergen (BE) in New Jersey, and Fairfield (FA) in Connecticut.

Figure 8-2

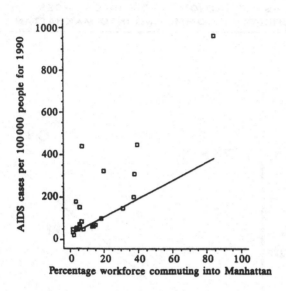

A. Cumulative AIDS cases per 100,000 people through 1990 for all the counties in the NYC SMSA as a function of the 1990 percent of their workforce commuting into Manhattan.

Note the seven data points well above the line.

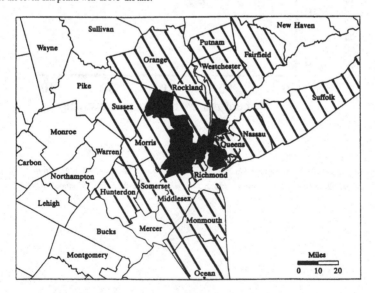

A. The map of the seven counties with data points above the line in a. (black) and the other SMSA counties (stripes). The seven counties form an extended epicenter.

Figure 8-3 PARALLEL REGRESSION LINES FOR THE 24-
COUNTY NYC SMSA FOR THE LOGARITHM OF THE CUMU-
LATIVE AIDS CASES PER 100,000 THROUGH 1990 AND OF
THE CUMULATIVE TUBERCULOSIS CASES PER 100,000
FROM 1985 THROUGH 1992

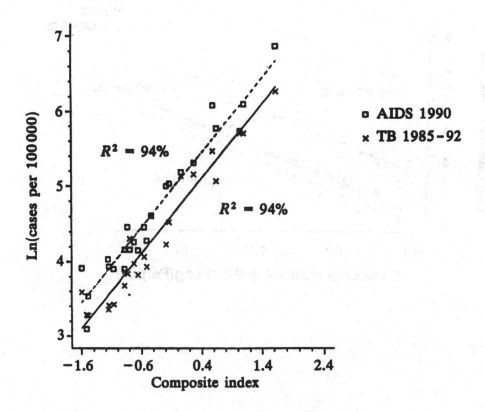

These are plotted against a composite index of the 1980 percent living in poverty and the 1980 commuter Markov-equi-
librium distribution per unit area of county.

X= 0.759 ln %pov + 0.197 ln (u/A).

Figure 8-4 PARALLEL LINES FOR AIDS, TB AND
VIOLENT-CRIME INCIDENCE PLOTTED AGAINST THE
COMPOSITE INDEX FOR POVERTY AND COMMUTING

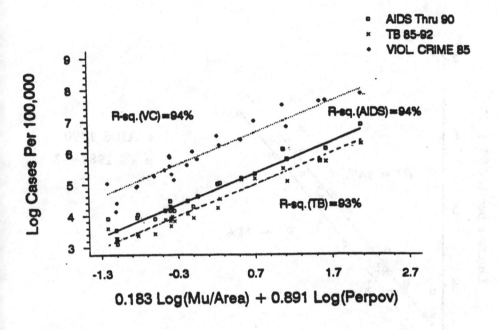

Figure 8-5 ANALYSIS OF VARIANCE SHOWING ACROSS-REGION STRUCTURES FOR AIDS, TUBERCULOSIS, LOW-BIRTHWEIGHT, AND VIOLENT CRIME

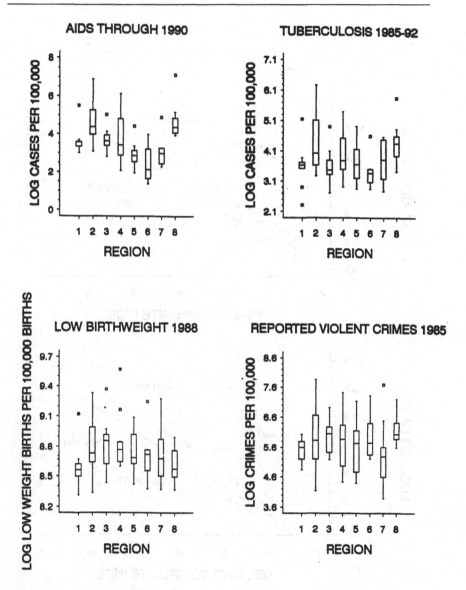

Clearly AIDS is the most region-dependent and violent crime the least.

1=Boston, 2=NewYork, 3=Philadelphia, 4=Washington, 5=Chicago, 6=Detroit, 7=St. Louis, 8=San Francisco.

Figure 8-6 HIERARCHICAL DIFFUSION OF AIDS AMONG THE 25 LARGEST US METROPOLITAN REGIONS

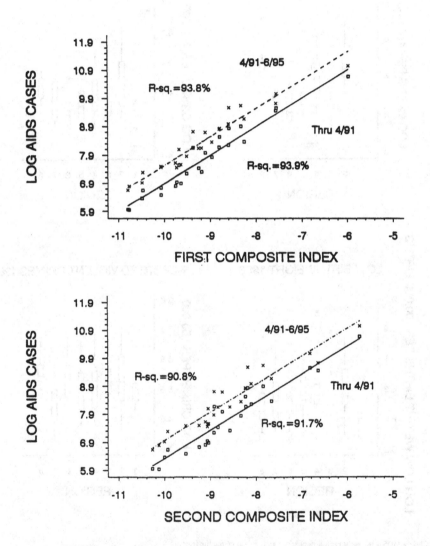

a. Fit of AIDS cases through April 1991 and between then and July 1995 to a composite index determined by MANCOVA: X= 0.41 log (P[New York]) + 0.26 log(P[San Francisco]) +1.09 log(violent crimes 1991/1990 population).

b. Same as a with X = 0.66 log (k(4))+1.19 log(1991 violent crimes/1990 population)

Figure 8-7 DIFFUSION OF VIOLENT CRIME THROUGH
THE 25 LARGEST US METROPOLITAN REGIONS

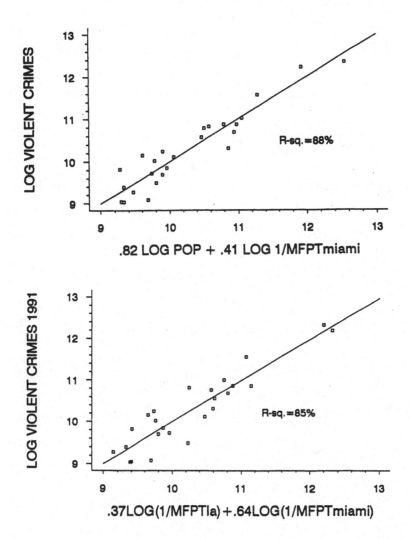

a. Regression of Log of 1991 violent crimes on the Log of the total population and the Log of 1 over the mean first-passage time from Miami to each metro region.

b. Same as a, using the mean first-passage times from Miami and Los Angeles as independent variates.

9

POLICY TO HEAL THE WOUNDS

THE CONTEXT OF OUR RECOMMENDATIONS

Successive governments for more than a quarter century have wracked America and its metropolitan regions through harmful inner city public policy. Although this nation now contains more wealth than it did during the Great Reform of 1880–1920, the culture, politics, social structure, and economic thrust essentially ensure the unfolding of the massive tragedy that we described here.

As we have documented, diseases and behaviors from poor, disrupted neighborhoods spread all the way to the national level and, we believe, even to the international level. Diffusion of pathologies from the other end of the income spectrum has also occurred. The fragmentation of poor and middle-class communities from the extensive migrations of the 1970s left individuals vulnerable to the alternative culture of survivalism, hoarding, acquisition-at-any-cost, and extreme individualism.

Studies in the 1960s and 1970s of the social structure of national elites who constitute the permanent government rendered a similar picture in several countries, including the United States: a small group (no more than about 1,000) of intensely interacting powerful individuals who bartered favors and continued accumulating power and wealth.[1] Loss of power and wealth automatically meant expulsion, by definition. Within the elite, small core groups engaged in close interactions. The only occasion for rendering service to the larger populace occurred in threatening circumstances when the accumulation produced excessive damage and riled the general population to rage and inflict warning wounds on the elite. The Great Reform and the New Deal exemplify the elite's socioeconomic fire brigade. Roger Starr's denial of community, with its widespread destructive results, may have deep roots in the culture and social structure of the elite. Lack of community is their sad, but lethal *modus vivendi*.

In our quarter century as scientists and political activists, we have often entertained the notion that if we could just find the right audience among the elected and appointed officials, we could present our data, analyses, and interpretations, and see them used to save lives, homes, families, public health, communities, and environmental quality

But going to health commissioners and legislators won't yield results without organized citizens. Elected and appointed officials have overt and covert agendas. Indeed, the permanent government rarely reaches the public eye. Only when public suffering becomes a threat in some way does the permanent government take action to reduce it. Science, even the very best and most sound, can't create public policy without political muscle.

POLICY I. ENACT THE 1989 NYAM DRAFT RECOMMENDATIONS

The policy recommendations that emerged from a 1989 New York Academy of Medicine conference entitled "Housing, Community, and Health" remain as sound as ever.[2] Philip Landrigan , Dean of Community Medicine at Mount Sinai Medical Center, chaired the conference and convened an ad-hoc working group to develop the recommendations that we stand by today. The following paragraphs relate these recommendations:

REBUILDING OF HOUSES

"A major need for amelioration of New York City's housing crisis is to build or rebuild thousands of units of decent, affordable low-income housing. . . . In summary, the Academy emphasizes that the only possible and practicable approach to providing housing for the homeless and inadequately housed is one that involves restoration of community and service infrastructure, as well as rebuilding the housing stock."

RESTORATION OF HARD MUNICIPAL SERVICES

1. "Following the recommendation of the Assembly Republican Task Force on Urban Fire Protection, the Academy of Medicine recommends the reopening of at least 45 fire companies, plus supervisory and support units, in the high fire-incidence areas of New York City. Additionally, the Academy recommends restoration of full staffing on all fire companies, re-establishment of an initial

response of three engines and two ladder companies on all first-alarm fires, and re-establishment of adequate policies for calling higher alarms and for relief of heavily worked fire companies at large fires."

Four other sub-recommendations followed: higher levels of sanitation service for high fire incidence, high-population density neighborhoods; a special hydrant and water-supply maintenance task force for these neighborhoods; special programs for housing-code enforcement and emergency repair for these neighborhoods; and fire prevention and sanitation-education programs as goals in themselves and as "one avenue of rebuilding the social network."

REBUILDING OF SOCIAL AND HEALTH CARE SERVICES

". . .while there is no question that high-level on-site medical and social care must be provided to homeless, sheltered, and inadequately housed persons, highest priority must be assigned to prevention of homelessness and to provision of permanent, decent, low-income housing. Pregnant women and families with children should receive highest priority for relocation to permanent housing. . . ."

Many subrecommendations on medical care and social services follow.

RE-ESTABLISHMENT OF COMMUNITY SOCIAL NETWORKS

"Reknitting of the social structure in communities to be rebuilt must be encouraged by an explicit community-organizing strategy."

Observations then follow on how hard services such as sanitation and police can play roles in community organizing. In particular, housing-construction rehabilitation must include a site-specific community-organizing plan. The plan must aim to insert the new residents into the community structure and to create such structures in neighborhoods where they were destroyed. Tenant councils and block associations, as well as churches, fraternal and political organizations, and quasi-official bodies such as the Police Precinct Councils and Community Planning Boards must be involved. Besides rebuilding of the social networks, the aim of the organizing is political and economic activity and participation in the Great Brawl of enterprise and demand for services and programs.

POLICY 2: REVIVE THE GREAT REFORM

The NYAM recommendations remain essentially sound policy as far as they go. They do not reflect what we now know about the depth, extent, and forms of psychosocial consequences of the slow disaster. We know now that intense community re-organizing, coupled with creation of economic opportunities, is necessary. We recommend revival of the type of missionary work and settlement-house activity which organized and adapted the masses of immigrants in the early twentieth Century.

The letters of Alice Hamilton, the environmental and occupational health physician, describe the urban slum of the Great Reform Era and the work of Hull House.[3] Doctors, nurses, and social workers went visiting home after home to improve them physically and to get into treatment all those with communicable or chronic diseases. The residents were educated about sanitation, ventilation, family planning and the programs of Hull House. Landlords were told to correct unsanitary and unsafe conditions. Special home visits focused on child nutrition, development, and immunization.

A wide variety of sectors participated in the housing, public health, educational, and community-building ferment: churches and ethnic organizations, political parties, medical and legal professionals, labor unions, patrician *noblesse obliger*s like the Junior League, and governmental officials. We need these kinds of elaborate, coordinated campaigns to improve living conditions and public health.

As during the Great Reform, extreme housing overcrowding must be reduced in all areas to below 3% of the dwelling units because concentrations of extremely overcrowded housing units over 3% lead to more and larger fires and increased incidence of substance abuse, violence, low-weight births, and contagious diseases. Yet, the resettlement must be accomplished without further disruption of social networks and with special efforts to increase the connectedness between existing social networks.

POLICY 3: END MASS CRIMINALIZATION

We recommend returning to the long-term solutions of the Great Reform to the problem of widespread crime: proper housing, strong social networks and community institutions, and good work opportunities. The involvement and coordination of churches and synagogues, labor unions, ethnic organizations, and settlement houses created the Iron Triangle of social, political, and economic activity for the immigrants and other marginalized sectors. Both street crime and government corruption declined during this period of intense participation and improvements in working conditions.

Even with the feverish prison-building in the late Cuomo regime, the Pataki regime has crammed the cells to overcrowded levels again. The New York City system, in order to house its own prisoners, evicted state prisoners who had been held in New York City facilities. The crime-and-punishment dilemma requires a cutting of the Gordian knot. Neighborhoods already destabilized will not recover if subject to high incidence of certain types of crimes, including drug dealing. Yet sending large proportions of the young men to prison, where they become criminalized and then return to the neighborhoods where they cannot get work, also leads to long-term destabilization. The get-tough wave of legislation fails to protect the neighborhoods as the long-term solutions would and, moreover, leads to prison for thousands of youths who do not commit violent crimes. These non-violent "criminals" also become criminalized in prison.

Recent declines in incidence of certain markers such as tuberculosis and violent crime (see next chapter) provided a context for a seeming validation of the public policies of policing both crime and disease, rather than investing in housing, housing preservation, and rebuilding of the social network. Within New York, political organizing and pushing for these long-term solutions fell to a level unequalled since before the turn of the century. The permanent government pumped out anecdotes to "prove" that apartheid actually works. However, the easily policed markers like substance abuse and AIDS among minority youth continue at unrelievedly high incidences and prevalences, belying the assertion.

POLICY 4: REBUILD COMMUNITY

Without commitment by New York City's citizens, elected government, and permanent government, urban decay with its many facets will simply continue. Failure to mitigate and rebuild will not be pretty, whether the present form of decay continues or jumps onto another track and presents us with unexpected consequences.

Social network and loose ties in a neighborhood mean more than the residents and local merchants. They encompass everyone who works, shops, eats, worships, or even walks in the neighborhood regularly. The civil servants assigned to a neighborhood—firefighters, police officers, sanitation workers, meter maids, teachers, doctors and nurses, rat-control officers, street pavers, building inspectors, EMTs, traffic-light repairers, etc.—are important to the social and economic life of the community they serve.

In the confines of their jobs, government workers in an area understand its ways and can operate there effectively, efficiently, and harmoniously. Surprises, and their consequent debacles, arise relatively rarely. The longtime workers understand how to talk with their "clients" and get the information to and from the neighborhood, information which must flow both ways for wholesome community life to continue securely and surely.

Certain restaurants, grocery stores, street corners, etc., mix workers and residents together. There's the stationary store where the teachers pick up their daily newspapers and say a few words to the merchant and his other customers. There's the really good restaurant/bar where the firefighters go after the day shift to have a beer and play a little pool with the young family men who live in the 'hood. It's all part of the dense, but loose weave of community, when no major disaster has shredded that weave.

We recommend that the worst-hit areas receive social, economic, and physical rebuilding. In particular, rapid reweaving of the social fabric must occur to stop the destructive feedback loops. More efficient social rebuilding may involve the kind of economic cooperatives which many international relief organizations encourage in disrupted Third World villages.

"Empowerment Zones" are not the answer, as they reopen these areas to corporate recolonization and exploitation under the guise of economic aid to increase employment. Empowerment Zones are predicated on the usual corporate-based economic structure and impose corporate culture whose individualistic orientation opposes collective continuity. Collective enterprises such as economic cooperatives would both build community stronger and faster *and* agree with many traditional ethnic cultures.

POLICY 5: REVIVE LABOR UNIONISM

American labor unions organized by and for immigrants in the first half of the twentieth Century provide a model for community-building. Not "merely" economic-bargaining organizations, they developed political, educational, health, consumer, sports, and cultural programs. Workman's Circle, the Educational Alliance, Consumers Union, and the legendary Broadway reviews Pins & Needles were legacies of the multi-faceted immigrant unions. The political organizing, in particular, left an illustrious monument to that generation of union activists: the 40-hour workweek, the minimum-wage concept, outlawing of sweatshops, worker's compensation, building and fire codes, and the right to engage in collective bargaining. Although patrician reformers lent respectability and some power to these causes and educated the upper classes about their necessity, the workers themselves provided the crucial forces and components to the fight to tame the excesses of late Industrial-Revolution America. The threat they represented forced the Great Reform and the New Deal.

In his election campaign and post-election statements, John Sweeney, the present AFL-CIO president, gave voice to the feelings of long-time union members and labor activists in his promise to renew the labor movement in the United States. The success or failure of this attempted renewal may save or doom not only the traditional working class but also the newly proletarianized professional and white-collar classes, even vulnerable rich sectors. Labor-movement renewal in all its aspects can form a vital core for reknitting the fragmented national social and political fabric. Endless analysis has revealed the economic side of the unraveling of America: the erosion of the value of real wages, the increasing hours of the average workweek, decreasing job security, an increasing incidence of bankruptcy, and the disappearance of "good" jobs. Nearly undocumented, the social and political segments of the locally-based national decay process grind on, having been initially triggered by the policy-driven city-to-suburb and region-to-region migrations of the 1970s and further exacerbated by the Reagan policies of the 1980s . The inter-relation of economics, social structure and function, and political structure and function lead to both hope and despair. Improvement in any aspect will improve the other two. Decay in any aspect will weaken the other two.

POLICY 6: TURN METROPOLITAN REGIONS INTO FUNCTIONAL CITIES

We recommend a metro-regional level of governance. Right now, the mayor and legislature of the central city essentially govern most American metropolitan regions, and the suburbanites don't even know it. They have no voice in electing these officials. They make sure that the State budget starves the City and that their own county and local township or village budget shares absolutely nothing with the City. In the light of what the previous chapters of this book describe, the lack of jurisdictional overlap and sharing dooms entire metro regions and the whole network to urban decay.

We can look to Toronto, Ontario and Portland, Oregon for forms of regional governance in which regional services such as sanitation, environmental quality, and transportation are managed at the regional level. The Tri-state Regional Plan Association, in the tradition of transportation engineers and planners for the past quarter-to-half century, gave birth to yet another plan for regional transportation, economic development, and natural preserves. It declared the wisdom of developing and implementing such plans on a metro-regional scale—long before the benefits of such plans were clear—whatever the details of the individually proposed plan. Transportation engineers have a pretty good handle on what can be done to move people and goods, given the patterns of population- and household-density and the geography of commerce and industry.

Regional socioeconomic and political planning may have been pursued in rare isolated instances but is not an accepted, respected activity. In the past, multi-faceted planning during various reforms encompassed neighborhood (settlement house catchment area) and city boundaries. Even though it addressed most facets, it reflected the upper-class view that the poor ethnic-minority population had to be transformed into culturally Anglo-Saxon, Protestant work-ethic, indi-vidualistic neighborhoods. Even within the Jewish sector, the older wealthy German- and English-Jewish community which followed Reform Judaism fash-ioned its aid programs for the Eastern European Jewish immigrants—Orthodox in religion and socialist in politics—to get them assimilated and quickly trans-formed into "good Americans." Local and regional planning must recognize the importance of cultural differences.

Just as some providers of medical care understand the necessity of culturally appropriate service, even to the point of working with traditional healers, pro-grams of social and economic development and redevelopment must include flexibility for cultural adaptation to target populations, even if the program ends up as something other than the usual corporate-based routine. Coordination between the region's developmental programs must occur to leverage scarce resources and to assure creation of larger social networks. Coordination of programs in different neighborhoods is also necessary to assure that a neighborhood that lags behind the others gets attention and doesn't bring the others down again. Coordination of programs adapted for the cul-tures of the neighborhood populations will challenge managers and evaluators and prove the mother of invention.

The knowledge and experience amassed since the Great Reform reveal that we cannot merely apply its approaches on the regional level. The outbreaks of the virulent xenophobia surrounding immigration indicate that the goal of assimilation and cultural uniformity and conformity left large sectors of the American population wounded, fearful, and alienated in the root sense of the word. These outbreaks occur periodically, for instance, during the McCarthy era and at the present time. They reflect the recurring tension between the reality of ethnic cultural heritage and the American dream of assimilation and belonging. Few of us are "real" Americans out of Betty Crocker's kitchen.

Preservation and building of metro-regional community depends on intermeshing neighborhood-level social networks. We recommend provision of adequate hard services to preserve the physical basis of stable neighborhoods as a first priority. That such services no longer seem an obvious necessity to most citizens and officials simply exposes the widening gap between reality and ideologically-warped perception. For fire service, a regional department is the wrong way to go. Fire service should go the other way: little self-sufficient neighborhood fire departments which draw on units from outside the neighborhood only rarely. For fire service, regional stability and well-being, paradoxically, require "neighborhoodization." Emergency services such as fire control, police, and ambulances should be designed for self-sufficient neighborhoods with provision for only rare reliance between neighborhoods.

Regionalizing municipal services must be limited to such interneighborhood ties as transportation, inter-library loans, committees on standards for municipal services, and the regional monitoring, planning, and oversight functions. These planning, monitoring and evaluation functions range from childhood immunization, housing codes and code enforcement, and fire-service delivery to bus routes and schedules. The most important of these functions focus on control over contagious urban decay processes and on encouragement of contagious community building and strengthening processes. The region is the upper end of that meso-scale on which contagious processes occur. Control over the neighborhood, city, and regional systems automatically translates into national public health, safety, and well-being. Toronto and Portland hint at the way to renewal on all levels.

THE POSSIBILITY OF RECOVERY

For many cities at the New York/Los Angeles end of the decay spectrum, the damage may be so thorough that rehabilitation is not economically or socially possible. The depth and extent of the multitudinous aspects of the decay may raise the ante for recovery to above the humanly feasible level, not just in terms of money and material, but also in terms of labor, love, and sustained human commitment.

We do not really know how to undo such a massive slow disaster, how to revive normal community life and reclaim the families and individuals who suffered their equivalent of carpet bombing and minefields.

Our policy recommendations could fail. But if anything can work to turn around the present ruins, these policies can. They rest on the history and trajectory of the events and systems described in detail in the previous chapters. The danger of doing nothing is too great to allow the processes set in motion by planned shrinkage to continue. Without strong action, the whole system may flip into a new domain with an even worse outcome for public health and public order.

10

THE 1990s
FIGHTING THE SYMPTOMS

By 1990, the New York City middle class was in a state of panic. Rampant murder and random gunfire, frightening contagious diseases, begging and homelessness, wordless screaming, and public hallucinating—in the subways and streets—all contributed to this panic. The public never traced this mayhem to a specific source but it did demand alleviation of the symptoms.

CRIME

In particular, the demand for more police and for patrolmen on the beat arose repeatedly. When Mayor Dinkins made a particularly lackluster statement after one of the many murders, his diffident delivery elicited sneers. Dinkins and his police commissioner responded by initiating "C-POP": community-program-oriented policing. Officers in C-POP walked an assigned beat and were expected to get to know the residents. Dinkins also greatly increased numbers of police officers, to about 35,000 by the end of his term. The 1993 Federal Crime Act supplied significant funds for some of the added force. Giuliani added still more annually, and the 1996 Police Academy graduates brought the force up to 38,000 (a ratio of one officer for less than 200 citizens!).[1]

Giuliani weakened C-POP and bolstered the "get-tough" side of the Police Department. The number of arrests for "quality-of-life" violations soared, as well as for other crimes. Jails became grossly overcrowded, and riots on Rikers Island reflected the deteriorating conditions. Thousands and thousands of young people entered the criminal-justice system, often for non-violent crimes like petty theft and graffiti vandalism.

In late July 1996, the Giuliani Administration won a court victory, having sued to apply a new law passed by the Gingrich Congress and Dole Senate. This law abrogates the court-monitored programs for overseeing conditions in jails and prisons.[2]

The freedom from the 1978 settlement agreement between the court and the City that established the court monitoring allowed gross prison overcrowding and all that overcrowding brings: violence, rape, transmission of diseases, drugs, and habits of domination and brutality. When released, the men and women kept under these conditions returned to their vulnerable neighborhoods with predictable outcomes.

When the late Dinkins and early Giuliani administrations implemented the policy of arresting the dope sellers, rather than concentrating on the kingpins, the drug trade did not abate. Violence escalated in the continual battle over territory. The arrests escalated turf battles that led to increases in violence. Giuliani also found that more and more police became involved in the drug trade, stealing from dealers and selling in the suburbs. New York police officers were arrested in Suffolk and Rockland Counties for selling dope. This would not do.

The policy appears to have tacitly reverted to not arresting the dealers. Open drug selling along the major avenues returned to the poor neighborhoods with a vengence in at least four of the five boroughs, but gunfire was less frequently heard in those neighborhoods. Also, the increase in arrests nearly depopulated entire neighborhoods of their male youth. Between these demographics and the greater stability, violent-crime incidence declined, as it did in most cities across the country, probably for the same reasons.

Approximately one out of every three-to-four young African-American males in New York City will spend time in prison before the age of thirty. Now, in the late 1990s, about one-fifth of the young males from poor neighborhoods are behind bars at any one time. Prison sentences are now longer, triggering a new wave of prison construction. As a result, we have the seeming paradox of decline in crime and an increase in prison population, but crime declines only temporarily, because of the increasing prison population. When the prisoners are released, they will have become criminalized. Because of the uniformity of sentence length for particular crime, releases of prisoners from the 1980s and early 1990s crime wave will occur rapidly and in large numbers. The "solution" will feed into the problem and enlarge it.

The neighborhoods beset by the open drug selling and the overt consequences (intimidation, demoralization, noise, litter, bizarre behavior, junkies nodding out, traffic from suburban junkies coming to buy, etc.) pressed the Mayor for a response. He went back to a previously scorned policy, special drug task forces which operate in a way similar to the previous generation.[3] As of summer 1996, the special task force STRIKE began operating in the "Dirty 30" (Manhattan's 30th Precinct), where police involvement with the drug organizations had allowed open selling on nearly every corner along Broadway between 135th and 155th Streets. The verdict on the effect is still not rendered, even after two years. Much of the street dealing simply moved down into the 26th

Precinct. Some citizens in the 30th Precinct say their blocks have been cleared; others, that the dealers simply moved to the other end of the block.[4]

So we had the seemingly contradictory situation in mid-1996 of declining violent crimes but still a very active and visible drug trade. The decline was indeed substantial, over 10% between 1993 and 1994 and between 1994 and 1995. The answer may be that the violence has turned inward and sustains the drug trade. Indeed, as gun-related deaths declined, drug-overdose deaths rose. This 1996 picture may be no real contradiction, but the natural consequence of all the previous events.

TUBERCULOSIS

Like violent crime, tuberculosis has declined greatly:

	1993	1994	1995
NEW CASES	3,235	2,921	2,100

The reported cases through mid-1996 indicate that the decline continues.[5] Certainly, this is good news and lifts a great burden from most New York City neighborhoods. However, like the decline in violent crime, the decline in new TB cases was achieved at great expense and effort, essentially by a disease police force. The beefed-up program of case-finding, directly observed therapy, and case retention until completion of treatment required a small army of case workers. At a conference on tuberculosis sponsored by *The Lancet*, the medical journal, in September 1995, the cost estimates per case bandied about by the New York City Department of Health representatives ran in the $20-40 K range. Infusion of massive federal, state, and city funds keeps this effort going.

In the absence of proper housing, housing-preservation service, and public social policy, such massive outlays of scarce public moneys must continue. The poor still suffer great residential instability, unhealthy working conditions, over-crowding at home and at work, and inadequate diet. They still want to discontinue taking the anti-TB drugs as soon as they feel the disease ebb because these drugs are toxic and make the patient sick, even non-functional. So the case workers must continue to track down their peripatetic and unwilling clients. Often the case worker must scour a large area to find his client. He may have to enter crack houses, gang headquarters, basements shared by many families, and sweatshops, all illegal premises, but ones which he cannot report.[6]

In order to keep the middle class safe from TB, continued illegal activity must go unreported in order to establish trust between the case worker and the client. Some of the illegal conditions like the housing arrangements and the sweatshops cause many of the TB cases, but will go unreported and unrelieved under this program of medicalization of a social disease. The case worker must simply witness his client ingest the pills.

Thus, the disorder of a quarter century not only spawned the TB cases, but also the life styles which would necessitate maximum staffing in order to treat the cases. Yet the eyes of this small army must remain averted even to those illegalities which foster transmission of the TB microbe and heightened susceptibility to infection and disease. Conditions which cause general public-health deterioration go unreported and even uncorrected when health department employees see them, even though many of these case workers care greatly about their individual clients and may spend their own money getting food, clothing, and other necessities for them.

The hardest-hit neighborhoods showed the following patterns in new TB cases per 100,000 from 1990–94:

AREA	1990	1991	1992	1993	1994
Central Harlem	233.4	220.8	221.7	169.7	113.4
East Harlem	124.2	93.5	95.1	70.7	69.9
Lower East Side	133.1	138.2	109.8	75.6	79.3
Morrisania	112.8	94.6	85.7	93.3	63.6
Bedford	112.7	112.5	100.9	83.3	77.3
Bushwick	85.0	66.3	74.5	69.6	61.9.

We should note that in 1991, the center of TB in the Bronx shifted to Mott Haven, which had incidences of 126.3 and 146.4 in 1991 and 1992, respectively, the latter higher than any other health district besides Central Harlem. Also to be noted is a shift in Brooklyn, although not one as dramatic as that in the Bronx: namely in 1992, the incidence in Fort Greene soared to 118.5 and remained high in 1993 (107.8). At 87.2, it was the highest in Brooklyn in 1994. This is very close to the TB rate in Croatia, about 88 new cases per 100,000, up from 45 before the current war.[7] Even with all the decline, the 1994 incidences of all thirty health districts remained above the national average of about 10. Only five districts had incidences below twice the national average. The citywide incidence was about 40, down from about 52 in 1992. TB has in fact declined, but without the maintenance of an expensive medical-enforcement army, it will return. As we mentioned above, the drug picture has not improved palpably, and neither have such TB-related factors as housing overcrowding and sweatshop employment.

The highest TB incidence in New York occurred in Central Harlem: 233 per 100,000. In 1992, approximately 4000 cases were reported. Approximately

one-quarter of the New York population receives some form of public assistance. If we designate that number as the highly susceptible sector of the population, this sector would generate slightly less than 4,200 cases at the maximum
rate of 233 per 100,000. It is entirely possible that the epidemic began to ebb
and settle into hyperendemicity because it had saturated the extremely susceptible population. There is a hint of this in the 1991 decline in the Central Harlem
rate *before* the beefed up "control" program was implemented. The shifts in borough top ranking in both Brooklyn and the Bronx also indicate more a geographic shift in the epidemic than the total success of the disease police. The
disease police may be taking credit for a trend which, at most, they accelerated.

The very steepness of the declines in TB and crime incidences point to gross
instability of the social system, in the absence of physical and socioeconomic
improvements. When TB is controlled because of improvements in living and
working conditions, the decline is slow but sure and lasting. During the entire
era between 1900 and 1970, murder incidence fluctuated around a very stable
average and indicated a fundamental social stability. The trends in murder incidence since 1975, first up and then down, point to a departure from that stability. In fact, in 1990, the number of extremely overcrowded housing units, a
determinant of both TB and violent crime, approximately doubled over that of
1970. The instability of the social indicators plus the worsening of living and
working conditions presage future new disasters. The urban decay "machine"
may be all wound up, poised for a new lurch with just a little push.

AIDS

Another disease which began to decline recently is AIDS. In 1993, over 13,000
cases of AIDS were reported; by 1995, a total of about 10,000 cases had entered
the CDC records.[8] This is a large decline. The decline continued through 1997
and, because of the new drug cocktails, accelerated between 1996 and 1997.
However, the AIDS rate among heterosexual minority youth keeps increasing, as
does their rate of HIV-seropositivity. This is another example of an epidemic
shifting between populations. It is possible that a decline in the absence of a
change in the backdrop may simply indicate a later and worse phase of the disease pattern. If the virus mutates to one more easily transmitted via heterosexual activity or if the heterosexually transmitted African and Asian strains are
imported, the larger context of physical and social decay and its behavioral fallout will force a massive heterosexual epidemic not confined to the poor minority communities but concentrated there.

COMMUNITY DESTRUCTION CONTINUES

The larger context of housing availability and housing preservation services has remained execrable. In 1990, the Dinkins administration began shifting the staffing levels on the fire engines with five-person staffs, so that if a firefighter was injured or sick, only four firefighters would work. Giuliani stopped this policy and practice but then tried to remove all the street fire-alarm boxes despite the fact that in many neighborhoods a high proportion of the residents do not have telephones on which to summon the Fire Department. The City Council refused to allow this total removal. After much back-and-forth and legal action, an agreement was reached whereby "only" one-quarter would be removed. A court suit on behalf of an organization of deaf and hearing-impaired people was still pending in mid-summer 1996, and Giuliani is using it as an excuse not to replace the boxes which were removed before the agreement. Thus, notifying dispatchers of a fire is now more difficult on the average.

Meanwhile, more housing-code-enforcement inspectors have been laid off under the cover of the recurrent "budget crisis." The other inspectors, those in the Buildings Department, who inspect new and renovated units during and after construction are also being laid off under a new program whereby the builders will inspect themselves![9] Thus, new housing may possibly be substandard and not conform to code, while old housing is rotting and not being maintained because there is no longer a mechanism to force maintenance.[10] Another ingredient in the recipe for a return of the Burnout.

Finally, sanitation service has been ruthlessly cut back.[11] In 1992, Dinkins slashed collection and street-cleaning personnel in the poor neighborhoods. The two most populous West Bronx Community Districts in 1991 each had about 100 garbagemen; in fiscal 1992, they each had 35. Because of a suit by the Bronx Borough President, sit-ins at the Commissioner of Sanitation's office by Harlem clergy, and the general outcry, a small readjustment was made in 1993. However, statistical tests show that the pattern of allocation in fiscal 1994 (July 1994–June 1995) was indistinguishable from that of 1992. That biomarker of bad sanitation, the rat, has surged in population in the affected neighborhoods. Even in middle-class neighborhoods like the one surrounding Columbia University, sightings of rats have become common. More trash lying around means more and larger trash fires. These extreme sanitation service shortfalls raise the probability of a return of the burnout of 1972–78.

The entire country still feels the effects of the Burnout, which rippled not only throughout the metro region but between metro regions. A new Burnout would add its impact onto those from the previous one. We cannot guarantee that these impacts would simply resemble those already seen, just as we could not predict

AIDS in 1979. The only thing we can say is that national literacy rate, family stability, job availability for minority youth, public-health status, and church attendence
will not increase in the event of a new Burnout. Everyone will suffer.

THE SPECTRE OF A REPETITION IN LONDON

In early 1996, the Tory government of John Major decided to trim the fire-service
budgets of thirteen of the thirty London boroughs and directed these borough councils to each eliminate a fire company.[12] Most of the thirteen companies planned for
elimination are what we call "combo units," engines equipped with ladders. The boroughs and the Fire Brigades Union have resisted the directive through political organizing like petitions (300,000 signatures) and large demonstrations. Because of the
popularity of fire service and, possibly, stepped-up IRA bombing activity, the central
government took a long time before it forced the boroughs to close the companies.

Because of the material we had sent the Fire Brigades Union about the devastating
effects of fire company closings in New York, the central government backed down
from the original number of cuts and forced only seven to close. In addition, the central government and boroughs established a system of monitoring such fire-service
indices as frequency and extent of temporary relocations, frequency and size of large
fires, fire-damage extent per year by area, and fire deaths and injuries of both firefighters and civilians. London responded somewhat to the New York disaster.

These closings come on top of two previous rounds of cuts, a very large one in
1979 and a relatively small staffing cut in 1986. The previous cuts and the rising fire
activity have begun to strain the service network in an all-too-familiar way: the company move-ups (temporary relocation) have left large areas inadequately covered in
case of a further fire or emergency. The company eliminations could send the system
into a New York-style process of rapid urban decay.

London is much more integrated economically and ethnically than New York, but
the Thatcher/Major years have frayed the physical and social structure. The deindustrialization reduced certain working-class areas such as Peckham to near slums. The
East End, which has always been a vibrant immigrant neighborhood, now boasts a
very densely packed Bengali population which may be living at many more people
per room than the public-health standards theoretically allow. Boarded-up flats and
stores dot the old working-class areas, especially the public-housing flats. The East
End is so overcrowded that even the sidewalks are almost impassable.

Up to now, fire safety has depended heavily on the building code, which
requires brick-and-mortar construction of flats, largely three-story construction,
and a high fire barrier between attached buildings. Brick walls extend above the
roofline between the buildings to shield one building from another. Now, however,

many American building technologies are being allowed under waivers. Warehouses used to be built as many compartments separated by fire-rated walls; now the huge one-room American warehouse is being allowed. American-style high-rise apartment and office buildings are also being constructed.

The Thatcher/Major deindustrialization has marked London, as well as the Midlands and the North. Between 1981 and 1991, ten of the thirty boroughs lost between 10 and 27% of their jobs.[13] London lost 12.9% of total jobs between 1981 and 1994. Unemployment rate is 11.9% in London, higher than for the UK as a whole, and inner London at 16.5% has a rate twice that of Great Britain. London also has a higher percent of its unemployed who were out of work for over a year (42%) than the nation (36%).

London has a shade under seven million people in it. Approximately 20% is non-white, largely Indian or other Asian and Caribbean. The international immigrants are young, largely between 15 and 44 years of age, prime child-bearing age. Indeed, London has a higher percent of its population in the 15–44 year old sector (23.7% of males, 23.4% of females) than the nation (21.6% of males, 20.8% of females). Although the rate of child-bearing is less than that of the nation as a whole, the large number of women of child-bearing age means lots of children, 15.41% of the births, compared with only 13.47% of the population in 1992. The immigrant populations have high fertility and lots of small children, which means housing overcrowding.

Housing in London is in flux. A program of privatization has led to a transfer of public housing to private hands. New units are not being built by the local author-ity, either. About 100,000 units net have disappeared from the social-rental sector. In April 1994, about five percent of the total housing stock was empty (143,000 dwellings). Additionally, about 8% (229,000 dwellings) are "statutorily unfit for human inhabitation." This is believed to be an underestimate.

In 1994, 31,239 households were accepted as homeless by the boroughs, a decline from the peak of 43,166 in 1992. However, it was well over double the number in 1986. If the housing market improves, more households will be evicted, as owners retake possession in order to sell.

The homelessness and vacancies are not uniformly distributed. Hackney, remarkably, had the highest number of homeless households in temporary accommodations and the second-highest percent of local authority stock vacant, as well as the second-highest percent of housing association stock vacant. In September 1994, 4,300 households in Hackney were in temporary accommodations; in April 1994, 7,000 dwelling units were vacant in Hackney, 4,200 under the local authority. Hackney also has the highest per-cent of its population receiving income support: 30.7% in 1993–94, not quite twice the London average (16.6%). Thus, the housing-related problems are geographically focused although London is much more integrated and mixed than New York.

Other social indices such as perinatal mortality rate and total- and violent-crime incidence per unit population also show great lack of homogeneity among the boroughs. Kingston-on-Thames had the lowest three-year average perinatal mortality rate (5 per 1,000 live births) and the lowest unemployment rate (6.3%). Its violent-crime rate (4.4 per thousand) was also low. Lambeth, on the other hand, had a high unemployment rate (18.7%), the highest perinatal mortality rate (10.2) and the highest violent crime incidence (12.4).

These indices represent conditions of populations ranging from 138,000 to 332,000 people, populations as large as small cities. More extreme values must characterize the individual neighborhoods (with populations of three to thirty thousand) within the boroughs.

Thus, certain areas are more vulnerable to urban decay than others, even in London. We do not know whether the concentrations of susceptible buildings and people are over the threshold for sustained contagious urban decay. But the central government seems willing to experiment.

If a new fire policy were to push London into contagious urban decay with its various physical, social, economic, public-health, and public-order deteriorations, the impact would not be contained within London, but would follow the New York example. The London metropolitan region would be dragged into the downward spiral, and the contagion would spread hierarchically to other cities in the UK. Because of the Thatcher/Major policies in the Midlands and North (deindustrialization and ghettoization of the long-term unemployed),[14] the cities of those areas would be extremely vulnerable. The EU would not get away unscathed because London is a linchpin in the European trade network. Other vulnerable cities on the Continent would catch the disease, just as New York and San Francisco spread AIDS to other North American cities. With the signing of the Maastricht Treaty, the EU functionally became a single system with massive flows of products and labor.

THE PERMANENT GOVERNMENT AND THE KILLING OF COMMUNITY

Roger Starr sneered at the idea of community. Yet our culture is based on very ancient visions of the supremacy of community over the mortal individual. The ritual of the red heifer in the Book of Numbers arouses frequent discussion and questioning among Christians, Jews, and Islamics who study the Bible. The entire nineteenth chapter of Numbers meditates on the red heifer which is to be sacrificed and burned with various herbs. The ashes then become a tool of ritual to be saved, a purification from the uncleanness of touching the dead.

Other sacrifices also took the lives of herd and flock animals. Animal sacrifice graphically demonstrated the mortality of the individual but the immortality of the herd. Breaking of the laws of community, in fact, required atonement by animal sacrifice. The ritual of the red heifer separated the dead individual from the immortal community, let the dead go, and maintained the human herd uncontaminated by death.

A raft of biblical laws severely limited accumulation of wealth and power, for example: the seven-year laws and the fifty-year jubilee. Every seven years, the slaves are freed. Every seventh year, the land must lie fallow and rest. No one can grind wealth from the land endlessly. Every fifty years, all property reverts back to its original owners. When the tribes entered the Promised Land, the area was divided up so that every family received a given acreage. The Law of Jubilee ideally reversed any buying and selling of land so that no one could amass property forever. The premise was that community is immortal and individuals are not.

The permanent government's denial of the existence of community, as exemplified by Roger Starr's sneering, ignores both the accumulated wisdom of the millennia and data and analyses of the social and economic sciences since their founding in the nineteenth century. Of course, Starr serves merely as the visible expressor of the policies and views of the local elite, some of whom, like Moynihan, also have achieved entrée into the national inner circle.

In our present political, economic, and social structure, candidates for office are largely chosen by financial contributors (what we call the permanent government), though they are formally elected into office by the populace, that small percentage of the eligible voters who exercise this right. We vote into office those who carry out the policies of the permanent government, and those policies become ours because we elected their executors. We vote into office those who destroy our homes and force us to migrate and thereby take away our vote, unless we take the trouble to re-register. We raise to power those who unravel our communities and thereby take away our collective power. We vote into office and render respectable and estimable those who drag us into the pit of substance abuse and promiscuity and thereby take away our esteem, community standing, and respectability. Our participation in the political process throws us out of the process and throws our sons into prison, away from normal participation. As Ewan McColl put it, "Through all their lives, they dug their grave."

CONCLUSION

There are those who look for an answer in harm reduction—providing medical care to the homeless, needle exchanges for addicts, condoms for the promiscuous, anti-TB drugs and other similar programs, all of which retain the basic structure and the grindingly murderous public policy. Although such programs are certainly necessary, the harm-reducers make them the ultimate goal and thus collaborate with those who destroy community.

In the long run, many of these programs will sour. Eventually, the microbes become drug-resistant; the addicts share needles at times when they cannot wait to get clean ones and do not have bleach at hand; the compulsive risk-takers have unprotected sex. Eventually, the "high-risk groups" multiply under the pressure of the grinding from the unreformed public policy. The epidemics of disease and behavioral problems then slide into new subpopulations before special harm-reduction programs can be designed and implemented for the new "high-risk groups."

Harm reduction as a policy is always falling behind. By itself, it serves only as a cosmetic containment device like that impressive big dome on the Chernobyl reactor before the run-away reaction and fire. It allows the middle class in the suburbs to rest easy in the knowledge that it is safe from the terrors of inner-city disease and crime. In this book, we have shown that the wounded ghettoes bleed all the way into New York's suburbs, all the way into other cities and their suburbs.

SIGNS OF HEALING OF COMMUNITY

Despite the continued policies for community destruction, the improvements seen in the rates of violent crime, tuberculosis, infant mortality, and low-birthweights indicate a general improvement in the social structure of poor communities in New York City and other large, old decaying cities. In chapter 7, we explained that infant mortality and low-birthweight rates were indicators of the efficacy of the benevolent community. The protection and guidance of pregnant women are fundamental to a shared future and to continuity. Low-birthweight rate was a strong predictor of intentional-death rate in the Bronx.

Thus, the fall in the incidences of all these related public-health and public-order problems signals to us that the healing of community began to manifest its power around 1993. If the rapid burnout-and-abandonment of low-cost housing can be prevented, the social networks will reknit. The same people will see each other on the block, in the stores, taking their children to school, and in the houses of worship. Just such simple continuity can give rise to conversation and friendships, to neighborliness, and to mutual support.

We do not believe that this fragile embryonic network can oppose the destructive influences of such anti-community policies as "welfare reform," the new apartment-vacancy-decontrol law, and the continued police predation on male youth. However, as a long as massive housing destruction does not occur, the network can become stronger and provide certain limited but important possibilities for the residents of poor neighborhoods.

If the anti-community policies were to be blunted—or indeed, reversed—the healing would accelerate and a yield a fully developed and functioning community of layers of social networks. A community backed by community-oriented (not community-based) programs and policies could solve a large portion of the problems now besetting the large cities.

That we can detect indications of community regeneration proves the immortality and bedrock-fundamental nature of human community. The "sick" communities targeted by planned shrinkage may have shifted geographically but, in regeneration, will likely outlive the cast of characters who sought to kill them: Ed Ignall of Rand (dead of leukemia), John O'Hagan of the New York Fire Department (dead of cancer), Homer Bishop of the Fire Department (dead of leukemia), John Lindsay, Abraham Beame, Ed Koch, Rudy Giuliani, and, of course, Roger Starr. Let the "sick" communities sprinkle these individuals with the ashes of the red heifer to cast out the dead. Let us all go back to saying "Good morning" at bus stops and newsstands. "Good morning" fights crime, keeps babies alive, and protects public health.

NOTES

NOTES TO INTRODUCTION TO PART ONE

1 Deborah Wallace. *In the Mouth of the Dragon: Toxic Fires in the Age of Plastics.* Garden City Park, Long Island. 1990, pp. 5–19.
2 Wallace. pp. 24–28 and 104–105.

NOTES TO CHAPTER 1

1 Joel Schwartz. *The New York Approach.* Columbus, 1993, p. 16.
2 Robert Fitch. *The Assassination of New York.* London, 1993, pp. 49–50.
3 John H. Griscom. *Sanitary Condition of the Laboring Class of New York.* Reprinted New York, 1970 (original publication date: 1845), p. 23.
4 David Rosner. 'Introduction' in David Rosner, ed. *Hives of Sickness.* New Brunswick, 1995, pp. 4–5.
5 Schwartz, p. 3.
6 Gretchen Condran. 'Changing Patterns of Epidemic Disease,' in *Hives.* pp. 32–36.
7 Rene and Jean Dubos. *The White Plague: Tuberculosis, Man, and Society.* New Brunswick, 1987, Chapter 1.
8 Planning Commission of New York City. *A Plan for the People of New York City,* 1969, p. 145.
9 David Durk and Ira Silverman. *The Pleasant Avenue Connection.* New York, 1976, pp. 94–98.
10 L. Hinkle. 'Closing Summary,' in L. Hinkle and W. Loring, eds. *The Effect of the Man-Made Environment on Health and Behavior.* DHEW, Publication No. (CDC)77-8318. Washington, 1977.
11 Rosner, pp. 9–14.
12 E. Blackmar. 'Accountability for Public Health: Regulating the Housing Market in Nineteenth-Century New York City, in *Hives.* pp. 42–64.
13 Griscom, pp. 42–58.
14 Fitch, pp. 37–49.
15 Fitch, pp. 60–61 and 108–111.
16 Fitch, p.279.
17 Fitch, pp. 18–19.
18 Schwartz, pp. 287–288 and p. 175.
19 Schwartz, pp. 295–305.

20 Schwartz, pp. 15–17, example of Greenwich Village.

21 Finch, pp. 132–138 and p. 149.

22 Schwartz, pp. 131–133.

23 Schwartz, p. 132.

24   Schwartz, p. 175.

25 Schwartz, p.175, pp. 202–203.

26 Schwartz, pp. 271–276.

27 Schwartz, pp. 290–292.

28 J. Leavitt. '"Be Safe. Be Sure." New York City's Experience with Epidemic Smallpox,' in *Hives*, pp. 95–111.

29 Schwartz, pp. 281–283.

30 Schwartz, p. 295.

31 Schwartz, p. 292.

32 Schwartz, p. 292.

33 B. Lopez. *Arctic Dreams*. New York, 1986.

34 R. Stone. *Dreams of Amazonia*. New York, 1985.

35 Fitch, p. 21.

36 R. Wallace, M. Fullilove, D. Wallace, and A. Flisher. 'The Long-Term Sociotemporal Diffusion of Disaster in the Bronx: 'Planned Shrinkage,' Violent Death, Substance Abuse, and the Dominion of Trauma,' in press. *Environment and Planning A*.

37 S. Roberts. 'A Critical Evaluation of the City Life Cycle Idea.' *Urban Geography*, vol. 12, no. 5, 1991.

38 J. Fried. 'City's Housing Administrator Proposes 'Planned Shrinkage' of Some Slums.' New York *Times*, 3 February 1976.

39 S. South. 'Metropolitan Migration and Social Problems.' *Social Science Quarterly*, vol. 68, 1987, pp. 3–18.

NOTES TO CHAPTER 2

1   Letters of Edward H. Blum to John T. O'Hagan (14 January 1970) and of Jan M. Chaiken to Daniel P. Moynihan (13 January 1970).

2   H. Rainie. 'US Housing Program in South Bronx Called a Waste by Moynihan.' New York *Daily News* 20 Dec 1978, p. 3.

3   'Text of the Moynihan Memorandum on the Status of Negroes.' New York *Times*, 30 January 1970, p. 3.

4   Appendix B to letter from Chaiken to Moynihan: 'Incidence of Fire Alarms.'

5   Joseph Fried. 'City's Housing Administrator Proposes "Planned Shrinkage" of Some Slums.' New York *Times*, 3 February 1976, p. B1 (front page, second section).

6   Roger Starr,. *Urban Choices: The City and its Critics*. Baltimore, 1969.

7   Susan Roberts. 'A Critical Evaluation of the City Life Cycle Idea.' *Urban Geography*, vol. 12, no. 5. 1991, pp. 431–449.

8   Institute of Urban Studies, Fordham University. *A Profile of the Bronx Economy*, 1967.

9   New York City Planning Commission. *Plan for New York City, A Proposal. 2. The Bronx*. 1969, p. 20.

10 R. Yin. *Urban Indicators: Fire Alarms and Reported Crimes*. Rand Institute document D20122-NYC. 1970.

11 M. Dear. 'Abandoned Housing,' in J. Adams, ed. *Urban Policy Making and Metropolitan Development*. Cambridge, Mass., 1976, pp. 59–99.

12. J. Odland, and R. Barff. 'A statistical model for the development of spatial patterns: application to the spread of housing deterioration.' *Geographical Analysis*, vol 14. 1982, pp. 326–339.

13 Women's City Club of New York. *With Love and Affection: A Study of Building Abandonment*. New York, 1977.

14 O. Moritz. 'Sees City Full of Ghost Towns.' New York *Daily News*, 3 August, 1970.

15 E. Blum. 'Measuring Fire Protection' in W. Walker, J. Chaiken, E. Ignall, eds. *Fire Department Deployment Analysis*. New York, 1979, pp. 39–46.

16 E. Ignall, K. Rider. 'A Simple Adaptive Approach,' in *Fire Department Deployment Analysis*. pp. 436–444.

17 R. Wallace. *The Fireboxes That Failed: A Study of the Emergency Reporting System in New York City*. Testimony before the New York State Senate Subcommittee on Fire and Police Protection of the Finance Committee, April 1976.

18 E. Blum. *Reducing False Alarms with Telephone-Type Street Alarm Boxes*. Rand Report WN-7566-NYC. 1971.

19 R. Wallace. *The Fireboxes that Failed*.

20 Conversation of RW with Frank Baraff, assistant to Manhattan Borough President Percy Sutton in 1973; J. Darnton. 'City's Fire Alarm Boxes Called Undependable.' New York *Times*, 20 December 1974, p. 1 and 38.

21 R. Wallace and D. Wallace. *Studies on the Collapse of Fire Service in New York City 1972–1976: The Impact of Pseudoscience in Public Policy*. Washington, D.C. 1977, pp. 12–15; R. Wallace. 'Fire Service Productivity and the New York City Fire Crisis: 1968–1979.' *Human Ecology*, vol. 9, no. 4, 1981, pp. 433–464.

22 P. Kolesar and W. Walker. *Firehouse Siting Model*. Rand report R-1618/2-HUD. 1976.

23 W. Walker to R. Archibald. 'Allocating Fire Companies to Divisions.' Rand memo NM-330, 16 April 1971.

24 Walker to Archibald, 16 April 1971.

25 Example: E. Ignall. 'The Fire Operations Simulation Model,' in *Fire Department Deployment Analysis*. p. 533 explains how parameters on an escalating fire were difficult to acquire and so the New York simulation model had no escalating fires!

26 K. Rider. *Creating Fire Department Demand Regions for New York City*. Rand report WN-9101-NYC. Sept. 1975.

27 Kolesar and Walker. *Firehouse Siting Model*.

28 P. Kolesar and W. Walker. *Measuring the Travel Characteristics of New York's Fire Companies*. Rand report R-1449-NYC.

29 C. Sarikcioglu (Head, Research Section) to H. Samuelson (Chief, Bureau of Plans and Surveys). 'A Brief Summary of Travel Time Study of Lower Manhattan.' Memo, June 1971.

30 US Department of Housing and Urban Development. Office of Policy Development and Research. Community Management and Productivity Improvement Research. Planning and Management Methods for the Deployment of Emergency Services. List of reports available in 1976.

31 'Report of the President's Commission on Bioethics and Use of Human Subjects.' *Federal Register*. vol. 47, no. 60, 1982. p. 13282.

32 D. Shalala to Congressman Ted Weiss. Letter, 22 May 1978.

33 Alan Siegel (Director, Division of Community Development and Management Research, HUD) to R. Wallace. Letter, 21 December 1976.

NOTES TO CHAPTER 3

1 R. Wallace. 'Contagion and Incubation in New York City Structural Fires 1964–1976.' *Human Ecology*, vol. 6, no. 4, 1978, pp. 423–433.

2 R. Wallace. 'Contagion and Incubation.'

3   N.T.J. Bailey. *The Mathematical Theory of Infectious Diseases and its Applications,* second edition. New York, 1975.

4   R. Abler, J. Adams, P. Gould. *Spatial Organization: The Geographer's View of the World.* Englewood Cliffs, NJ. 1971.

5   A. Cliff, P. Haggett, J. Ord, G. Versey. *Spatial Diffusion: An Historic Geography of Epidemics in an Island Community.* London, 1981.

6   R. Wallace, D. Wallace. 'Origins of Public Health Collapse in New York City: The Dynamics of Planned Shrinkage, Contagious Urban Decay, and Social Disintegration.' *Bulletin of the New York Academy of Medicine,* vol. 66, no. 5, 1990, pp 391–434.

7   R. Wallace. 'The New York City Fire Epidemic as a Toxic Phenomenon.' *International Archives of Occupational and Environmental Health,* vol. 50, 1982, pp. 33–51.

8   R. Wallace. 'Recurrent Collapse of the Fire Service in New York City: the Failure of Paramilitary Systems as a Phase Change.' *Environment and Planning A,* vol. 25, 1993, pp. 233–244.

9   R. Wallace, D. Wallace. *Studies on the Collapse of Fire Servie in New York City 1972–1976: The Impact of Pseudoscience in Public Policy.* Washington, 1977, pp. 50–69.

10 R. Wallace. 'Urban Desertification, Public Health, and Public Order: Planned Shrinkage, Violent Death, Substance Abuse and AIDS in the Bronx.' *Social Science and Medicine,* vol. 31, 1990, pp. 801–813.

11 Wallace and Wallace. *Studies on the Collapse,* pp. 64–71.

12 R. Wallace. 'Recurrent Collapse of the Fire Service in New York City.'

13 Abler, Adams, Gould, pp. 391–397.

14 D. Wallace. 'The Tuberculosis Resurgence in New York City as a Mixed Hierarchically and Spatially Diffusing Epidemic.' *American Journal of Public Health,* vol. 84, no. 6, 1994, pp. 1000–1002.

15 D. Wallace, R. Wallace. 'Structural Fire as an Urban Parasite: Population Density Dependence of Structural Fire in New York City and its Implications.' *Environment and Planning A,* vol. 16, 1984, pp. 249–260.

16 N.T.J. Bailey. *The Mathematical Theory of Disease.*

17 M. Burnet, D.O. White. *Natural History of Infectious Disease,* fourth edition, London. 1978, p. 15.

18 Wallace and Wallace. 'Origins of Public Health Collapse in New York City.'

19 R. Wallace, D. Wallace. 'Urban Fire as an Unstabilized Parasite: the 1976–1978 Outbreak in Bushwick, Brooklyn.' *Environment and Planning A,* vol. 15, 1983, pp. 207–226.

20 Wallace and Wallace. 'Urban Fire as an Unstabilized Parasite'.

21 D. Wallace. 'Application of Ecological Analytical Approaches to Public Health.' *Proceedings of the 25th National Conference on Records and Data.* Sponsored by the National Center for Health Statistics (CDC), 1995.

22 NYC Dept. of Health. 1990 Census data aggregated by health area. Received by RW on diskette from NYC DOH Bureau of Biostatistics.

23 R. Wallace. 'Homelessness, Contagious Destruction of Housing, and Municipal Service Cuts in New York City: 2. Dynamics of a Housing Famine.' *Environment and Planning A,* vol. 22, 1990, pp. 5–15.

24 C.B. Stack. *All Our Kin: Strategies for Survival in a Black Community.* New York. 1974.

25 I. Susser. *Norman Street: Poverty and Politics in an Urban Neighborhood.* New York. 1982.

26 Stack. *All Our Kin.*

27 D. Massey, F. Espana. 'The Social Process of International Migration.' *Science,* vol. 237, 1987, pp. 733–737.

28 H.N. Vyner. *Invisible Trauma: The Psychosocial Effects of the Invisible Environmental Contaminants.* Toronto, 1987.

29 W. Kinson, R. Rosser. 'Disaster: Effects on Mental and Physical State.' *Journal of Psychosomatic*

Research, vol. 18, 1974, pp. 437–456.

30 R. Wallace, M. Fullilove, D. Wallace. 'Family Systems and Deurbanization: Implications for Substance Abuse,' in Lowinson, Ruiz, Millman, Langrod, eds. *Substance Abuse: A Comprehensive Textbook*. Baltimore, 1992, pp. 944–955.

31 "Indian Plague." *New Scientist*, vol. 143, no. 1944, p. 11.

NOTES TO CHAPTER 4

1 E. Wichen. *Tuberculosis in the Negro in Pittsburgh*, a report of the Tuberculosis League of Pittsburgh. Pittsburgh, 1934.

2 G.P. Youmans. *Tuberculosis*. Philadelphia, 1979, p. 112.

3 Youmans, p. 357.

4 H.A. Wilmer. *Huber the Tuber, A Story of Tuberculosis*. Published by the National Tuberculosis Association. New York, 1943. This is the clearest explanation. A more "scientific" explanation is in Youmans, pp. 317–326.

5 CDC. "A Strategic Plan for the Elimination of Tuberculosis in the United States." *Morbidity and Mortality Weekly Report*, vol. 38, No. S–3, 1989.

6 S. Grzybowski. *Tuberculosis and its Prevention*. St. Louis. 1983.

7 W. Pagel, F. Simmonds, N. MacDonald, E. Nassau. *Pulmonary Tuberculosis*. London. 1964.

8 Youmans, pp. 358–362.

9 G. Condran. "Changing Patterns of Epidemic Disease in New York City." In D. Rosner, ed. *Hives of Sickness*. New Brunswick, 1995, pp. 27–41.

10 Task Force on Tuberculosis Control. *Future of Tuberculosis Control. A Report to the Surgeon General*. Public Health Service Publication No. 1119. Washington, D.C., 1963.

11. Task Force on Tuberculosis in New York City. *A Plan to Control Tuberculosis in New York City*. Published by the NYC Health Services Administration. New York, 1968.

12 CDC, 1989.

13 D. Wallace. R. Wallace. "Structural Fire as an Urban Parasite: Population Density Dependence of Structural Fire in New York City, and its Implications." *Environment & Planning A*, vol. 16, 1984, pp. 249–260.

14 Source of tuberculosis case and incidence data in this chapter: New York City Department of Health. Mainly from the annual reports of the Bureau of Tuberculosis Control.

15 E. Drucker, P. Alcabes, W. Bosworth, B. Sckell. "Childhood Tuberculosis in the Bronx, New York." *The Lancet*, vol. 343, pp. 1482–1485.

16 D. Wallace. "The Resurgence of Tuberculosis in New York City: a Mixed Hierarchically and Spatially Diffused Epidemic." *American Journal of Public Health*, vol. 84, pp. 1000–1002.

17 D. Wallace. "Ecological Analytical Approaches for Public Health Research." *Proceedings of the 25th Conference on Data and Health Records*. CDC, National Center for Health Statistics. Washington, D.C., 1995.

18 F.G. Hofman. *A Handbook on Drug and Alcohol Abuse: The Biomedical Aspects*. New York, 1975; R.F. Johnston. *Drug Abuse, Clinical and Basic Aspects*. St. Louis, 1977.

19 N. Firooznia, R. Seliger, R. Abrams. "Tuberculosis in Drug Users." *Radiology*, vol. 109, 1973, pp. 291–302.

20 B. Rabin, M. Lyte, L. Epstein, A. Caggiula. "Alteration of Immune Competency by Number of Mice Housed per Cage." in B. Janokiv, B. Markovic, N. Spector, eds. *Neuroimmune Interaction: Proceedings of the Second International Workshop on Neuroimmunomodulation. Annals of the New York Academy of Sciences*, vol. 496, New York, 1987.

21 J. Grosset. "Treatment of Tuberculosis in Developed Countries." In *The Challenge of Tuberculosis: Statements on the Global Control and Prevention of Tuberculosis*. Preceedings of The Lancet

Conference. 1995.

22 P. Simone. "Drug Toxicity" in Briefing Papers for the New York Academy of Medicine Course on Clinical Management and Control of Tuberculosis. 9–11 March, 1992; M. Steele, R. Burk, R. DesPrez. "Toxic Hepatitis with Isoniazid and Rifampin, a Meta-Analysis." *Chest*, vol. 99, 1991, pp. 465–471; W. Lee. "Drug-Induced Hepatotoxicity". *New England Journal of Medicine*, vol. 333, 1995, pp. 1118–1127.

23 M. Iseman. "The Treatment of Multidrug-Resistant Tuberculosis." *New England Journal of Medicine*, vol. 329, 1993, pp. 784–791.

24 N. Gnanadesigan, P. Davidson, L.Q. Hanh, A. Balanon, E. Alkon. "Reliability of Death Certificates as a Source of Tuberculosis Mortality Data." Poster exhibited at The Lancet Tuberculosis Conference, Washington D.C., 1995.

25 H. Rider. "Risk Factors for Tuberculosis Defined." Address before The Lancet Conference, Washington D.C., 1995.

NOTES TO CHAPTER 5

1 C. Winick. "Epidemiology of Alcohol and Drug Abuse," in Lowinson, Ruiz, Millman, Langrod, eds. *Substance Abuse: A Comprehensive Textbook*. Baltimore, 1992, p. 22.

2 H. Vyner. *Invisible Trauma, The Psychosocial Effects of the Invisible Environmental Contaminants*. Toronto, 1987.

3 G. Pappas. *The Magic City: Unemployment in a Working-Class Community*. Ithaca, 1989, p. 89.

4 R. Wallace. "Urban Desertification, Public Health, and Public Order: 'Planned Shrinkage', Violent Death, Substance Abuse, and AIDS in the Bronx." *Social Science and Medicine*, vol. 31, 1990, pp. 801–813.

5 Wallace. "Urban Desertification."

6 C. McCord and H. Freeman. "Excess Mortality in Harlem." *New England Journal of Medicine*, vol. 322, 1990, pp. 173–177.

7 J. Collins, Jr. "Alcohol Use and Criminal Behavior." in J. Collins Jr. ed. *Drinking and Crime*. New York, 1981.

8 R. Wallace. "Expanding Coupled Shock Fronts of Urban Decay and Criminal Behavior: How U.S. Cities are Becoming 'Hollowed Out'." *Journal of Quantitative Criminology*, vol. 7, 1991, pp. 333–355.

9 R. J. Lifton. *The Broken Connection: on Death and the Continuity of Life*. Chapter 13: 'Survivor Experience and Traumatic Syndrome.' New York, 1980.

10 Dr. Mindy Fullilove. Personal communication, 1993.

11 R. Wallace, M. Fullilove, D. Wallace. "Family Systems and Deurbanization: Implications for Substance Abuse," in Lowinson, Ruiz, Millman, Langrod, eds. *Substance Abuse: A Comprehensive Textbook*. Baltimore, 1992, pp. 944–955.

12 E. Currie. *Reckoning: Drugs, the Cities, and the American Future*. New York, 1993, pp. 85–91.

13 Currie, pp. 113–116.

14 R. Wallace. "A Synergism of Plagues: 'Planned Shrinkage, Contagious Housing Destruction, and AIDS in the Bronx." *Environmental Research*, vol. 47, 1988, pp. 1–33.

15 Currie, pp. 23–33.

16 T. Williams. *The Cocaine Kids*. New York, 1989.

17 Currie, pp. 253–259.

18 Eddie Ellis. "85% of Prisoners Black or Latino; 75% of State's Entire Prison Population Comes from Just Seven Neighborhoods in New York City," in *The 12% Problem: Continuing Dilemma of Caribbean Prisoners*. Position paper for the Caribbean/African Unity Conference, Greenhaven Correctional Facility, November 3, 1990.

19 Currie, Chapter 2, "Roots of the Drug Crisis," pp. 36–74.

20 Currie, pp. 158–163.

21 Currie, pp 116–119.

22 Currie, pp. 70–71.

23 Currie, pp. 217–218.

24 Currie, pp. 280–283.

25 G. P. Kane. *Inner City Alcoholism, An Ecological Analysis and Cross-Cultural Study*. New York, 1981.

26 Wallace, Fullilove, and Wallace. "Family Systems and Deurbanization."

27 A. Pogrebin. "Neglected Zone: 135th–145th Street." New York *Times*, 6 June, 1996, p. B1 (front page of Metro Section); Meetings of West Harlem/Morningside Heights Sanitation Coalition, November 1995–July 1996 (of which DW is an organizer).

NOTES TO CHAPTER 6

1 The information on AIDS and the human immunodeficiency virus can be found in any textbook or public-education pamphlet on AIDS. Good information can be found in several books available on emerging infections.

2 P. Ewald. "The Evolution of Virulence." *Scientific American*, vol. 86, 1993. pp. 86–93.

3 P. Gould. *The Slow Plague*, Cambridge, Mass., 1992.

4 R. Wallace. "Social Disintegration and the Spread of AIDS II. Meltdown of Sociogeographic Structure in Urban Minority Neighborhoods." *Social Science and Medicine*, vol. 37, no. 7, 1993, pp. 887–896.

5 R. Wallace. "A Synergism of Plagues: 'Planned Shrinkage,' Contagious Housing Destruction, and AIDS in the Bronx." *Environmental Research*, vol. 47, 1988, pp. 1–33.

6 "The First 500,000 AIDS Cases—United States, 1995. *Morbidity and Mortality Weekly Report*. vol. 44, 24 November, 1995, pp. 849–853; "Update: Mortality Attributable to HIV Infection Among Persons Aged 25–44 Years—United States, 1994." *Morbidity and Mortality Weekly Report*, vol. 45, 16 February, 1996. pp. 121–125.

7 P. Gould. *The Slow Plague*, cover maps.

8 R. Wallace and M. Fullilove. "AIDS Deaths in the Bronx, 1983–1988: Spatiotemporal Analysis from a Sociogeographic Perspective." *Environment and Planning A*, vol. 23, 1991, pp. 1701–1723.

9 E. Schoenbaum. "High Prevalence of HIV Antibody in Heterogeneous Populations in the Bronx, New York City." Presented at Fourth International Conference on AIDS, Stockholm, 13–16 June 1988. Obtainable from University Publishing Group, 107 E. Church St., Frederick, Md. 21701.

10 R. Wallace. "Social Disintegration and the Spread of AIDS: Thresholds for Propagation Along 'Sociogeographic' Networks." *Social Science and Medicine*, vol. 33, 1991, pp. 1155–1162.

11 D. Wallace and R. Wallace. "Structural Fire as an Urban Parasite: Population Density Dependence of Structural Fire in New York City, and its Implications." *Environment and Planning A*, vol. 16, 1984, pp. 249–260.

12 Schoenbaum, 1988.

13 R. Wallace. "Urban Desertification, Public Health, and Public Order: 'Planned Shrinkage', Violent Death, substance Abuse and AIDS in the Bronx." *Social Science and Medicine*, vol. 31, 1990, pp. 801–813.

14 M. Smallman-Raynor, A. Cliff, P. Haggett. *London International Atlas of AIDS*. London, 1992.

15 R. Wallace. "Traveling Waves of HIV Infection on a Low Dimensional 'Socio-Geographic' Network. *Social Science and Medicine*, vol. 32, 1991, pp. 847–852.

16 J. Potterat, R. Rothenberg, D. Woodhouse, J. Muth, C. Pratte, J. Fogle. "Gonorrhea as a Social Disease." *Sexually Transmitted Diseases*. vol. 21. 1985. pp. 25–32.

17 R. Wallace's three papers above on social disintegration, traveling waves, and spread of AIDS.

18 D. Wallace. "Roots of Increased Health Care Inequality in New York." *Social Science and Medicine*, vol. 31, 1990, pp. 1219–1227.

19 The Lancet Conference, 14–15 September 1995, Washington, D.C., "The Global Challenge of Tuberculosis." Presentations by H. Rieder ("Risk Factors for Tuberculosis Defined") and J. Ellner ("Regulation of the Human Cellular Immune Response in Tuberculosis"). Conference abstracts available from The Lancet editorial office, London.

20 Dr. Susan Hunter, demographer for Save The Children Foundation project in Uganda. Personal communication, 1989–1990.

21 J. Catania, T. Coates, R. Stall, et al. "Prevalence of AIDS-Related Risk Factors and Condom Use in the United States." *Science*, vol. 258, 1992, pp. 1101–1106.

NOTES TO CHAPTER 7

1 G. Rushton. "Geography of Birth Defects in Des Moines." In *Proceedings of the 25th Public Health Conference on Records and Statistics.* National Center for Health Statistics, CDC, 1995.

2 "Asthma—United States, 1982–1992". *Morbidity and Mortality Weekly Report.* vol. 43, 1995, pp. 952–954.

3 C. McCord and H. Freeman. "Excess Mortality in Harlem." *New England Journal of Medicine*, vol. 322. 1990, pp. 173–177.

4 National Center for Health Statistics. *Healthy People 2000 Review, 1992.* Hyattsville, 1993, pp. 83–88.

5 R. Wallace. "Urban Desertification, Public Health, and Public Order: 'Planned Shrinkage,' Violent Death, Substance Abuse and AIDS in the Bronx." *Social Science and Medicine*, vol. 31, 1990, pp. 801–813.

6 K. Fiscella. "Racial Disparities in Preterm Births: the Role of Urogenital Infections." *Public Health Reports*, vol. 111, 1996, pp. 104–113.

7 C. Stack. *All Our Kin: Strategies for Survival in a Black Community.* New York, 1974.

8 R. Sampson. "The Impact of Housing Policies on Community Social Disorganization and Crime." *Bulletin of the New York Academy of Medicine*, vol. 66, 1990, pp. 526–533.

9 N. Denton and D. Massey. *American Apartheid: Segregation and the Making of the Underclass.* Cambridge, Mass., 1992.

10 R. Wallace, M. Fullilove, and A. Flisher. "AIDS, Violence, and Optimal Behavior Coding: Information Theory, Risk Behavior and Dynamic Process on Core-Group Sociogeographic Networks." *Social Science and Medicine*, vol. 43, no 3, 1996.

11 D. Wallace and R. Wallace. *American Journal of Public Health*, in press. 1998.

12 R. Wallace, A. Flisher, R. Fullilove. "Marginalization, Information, and Infection: Risk Behavior Correlation in Ghettoized Sociogeographic Networks and the Spread of Disease to Majority Populations." *Environment and Planning A*, in Press. 1997.

13 E. Wiesel. "Cain and Abel: the First Genocide." *Messengers of God.* New York, 1994, pp. 37–64.

14 H. Needleman, J. Riess, M. Tobin, G. Biesecker, J. Greenhouse. "Bone Lead Levels and Delinquent Behavior." *Journal of the AMA*, vol. 275, 1996, pp. 363–369.

15 N. Moss and N. Krieger. "Measuring Social Inequalities in Health: Report on the Conference of the National Institutes of Health." *Public Health Reports.* vol. 110, 1995, pp. 302–305.

16 Wallace, Fullilove, and Flisher. *Social Science and Medicine*, 1996.

NOTES TO CHAPTER 8

1 N. Denton and D. Massey. *American Apartheid: Segregation and the Making of the Underclass.*

Cambridge, Mass., 1992.

2   US Bureau of the Census. Journey-to-Work Matrices from the 1980 and 1990 Census. Washington, Dept. of Commerce.

3   R. Wallace and D. Wallace. "The Coming Crisis of Public Health in the Suburbs." *The Milbank Quarterly*, vol. 71, 1993, pp. 543–564.

4   R. Wallace, D. Wallace, H. Andrews, R. Fullilove, and M. Fullilove. "The Spatiotemporal Dynamics of AIDS and TB in the New York Metropolitan Region from a Sociogeographic Perspective: Understanding the Linkages of Central City and Suburbs." *Environment and Planning A*, vol. 27, 1995, pp. 1085–1108.

5   R. Wallace, D. Wallace, H. Andrews. "AIDS, Tuberculosis, Violent Crime, and Low Birthweight in Eight US Metropolitan Areas: Public Policy, Stochastic Resonance and the Regional Diffusion of Inner-City Markers." *Environment and Planning A*, vol. 29, 1997, pp. 525–555.

6   D. Wallace and R. Wallace. "Global Implications of TB Metropolitan Regional Structure in the USA." Poster Session at The Lancet Conference 1995: "The Challenge of Tuberculosis." Washington. 14–15 September. Abstract published in conference booklet, p. 14.

7   R. Wallace, Y-S. Huang, P. Gould, and D. Wallace. "The Hierarchical Diffusion of AIDS and Violent Crime Among US Metropolitan Regions: Inner City Decay, Stochastic Resonance, and Reversal of the Mortality Transition." *Social Science and Medicine*, in press.

8   A. Ives. "Measuring Resilience in Stochastic Systems." *Ecological Monographs*, vol. 65, 1995, pp. 217–233.

NOTES TO CHAPTER 9

1   R. Alba and G. Moore. "Elite Social Circles." Chapter 12 in R. Burt and M. Minor, eds. *Applied Network Analysis: A Methodological Introduction.* New York. 1983.

2   Committee on Public Health, New York Academy of Medicine. *Housing and Health: Interrelationship and Community Impact. Bulletin of the New York Academy of Medicine*, vol. 66, no. 5, 1990.

3   B. Sicherman. *Alice Hamilton, A Life in Letters.* Cambridge, Mass., 1984.

NOTES TO CHAPTER 10

1   Office of the Mayor. Executive Budget, Fiscal Year 1996. New York, February 1995.

2   P. Moses. "Jail Rules Rejected by Court." *Newsday*, 24 July 1996, p. A8.

3   Information on drug strike forces came from Peter Powers, deputy mayor, at June 1996 meeting of the West Harlem/Morningside Heights Sanitation Coalition.

4   Discussion among block association leaders at the July 1996 meeting of the West Harlem /Morningside Heights Sanitation Coalition.

5   TB data for 1990–1995 from the annual reports of the New York City Bureau of Tuberculosis Control. Data on 1996 is from *Morbidity and Mortality Weekly Reports*.

6   Lee Reichman described how a TB case worker in Newark, N.J. hunted for his addict client in crack houses. Discussion at The Global Challenge of Tuberculosis Conference, sponsored by *The Lancet*, 14–15 September 1995, Washington D.C.

7   I. Puljic, Z. Trkanjec, and J. Tekavec. "Tuberculosis—Consequences of War". Poster at The Global Challenge of Tuberculosis Conference, sponsored by *The Lancet*, 14–15 September 1995. Washington, D.C.

8   AIDS case numbers from the end-of-year issues of *Morbidity and Mortality Weekly Report* for 1993

and 1995.

9 Office of the Mayor. Executive Budget. Fiscal Years 1994, 1995, and 1996. New York, February 1993, February 1994, and February 1995.

10 D. Sontag. "A Weak Housing Agency Seems to be a Step Behind". New York *Times*, 7 October 1996. Begins front page, ends p. B5.

11 Office of the Mayor. Executive Budget: Geographic Spending. Fiscal Years 1992–1994.

12 Information on fire service cuts, relocation crises, and London building code from Raymond Mooney and James Fitzpatrick, London Regional Office, Fire Brigades Union and from tour of London Fire Control Centre.

13 Socioeconomic and demographic data on London taken from London Research Centre. T. Travers and M. Minors, eds. *London 95*. vol. 1, London, July 1995.

14 R. Hudson. "Deindustrialization and Ghettoization of the Longterm Unemployed in the Midlands and North," presented at the International Conference on the MetroRegion Impacts of the Maastricht Treaty: Geographic Inequalities. Syros, Greece, 1–5 September 1994.

INDEX